THE ENTREPRENEUR'S GUIDE TO
Doing Business with the Federal Government

A HANDBOOK FOR
SMALL AND GROWING BUSINESSES

CHARLES R. BEVERS
LINDA GAIL CHRISTIE
LYNN ROLLINS PRICE

Prentice Hall Press
New York   Toronto   London   Sydney   Tokyo

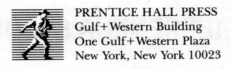

PRENTICE HALL PRESS
Gulf+Western Building
One Gulf+Western Plaza
New York, New York 10023

PRENTICE HALL PRESS and colophon are registered
trademarks of Simon & Schuster, Inc.

Library of Congress Cataloging-in-Publication Data

Bevers, Charles R.
  The entrepreneur's guide to doing business with
the federal government.

    Bibliography: p.
    Includes index.
    1. Government purchasing—United States.   2. Public
contracts—United States.   3. Small business—United
States.   I. Christie, Linda Gail.   II. Price, Lynn
Rollins.   III. Title
JK1671.B48   1989   353.0071'2   88-35746
ISBN 0-13-423328-X

Manufactured in the United States of America

      10   9   8   7   6   5   4   3   2   1

                First Edition

This book is dedicated to the federal government,
without which the following wouldn't have been necessary.

Advisory

The names, characters, places, dialogue, and situations in this book are either the product of the author's imagination or are composites of certain situations and conversations, with names disguised.

The preparation of this book involved an intensive review of government procurement procedures. However, government regulations, procedures, forms, instructions, and guidelines are constantly being revised, and procedures and requirements vary from one government agency to another. Also, due to the extensive cost of duplicating written information, the government often depletes its stocks of old forms and publications before ordering new ones.

Therefore, while I have made every attempt to ensure the validity of the information in this book, the accuracy and completeness of all statements, information, and/or recommendations contained herein are not guaranteed. In all cases you should consult the appropriate contracting officer or a legal or accounting professional.

This book is designed primarily to teach the general guidelines of small business procurement. Remember that each individual procurement is a self-contained contract that must be followed to the letter. Only the contracting officer has any legal authority to provide detailed instructions to you, and even those instructions will change from time to time as new legislation and requirements are adopted. You *must* be flexible. As one contracting officer says, "Dealing in federal procurement requires a tolerance for ambiguity." A good sense of humor doesn't hurt, either.

Contents

Meet the World's Largest Customer

There's a $240-billion market out there with your name on it! When was the last time you considered doing business with the government or with one of its prime contractors? Uncle Sam wants your business—especially if you're a small business.

What you need to know to win that business is what this book is all about. I'll share with you practical tips I've learned after eighteen years of working in federal procurement—from inside, as a procurement officer, and from outside, as a business owner and consultant. Step by step, I'll be your guide on a procurement journey that will teach you how to *use* federal business to reinforce and even promote your commercial business goals.

I'll begin by dispelling the old myths about doing business with the federal government. I'll help you examine what your company can gain—and lose—from federal business. Then I'll show you how to research the many federal markets, uncovering astounding market "secrets" about your competitors and the government. Next, I'll teach you how to target and penetrate the best federal markets for your company. Then, after demystifying federal business procedures and requirements, I'll explain how to prepare a competitive bid and perform successfully to enhance your chances of winning future contracts. Finally, I'll teach you strategies to uncover future trends and opportunities so you can be one step ahead of your competition.

There's more to this book than strategies for winning government contracts. A procurement adage says it best: "Once you learn how to do business with the government, you can do business with anyone." To this end I dedicate this book. May it serve as a guide for any business striving to be the best it can be. Of course, the proof is in the resulting profits. So let's get down to business. You *do* want a piece of that $240-billion pie, don't you?

—Charles R. Bevers

Why You Need This Book

"My father told me not to do business with the government if it was the last customer on earth."

The senator's comment seemed ironic, considering that he was the sponsor of a state conference on "How to Do Business with the Federal Government." It was also ironic that the sponsoring state and city, touted nationwide for their spirit of entrepreneurism, had forfeited 70 percent of their small business federal contracts to other states that year. But irony was what this conference was all about—and what this book is all about. Isn't it ironic that your small business hasn't pursued the biggest market in the nation, or, for that matter, the biggest market in the world? Last fiscal year alone, small businesses received over $200 billion in government contracts. Did you get your share of the pie?

"I've heard it all before," you say?

"Why, I know someone who spent a fortune trying to land a government contract, and lost his own customers in the meantime."

"What could I possibly have that the government wants?"

"I have all the business I can handle now, and I'm too independent to do business with those regulating feds."

If you have used one or more of these excuses for not pursuing your share of the world's largest market, you are not alone. In my eighteen years as an industrial government procurement specialist, I have listened repeatedly to such objections.

After I left active military duty, I became a procurement consultant in the civilian sector almost by accident. I was working as a technical project control administrator when the oil economy bottomed out in the mid-eighties. My state was hit hard. Faced with losing some or most of their business, my friends lamented, "If we just had some government contracts," "If we just knew how to work with government contracting personnel." I had seen it happen before. During the good times we become complacent. We rationalize, "We're doing fine, so why should we expand into other markets?" It's the put-all-your-eggs-in-one-basket syndrome.

I quickly found myself leading my friends in small business through the procurement process, step by step. It was then that I realized how the process I took for granted could be intimidating to small businesses, which are so often preoccupied with the daily challenge of meeting the payroll. I also realized that the prospect of actually winning a contract could be just as frightening as the procurement process.

"Do you think I can really measure up?" asked one business owner when she realized that success on a first contract almost assured her future contracts. Another businessman feared that the process of qualifying for government contracts would surely expose some insurmountable shortcoming.

Both of these small businesses lived through the first contract and went on to win other contracts. But their fears were real—just as real as their ultimate successes.

For most of these small companies, hiring a full-time government procurement specialist was out of the question. The investment in time and money was just too much. These businesspeople also realized that after they landed their first few contracts, they could repeat the process on their own.

It was at this point that I began to consider writing a book. Why couldn't I share my inside information to help small businesses realize that doing business with the federal government can mean the difference between a break-even business and a business operating in the black? I could explode those old fears, those old myths, and then, step by step, lead businesses through the federal procurement maze. Like Dorothy in *The Wizard of Oz*, I had been down the yellow brick road, and I knew that there were rewards at the end of the journey.

Let me show you how to travel down the yellow brick road. I've got a map and it's written in your language. Like any good map, it provides you with a starting point and a destination. In fact, it may reveal more than one destination, for the road to the federal market may lead to other lucrative markets—city, state, even international—for products and services you've never even dreamed of. My *Entrepreneur's Guide* will show you a strategy for getting to your destination the easiest and fastest way possible. My strategy includes specific directions for doing business with the federal government. You will learn what the government is buying, how to develop your own market plan, how to make contact with your customer, how to prepare a bid for a contract, and how to fulfill your contract.

And what about the senator whose father warned him never to do business with the government? He now jokes about it, obviously enjoying the irony. "I ignored my father's admonitions. I did business with the federal government. I learned that there was 'nothing to fear but fear itself.' "

So let's not waste time. There are government contracts out there waiting for you. Let's begin the journey. If you pass *Go,* you may collect much more than two hundred dollars.

—Charles R. Bevers

1

Seven Myths That Paralyze, Seven Steps That Mobilize

You may think this is another one of those quick-and-dirty how-to, ten-steps-to, you-can-do-it-too, dream-your-way-to-overnight-success books on a subject that has been beaten to death.

Wrong! The subject of government procurement has received very little attention. Reviewing the published material, I found that what little has been written is so skeletal or so specialized that it's no wonder a small businessperson like yourself might dismiss the federal market altogether.

This book is for you, the small businessperson, who has worked hard to get where you are today. It is written for someone who is much too intelligent to be seduced by flip success formulas and much too busy to decipher technical mumbo jumbo.

What distinguishes this book is the commonsense, step-by-step approach I recommend for doing business with Uncle Sam. I have helped small businesses win government contracts and helped the government award federal contracts to small businesses. Let me be your guide to a subject that has been muddied by misconceptions and myths since the private sector first agreed to do business with the public sector.

Right now you're probably poised on the outside of the procurement process looking in, with a lot of healthy skepticism and distrust influencing your view. There's no better place to begin than by confronting your fiercest objections to doing business with the federal government. Although I call them the "seven myths that paralyze," I do not dismiss these perceptions. In fact, I will approach this whole procurement business from *your* point of view, that of the doubting Thomas who would like to be proven wrong—especially if it proves profitable.

MYTH #1: "THE GOVERNMENT WON'T BUY MY WIDGET"

Recently I had lunch with a procurement officer at a local military base. Finishing up a particularly good piece of pie, I commented, "Great pumpkin pie."

"Thanks, but actually it's sweet potato pie. We have a contract with a local bakery, and the potatoes are grown locally, too," he explained.

Even after eighteen years as a procurement officer, I am still surprised at the variety and volume of products and services that the federal government purchases. As with the sweet potato pie, I am often amazed by the government's unique appetite and specialized needs.

If I can still be surprised, it is no wonder that so many companies still believe that the government has no use for their products. Of all the reasons for not doing business with the government, this is what I hear most often.

Unfortunately, when people think of government procurement they usually visualize the items available in army surplus stores. It's true, a large portion of what the government buys is for defense. But if you think that canteens and uniforms are representative, think again.

In any given year, the federal government, or one of its 1,200-plus large (prime) contractors, buys most tangible products and services produced in the United States. Have you ever visited a military base or post? A brief tour will uncover a huge number of opportunities. (See appendix 3 for a summary of government procurement activity and appendix 4 for information on prime contracting opportunities.)

Entering the gate, you notice the gate and the guard. Someone had to build the gate; someone had to supply the parts. Someone also provides for the guard: what he eats, what he wears, even who cuts his hair and does his laundry.

Then you pass an army car with its hood up. "No doubt it needs repair," you muse. Who stocks and supplies the repair parts? Driving down the road, you pass barracks surrounded by flowers and trees. Did a nursery supply those perennials? Are those barracks prefabricated, or is everything from the lumber to the paint purchased separately?

Now you pull up to the post exchange and get permission to enter. What do we have here? It's a regular shopping mall, with various specialty stores selling everything from cameras and film to eyeglasses. There's even an ice cream parlor.

Hold on—it's just dawned on you that all of these items could be supplied by small businesses! And this is just the beginning. There's much more here than meets the eye. As you leave the commissary you notice two delivery trucks unloading frozen chickens and bread. Finally, on your way out of the base you drive past a fast-food drive-in and a convenience store.

"This is all fine and good," you say. "But my company doesn't produce a product. I provide a service." Don't fret, the government hasn't forgotten you. In fact, currently the government is expanding its range of contracts with commercial businesses in such diverse areas as security, travel agent services, park management, data entry, space planning, food services, and printing. Because the size of the armed forces is shrinking, many jobs formerly done by servicemen are now subcontracted. Even traditional duties such as kitchen patrol usually are subcontracted.

Remember the military base? Maybe you could have constructed that gate, those barracks. Could you repair them? What about creating or maintaining the landscaping? Even the post security guard may have been a civilian. One franchised doughnut maker I know relocated his shop inside the base. "Soldiers eat an incredible amount of doughnuts," he says.

MYTH #2: "THERE'S NO BUSINESS FOR SMALL BUSINESS"

Okay, so now you're persuaded that the government might buy your widget or your service, but let's face it, you're just a mom-and-pop shop and there's probably not enough government business out there for the little guy to make it worth your while.

On the contrary. Now more than ever, the federal government is turning its eye—and its business—to small business. In fiscal year

1984 the government awarded small businesses $23.8 billion in contracts. At the same time, the government's large-dollar prime contractors awarded another $18 billion in contracts to small business, for a combined total of $41.8 billion. Award amounts are increasing each year. By fiscal year 1986 the combined total had increased to $200 billion.

Decreed by Congress, the "smaller is better" battle cry echoes throughout the ranks of more than two thousand federal agencies. Also, several laws provide all kinds of incentives for all kinds of small businesses, including minority- and women-owned businesses, as well as firms owned by individuals from "economically or socially disadvantaged" groups. (See exhibit 1-1 for a description of small business procurement opportunities.)

━━━━━━━━━━━━━━━━━ **EXHIBIT 1-1** ━━━━━━━━━━━━━━━━━

SMALL BUSINESS PROCUREMENT OPPORTUNITIES

If you make it your business to understand small business procurement laws and opportunities, you'll realize that the government has made provisions, established grants, and set aside procurements for small businesses. Just consider these possibilities:

Contracts for Small Business Classifications

Under the Small Business and Small Business Investments Acts, Congress established the Small Business Administration (SBA) to oversee the small business needs of the nation. In 1978 Congress passed Public Law 95-507 to amend and strengthen the Small Business Act. This law provides contracting opportunities to (1) small businesses, as well as to small businesses that are designated as (2) socially disadvantaged, (3) economically disadvantaged, (4) women-owned, (5) 100 percent minority-owned, (6) located in surplus labor areas, and (7) disadvantaged. These set-asides are also detailed in part 19 of the *Federal Acquisition Regulations* (*FAR*) and may include a "total" or "partial" amount of the solicitation in these areas:

1. *Contracts for small businesses.* Broadly defined, a small business is a concern, including its affiliates, that is independently owned and operated and is not dominant in the field in which it is bidding on government contracts.

Although size criteria vary according to the type of product or service, size generally is measured by number of employees and volume of gross receipts averaged over the past three years. This usually translates to fewer than 500 employees with average sales of under $3.5 million.

To learn if you qualify, contact the SBA's *small business specialist* and give him or her your Standard Industrial Code (SIC). In turn, the specialist can tell you about the small business qualifications that pertain to your type of business.

2. *Contracts for small socially disadvantaged businesses.* The government has special set-asides for small businesses designated as socially disadvantaged. A small socially disadvantaged business is a small business that is 51 percent owned and managed by one or more individuals who have been subject to racial or ethnic prejudice or cultural bias because of their identities as members of a group without regard to their qualities as individuals.

3. *Contracts for small economically disadvantaged businesses.* Partial or total set-asides also include small businesses that are economically disadvantaged. Economically disadvantaged businesses are 51 percent owned and managed by socially disadvantaged individuals whose ability to compete in the free enterprise system is impaired due to diminished opportunities to obtain capital and credit, compared to others in the same line of business.

4. *Contracts for small women-owned businesses.* To qualify for this designation, you must be a small business that is at least 51 percent owned, controlled, and operated by a female U.S. citizen.

5. *Subcontracts for small 100 percent minority-owned businesses.* These contract set-asides are available for small businesses that are 100 percent owned and operated by individuals who can certify that they are members of named groups (black Americans, Hispanic Americans, native Americans, Asian-Pacific

Americans, Asian-Indian Americans) that are socially and economically disadvantaged.

6. *Contracts for small businesses in surplus labor areas.* There are special set-asides for small businesses located in geographical areas that have high unemployment as defined by the U.S. Department of Labor.

7. *Contracts for small disadvantaged businesses.* If your small business is both socially and economically disadvantaged *and* at least 51 percent owned and operated by a minority group, you may qualify for yet another set-aside designation, called *8A.* If this sounds like a small niche, consider that in fiscal 1986, $7 billion in procurement went to this group alone.

More Small Business Opportunities

In addition to the special contract opportunities listed above, the government has provided:

1. *Incentives for primes.* Public Law 95-507 establishes special contract clauses to encourage prime contractors to increase the number of subcontracts to small *and* minority businesses. For example, most Department of Defense contracts of more than $10,000 have a subcontract clause pertaining to small businesses, and still larger contracts require written plans for subcontracting to small businesses. (See appendix 4, on prime subcontracting procedures.)

2. *Competition in contracting.* In 1984 Public Law 98-369 provided for "competition in contracting," thus creating a position for a "Competition Advocate" in Washington, D.C., with representation in every buying agency. The advocate's role is to challenge barriers to competition and to promote full and open competition in the acquisition of supplies and services by the federal government.

3. *Grants for research.* In 1982 the Small Business Innovation Research Law (SBIR) set goals for awarding research and development grants to small businesses (Public Law 97-219). These grants are used to develop technology that meets federal research and development objectives. (See appendix 5, on SBIR procedures.)

4. *Embassy construction contracts for small businesses and small minority-owned businesses.* The 1986 Omnibus Diplomatic Security and Anti-terrorism Act (Public Law 99-661) established a 10 percent goal for American minority contractors for embassy design and construction. The law also established an additional 10 percent goal for American small business contractors for diplomatic construction projects.

5. *Procurement data.* Responding to Public Law 93-400, a system was established for collecting, developing, and disseminating procurement data. The Federal Procurement Data System began data collection in fiscal year 1979, one year after the law passed. The Federal Procurement Data System's standard report is used to analyze the impact of congressional and presidential initiatives in socioeconomic areas such as small business. A copy of this report is available upon request. (See bibliography: *Federal Procurement Data System, Standard Report.*)

If you think these incentives don't work or don't include you, consider these percentages: In 1986 the federal government spent approximately 45 percent of its procurement budget with small business. Additionally, the government's large-dollar prime contractors awarded 40 percent of their federal contract monies to small businesses. And if you think that all government contracting actions are multimillion-dollar deals rather than small transactions, prepare for another surprise: *Approximately 98 percent of all government contracts are for $25,000 or less.*

Elena Jimenez recently benefited from several of these government incentives. As the woman owner of a small accounting firm with fifty employees (including her husband), she qualified for the small business category (Federal Law 95-507). As a Hispanic owner she is classified as both a "minority" and an "economically and socially disadvantaged" business (Federal Law 99-661).

"I could have set up my business with my husband as an equal partner, but I didn't," Jimenez says. "Establishing myself as the majority owner and manager was no accident. I planned to go after government contracts in high-speed data entry, and a woman-owned, disadvantaged small business is the fast track."

Jimenez also hires and trains minority employees. This way she qualifies for federal tax breaks and salary subsidies.

If Jimenez had been the owner of a high-tech company, she might even have qualified for incentives under a third law (97-219). Passed in 1982, this law requires that all federal agencies with research budgets over $100 million must reserve approximately 1.5 percent of their research budget for the Small Business Innovation Research program (SBIR). The law encourages the government to use small businesses to meet federal research needs for technological innovations. Under this law the federal government grants hundreds of millions of dollars to small business for research and development projects. (See appendix 5 for SBIR opportunities and procedures.)

MYTH #3: "I CAN'T COMPETE AGAINST BIG BUSINESS"

Set-asides and incentives ensure that you don't have to compete against big businesses. Even if you decide to compete against large businesses, the odds favor you. Statistics show that a small company can beat a large company's price on an identical product by at least 40 to 50 percent, because of lower labor and overhead costs.

No matter whom you decide to compete against, when the size of the contract increases, the amount and complexity of the competition increase. Do you realize that the government can make purchases of goods and services for less than $1,000 by obtaining no more than one verbal quote? And for purchases between $1,000 and $25,000, the government need obtain only three verbal or written quotes. With a few exceptions, contracts over $25,000 must be advertised in a Department of Commerce tabloid called the *Commerce Business Daily* (CBD). (See exhibit 1-2 for a sampling of CBD ads.)

While Jimenez set out to win federal contracts even before she set up her accounting business, many other small businesses approach bidding from the back door, even using the government to open new commercial markets. Tom Burris, the president of a small company specializing in optical data scanning, had more than one reason for not doing business with the government. Says Burris, "I had this idea for building an enhanced document scanner, but I didn't have the time or money to develop the prototype. I wasn't

======== **EXHIBIT 1-2** ========

Samples of CBD Ads

WE WANT YOU!

"Want ads for small business products and services" is one way to describe the contents of the daily tabloid publication called the *Commerce Business Daily* (CBD). (See bibliography for ordering information.) Just what kinds of products are solicited in the CBD on any given day? Let's take a look at a few:

SERVICES

- Tree trimming and thinning for local flood control on government land
- Tree planting on federal highways
- Checking farmland to ensure it is not planted in crops that the government is paying farmers not to grow
- Operating base laundry and dry cleaning services
- Picking up garbage and trash at federal buildings
- Mowing and flower bed cleanup and maintenance
- Shelf stocking at commissaries and post exchanges
- Underwater diving for quality assurance in construction projects
- Word processing
- Developing curricula for all kinds of training
- Weather observing for Washington state coastline

PRODUCTS

- Foodstuffs: dehydrated potatoes, paprika, wheat flour, margarine, cake mix, cherry pie filling
- Clothing: hats, shoes, items from head to toe
- Office supplies: furniture, textbooks, mail room supplies
- Miscellaneous: conveyer check-out counters, paintbrushes, paint, plastic trash bags, food serving trays, safety eyeglasses, key chains, steam cookers, can openers

afraid of competing with the big boys, but I figured they could develop the technology and market it faster than I could.

"Enter the Small Business Innovation Research program. Through my local small business assistance program I heard about these small business grants to solve technical problems. The SBIR solicitation brochure indicated that the government needed tons of printed documents converted to digital data, so I applied for an SBIR grant, got it, and used the money to define a prototype document scanner."

Financed by the SBIR grant, Burris quickly got his idea off the drawing board and developed a prototype to market both to the government and commercially.

Burris realizes now that his fear of big business finishing first was groundless. In fact, small technical businesses often make better and faster use of available technology than big businesses and can also adapt more quickly to changing markets. Big business bureaucracies can bog down during the development of technology. They support large overheads, are too busy defending their market shares, and have cumbersome layers of management. The government SBIR program is capitalizing on this discovery.

By concentrating on specific areas of expertise, small businesses find that they can compete for an increased share of the procurement pie. John Menke, an auto parts store owner, says, "I learned a lesson from the full-service filling stations of bygone years. When they broke up, they were replaced by a multitude of specialty shops, such as parts supply, auto tune-up, quick lube, and muffler shops. Like the filling stations, I realized I couldn't do everything, so I concentrated on my most profitable area—supplying auto parts. Now I supply parts for local repair shops *and* for the government."

Contracts Go Begging

A classic example of opportunity knocking, John Menke's situation also illustrates what a midwestern base commander calls "contracts that go begging." One day the commander, who was contracting with a California firm to obtain military auto parts, wondered, "Why couldn't a local company provide the same service?" The commander went shopping. He found Jim Youell's shop less than five miles away from the base, so he encouraged Youell to consider government contracting. Since Youell already stocked most of the parts the base needed, all he needed was another panel truck to handle the additional deliveries. Now the commander enjoys quick response from a local supplier, and Youell enjoys the extra profits from doing business with the government.

MYTH #4: "I'LL NEVER RECOVER MY INVESTMENT"

You've already learned that there are few fast tracks to fortune. The same lesson applies in doing business with the federal government. It takes time and effort to build a good business relationship.

"I lost the first contract I bid on," says John Wooley, who repairs roofs for government facilities. "I barely broke even on the second contract because I had to buy extra equipment and train new personnel. But that third contract made up for everything. Besides, who can beat payment in thirty days?"

Payment in thirty days! Not only is it the government's policy to pay within thirty days of acceptance of a qualified billing invoice, but if it fails to pay within forty-five days, it must pay interest on the unpaid balance.

Admittedly, you should approach the government market with all the business acumen you bring to any new market, together with a special knowledge of the idiosyncrasies of the federal market. I tell most businesspeople that the best approach is conservative, based on six months of market research. *I also advise them never to expect government business to save a failing business or provide windfall profits.*

Ideally, *you should go into business with the government to supplement or expand an existing production base or balance production cycles.*

The auto parts store owner, for instance, already had most of the parts the base needed. All he lacked was an extra delivery truck and a driver. Sure, he invested more money, but the truck and driver allowed him to serve several more garages and repair shops in neighboring towns.

Similarly, the roofing contractor knew that his investment in equipment and employee training would pay off immediately by providing larger in-town and out-of-town commercial jobs. What he didn't predict was landing out-of-town commercial jobs while working on out-of-town government jobs. While eating breakfast at a small-town café, he contracted for three other roofing jobs on buildings in the same block.

Four small specialized companies were frustrated because the government's solicitation actions were so inclusive, requiring not only a product but also installation, development of instructors' courses, development of operating specifications, and long-term maintenance. None of the fledgling companies could supply all these facets. Then an enterprising owner suggested a joint venture.

"The joint venture bid required us to submit an explicit statement of work [SOW] detailing which company was responsible for what," explains owner Mark Townsend. "We also decided the company that qualified as 'small and disadvantaged' would be the lead bidder, and the rest of us would be subcontractors." By consolidating the four small businesses into one common office area, the companies could show their customers the full range of their joint capabilities and simultaneously save costly overhead. Their first contract proved the coalition could work together for everyone's financial gain—without anyone's having to expand.

Expanding a service or inventory to include both commercial and government customers (as did the parts store and roofing contractor) and organizing a joint venture (the technology companies) are two innovative ways of recovering the investment often required to compete for government contracts.

MYTH #5: "THE BUREAUCRACY WILL BURY ME"

Perhaps small business's biggest complaint is the complex nature of the federal procurement system. Let's face it, 4,000 federal acquisition regulations plus more than 2,000 federal buying offices and 1,200 prime contractors' buying offices can add up to an infinite amount of "how tos" and "wherefores." (See appendix 7 for a summary of the *Federal Acquisition Regulations'* major topics.) Since each government agency buys independently, and each contracting officer has a different personality, *there is no single path leading to the federal marketplace.*

Nonetheless, the complexity and immensity of the system can work to your advantage. For instance, each government purchasing agency and prime contractor has its own "bidders' list" of qualified contractors and suppliers. This means, for example, that even if your competitor wins a contract from his local air force base down the road, he will not necessarily win another contract from the U.S. Postal Service across the street. Typically, a business competes until it becomes comfortable—or complacent—allowing new opportunities to slide. If you register on multiple bidders' lists *and* keep following up on your leads, your tenacity will be rewarded.

"I tried selling to our local army post," says a manufacturer of small stranded steel cables, "but the contracting officer told me I should be manufacturing 'wire rope.' He suggested I contact the Defense General Supply Center in Richmond, Virginia. When I did, the official told me they bought lots of wire rope. I knew 'wire rope' was just another name for stranded steel cables. By changing the name of my product, I discovered an opportunity to sell not only wire rope but also the corresponding assemblies, like clamps and pulleys."

Businesspeople are often overwhelmed by bureaucracy, government regulations, and procedures. But actually, these government regulations and procedures can empower you. As you have already seen, the laws provide opportunities, set-asides, and incentives where they wouldn't ordinarily exist. In addition, procurement regulations ensure free and open competition. This means that if your bid is the most competitive—based on responsiveness, responsibility, and price—it must be accepted.

Another complaint I've heard is that it is too difficult to meet the demanding federal standards for employee skills or product and service specifications. Keep in mind that often such products go all over the world and are used under the most challenging conditions. Sometimes human lives depend on the government's quality standards.

Surprisingly, many companies discover that while becoming certified for government work may seem arduous, there are often unforeseen benefits. Says one contractor who owns a small-town welding company, "To qualify for some government contracts I decided to stretch my budget and invest in state-of-the-art welding equipment and specialized personnel training. When the local oil business went bust, I had my government contract work to fall back on. And when out-of-state commercial customers found out I was certified for government work, I was usually hired on the spot."

MYTH #6: "THEY'LL TAKE OVER MY BUSINESS"

Many people still suspect that doing business with the federal government means that the government will try to run their business.

"I've always cherished my independence and the free enterprise system. I thought the government would bury me," states machine shop owner Bill Dawson. "So the day my partner approached me about competing for a government contract, frankly, I was worried.

"But when we had the opportunity to discuss what was involved with a government 'small business specialist' [SBS] we couldn't resist the opportunity." Dawson discovered that the SBS works for the Small Business Administration (SBA) and is available to meet with small companies to review the government procurement system. (See exhibit 1-3 for a summary of other SBA services.) Says Dawson, "After a long discussion with the SBS about the ins and outs of government contracting, we realized our main concern was whether our product and manufacturing procedures could meet government qualification standards. So we invited a government quality assurance representative [QAR, or Q] to preview our manufacturing process. He gave us a set of survey forms that showed us what the government inspectors would look for—*if* any came!"

==================== **EXHIBIT 1-3** ====================

Small Business Administration

HOW CAN IT HELP YOU? JUST COUNT THE WAYS . . .

Charged under the law to ensure that a fair portion of the government's procurement funds go to small and minority businesses, the Small Business Administration (SBA) provides management consulting and financial assistance to small businesses—at no charge. This assistance includes

1. Financial assistance and leads by:
    - Providing development funds
    - Helping to obtain surety bonds
    - Helping to secure lines of credit
    - Obtaining disaster assistance
    - Funding minority small business investment companies that invest in start-up and expansion
    - Providing a conduit for 8A funding by guaranteeing small disadvantaged business set-aside contracts
2. Training and management counseling for business development through:

- College-level Small Business Institutes (SBI). Located at approximately five hundred college campuses, SBIs provide management counseling through the services of senior and graduate students of business administration. Counseling is provided at the business site and is monitored by faculty advisors.
- Small Business Development Centers (SBDC). Based at universities throughout the country, SBDCs provide free managerial, technical, and other specialized help to small businesses.
- Small Business Administration management courses. These courses are jointly sponsored by the SBA, educational institutions, chambers of commerce, and trade organizations to teach planning, organization, and control of a business, in contrast to administration of daily activities.
- International trade conferences.
- Management, marketing, and technical publications (see bibliography).
- Small Business Innovation Research Assistance (SBIR) guidelines (see appendix 5 for a detailed discussion of SBIR).
- Service Corps of Retired Executives (SCORE) and the Active Corps of Executives (ACE), which provide free counseling and assistance to small businesses in a variety of areas, from administration of daily activities to long-range management techniques.

3. Certification (by Certificate of Competency) of small and small disadvantaged businesses to guarantee contract performance (see chapter 7).

4. Management of the Procurement Automated Source System (PASS), a computerized referral system of the names and capabilities of small businesses desiring federal contracts, used by federal agencies and prime contractors to locate potential small businesses when the bidders' lists are inadequate (see chapter 5 for an explanation of PASS).

5. Overseeing government agency compliance with Congress's provisions for small businesses, including the use of "advocates" who monitor contract awards for potential set-asides.

Dawson learned that more elaborate contracts require compliance with more complex administrative procedures and regulations, but contracts for less than $25,000 require only "simplified procedures," which are similar to "normal" business practices.

Says Dawson, "Our company's product easily met the government's qualifications. We won our contract, manufactured the product, and shipped it without the government even coming to the plant!"

For contracts requiring more complex specifications, a company will need to develop a quality assurance (QA) manual. The QA manual is a structured, comprehensive set of quality control procedures and policies. But most companies eventually praise the benefits of creating such a manual. Says Rowena Mills, a laminated Plexiglas manufacturer, "When we began to follow the procedures in our new QA manual, we reduced production costs by cutting down on rejects and rework. We now have a quality circle of checks and balances to improve product reliability." It didn't take long for her existing customers to realize the improvement, and her commercial business expanded by 25 percent within two years.

"In addition," Mills says, "we attached a summary of our new QA manual to a four-color sales brochure with photos depicting the full range of our production capability. We used the entire package as a marketing tool for attracting government and commercial business contracts."

Both Dawson and Mills realized that an efficient production department that maintains a schedule and good quality control should have no problems if a government industrial specialist (IS) arrives to review its manufacturing methods and facilities. Recalls Mills, "The specialist was only interested in our ability to produce a quality product in a timely manner. He wanted to know if we had adequate equipment, if we had all our materials on hand, and if we had a firm written quote from the vendor supplying the materials. He also made sure that we had adequate, skilled manpower and the ability to pack and crate the order. His concerns were reasonable."

MYTH #7: "THERE ARE TOO MANY HIDDEN RISKS"

"Doing business with the government is risky, but no more risky than going into business in the first place!" Susan Rupp paused a moment, and added, "And certainly no more risky than specializing in commercial printing jobs in a failing local economy."

Gene Case, Susan's former competitor, had learned that the hard way. A couple of years ago Gene decided to stick with a sure thing and continue concentrating on local printing and reproduction services in what he thought was a "thriving" economy, while Susan—who took my advice—expanded her customer base by bidding on solicitations from a variety of government agencies. When the local economy declined and competition increased, Gene lost most of his commercial orders and desperately sought government business. But he was two years behind in the bidding process. Meanwhile, Susan had expanded her business.

As a small businessperson, you no doubt have heard many of the same warnings as Susan and Gene about going into business with the government. If you think back, you probably can remember hearing many of them about going into business in the first place: "Competition is just too tough." "It's too hard to get a loan." "No one wants to do business with a small business anymore." You remember all the warnings, don't you?

Risky business, business is. After all, of the seven hundred thousand business start-ups in 1984, over 80 percent had failed by the end of 1987.

But knowing the risks did not stop you from going into business, did it? Nor has it decreased the number of business start-ups nationwide. Within the last ten years, new business start-ups have more than doubled, and the majority of new jobs have been provided by small business.

Now you're hearing many of those same warnings against going into business with the world's biggest customer—the federal government. Yes, there are true stories of businesses that received government contracts, defaulted, and lost money. There is always a risk when any seller fails to furnish a quality product or service on time and according to specifications. In such a situation, the government can not only terminate the contract but also "buy against it" by going to another contractor and charging the original contractor the difference between the original bid and the new bid.

Also, there are true cases of companies bidding for and receiving contracts, only to have the government "terminate" their contracts "for the convenience of the government" (TFC). Translated, this means that the government has determined that it does not need the product or service it contracted for and will pay the company's expenses to date, plus a reasonable profit.

I remember one rag manufacturer that got a one-year contract to supply an air force base with a large quantity of shop rags. After the first delivery, the contracting officer terminated the remainder of the contract. Why? The contract had not specified the composition of the rags. When the air force base realized that it had purchased nonabsorbent nylon rags to clean up oil spills, it had no choice but to cancel the remainder of the contract. Although this case is exceptional, you need to be aware that most contracts have provisions for termination. In the case of the rag manufacturer, the government compensated the owner for his costs plus a reasonable profit.

For one company owner, "reducing risk" on his first contract bid meant padding the figures to buffer potential losses from volatile material costs. "I padded my first bid knowing full well I probably would not win the contract," admits the contractor. He continues, "I lost the first contract, but the next time I bid more responsibly. When I understood what the risks were, I won the second contract."

How did he learn what the risks were? "I attended a federal procurement seminar and discovered that the government publishes volumes of information that make it possible to understand and capture the varied procurement markets. I was able to learn everything I needed to know about past and future procurement activity. What would be considered privileged information in the private sector is published information in the public sector," he says.

He adds, "I also discovered that the local Small Business Administration office could help me with financing and management counseling. All the help I needed was right at my fingertips!"

SEVEN STEPS THAT MOBILIZE

Does one or more of these myths sound familiar? I thought so. More important, are you beginning to see another side of the story? I hope so.

Now that you've begun to understand the seven myths that can paralyze your desire to do business with the federal government, let's take a look at the seven steps that can mobilize your desire. These seven steps add up to a commonsense strategy for doing business with the federal government.

Step #1: Analyze Your Markets (Chapters 2, 4, and 5)

Before you can decide whether you want to do business with the government, you need to determine whether there is a federal market for your product or service. The first step will guide you through the process of analyzing your company to determine whether you should enter the federal market. I'll show you how several companies redefined their products and services to land government contracts. You'll also learn how to find out precisely what, where, and how much the government is buying. I'll help you translate government codes and acronyms (see appendix 2: Government Acronyms and Abbreviations Glossary) to reveal valuable past and future procurement information, including who won previous bids, what the government paid, what the requirements were, what the buying forecasts will be for the next two years—the past, present, and future "insiders' information" you must know to win government contracts.

Step #2: Determine Whether You Want to Bid (Chapter 3)

Now that you realize there's a government market for your product, are you ready to do business with the government?

Hold on! The second step in my seven-part strategy helps you analyze why you should—or shouldn't—do business with Uncle Sam. First you need to know whether doing business with the federal government will be profitable—in both the short term and the long run.

Discover those hidden costs of doing business with the government. Learn how to determine whether the federal market can complement or promote your company's major goals, such as quality improvement, product development, cost reduction, and better project management.

Step #3: Get on "The Lists" (Chapters 4 and 5)

When you've determined that government business is for you, you need to learn the easiest ways to penetrate the procurement bureaucracy to get—and stay—on the government's "bidders' lists" of qualified contractors. I'll show you how to uncover profitable markets your competitors may have overlooked. In the process, I will teach you the protocol for contacting government procurement officials and the secrets of building a good relationship with them.

Step #4: Capture Your Market (Chapters 6 and 7)

Once you've made contact and established yourself on bidders' lists, the government should be knocking on your door, right? Don't bet on it. This is where the real test begins. So how do you get the edge on the competition? Obviously, what might work for capturing a commercial market will not work for the federal market. You can't take out a full-page ad in the *Wall Street Journal* to solicit government business. Step #4 will help you adapt your current market plan to include—and capture—government business, from establishing your reputation *before* you get on the bidders' list to preparing for a preaward survey.

Step #5: Conquer the Contract (Chapter 8)

You'll remember the day your first solicitation arrives almost as well as you remember the day you sign your first contract. Most people describe their response as a moment of elation followed by an eternity of panic. In chapter 8 and appendix 11, you'll discover the effective way to read, understand, and respond to a solicitation and contract form before it arrives in the mail.

Step #6: Fulfill the Contract (Chapter 9)

Just because you win and understand your contract doesn't mean you can perform it successfully. Since you may get only one chance to prove yourself to the government, you won't want to blow it. I'll teach you how to administer your contract, interact effectively with government contract officials, keep on schedule, maintain quality control, and handle contract disputes.

Step #7: Preparing for the Future (Chapter 10)

Now that you've successfully completed your first contract, are you ready for another? I'll teach you strategies for identifying future procurement opportunities and creating your own opportunities so that you can keep one step ahead of your competition.

*   *   *

So now let's begin our journey. With a seven-step strategy mapping the way to procurement, you already have a head start.

If you're still skeptical, read on. You're going to meet your old skeptical self in the pages of this book. And you're going to meet— and learn to understand—the government. Give yourself a chance to get to know the biggest customer on earth. Uncle Sam has deep pockets. And he wants to get to know you.

Let's start by taking a look at some companies, just like yours, that took that first step—and never looked back.

Note: Samples of standard government procurement forms and government acronyms and abbreviations are included in appendix 1 and 2 at the back of the book. The reader is advised to refer to these appendices as required.

2

Analyzing Your Product, Company, and Markets

Before you weigh the economic pros and cons of doing business with the government, before you even start to explore the myriad federal markets, take another close look at your company. Do you really know your own business? You may be in a business that you are not aware of.

It's true. Many companies have not clearly defined their product or service. When they take a second look at their production facilities, their labor skills, their market area, and even their products and services, often the results prove profitable—not only in procuring federal contracts, but also in capturing commercial markets.

In this chapter we will take a look at companies that took a second look at themselves to discover that they had more to offer than they had ever dreamed. By redefining their businesses, they gained market share—and in some cases took on new markets—to become successful in both government and commercial arenas.

ANALYZE YOUR PRODUCT

"It Dices, Chops, and Minces."

When I think of product analysis, I am reminded of the TV ads for those amazing kitchen gadgets, small enough to fit in one hand, that in sixty seconds diced, minced, and chopped everything from eggs to whole, undressed fish. Only after you ordered this gadget did you realize that there was little distinction between dicing, chopping, and mincing. But you didn't care. The gadget was handy, and you were always finding new uses for it.

Like the company that discovered its gadget could chop and could also dice and mince, some of the most successful businesses I've ever worked with have learned to take a second look at their product or service. Consider the company that *thought* it manufactured heat exchangers for the petrochemical industry. One day, a welding supply salesman visited the plant. As he was leaving, he turned to the manager and asked, "Could you produce steel work stands?" The salesman explained that he had just visited a prime contractor in the aerospace industry who wanted to subcontract the manufacturing of customized steel work stands for assembling and storing jet engines.

At first the plant manager was skeptical, but the next day he called the prime contractor's small business representative. The representative confirmed the need and helped the company set up its welding certification test and get on the bidders' list. The plant manager assembled the company's quality procedures and sales brochure, contacted the prime buyer, and provided him with documented qualifications and a bid estimate. The prime contractor subsequently awarded the manufacturer a contract to produce work stands. Later, the manufacturer won contracts to manufacture assembly work tables.

Another small business *thought* it made offshore drilling platform monitoring systems. When it redefined its job as "designing and installing critical data monitoring systems," it landed local and federal government contracts: two with the public schools and local city government for heating and cooling system controls, and another contract with the U.S. Navy for a fuel distribution monitoring system.

ANALYZE YOUR PRODUCTION FACILITY

"For Lease: Manufacturing Plant. Inquire Within."

If you work in government procurement long enough, you get a firsthand look at what was once referred to respectfully as "Yankee ingenuity." One of the most inspiring examples of such ingenuity was dramatized by a machine shop that refused to die—even when advancing technology, competition, and economic vicissitudes threatened it through the years.

Precision Manufacturing began as a modest, all-purpose machine shop that prided itself on producing excellent work in a timely manner at an economical price. Perhaps its greatest source of pride was its production facility. The conservative owners had bought and paid for their buildings and equipment, and kept them well maintained. Over the years their work had focused on the strict machining of electromechanical devices. Then, in a bold expansion, the shop launched into the specialized market of repairing electro-mechanical devices. Accordingly, the owners purchased electrical test benches with such equipment as oscilloscopes, amp meters, and logic analyzers. Ever adapting to changing markets, the company soon realized that with a modest investment in new equipment, it could easily repair hydraulic components.

During this time, Precision Manufacturing did government contract work. As you may guess, however, the company did not limit itself to government work. It still concentrated on the production and repair of basic units—a market that would not interfere with its government business.

If the story of Precision Manufacturing sounds a bit too easy, hang on. This "free enterprise" fairy tale has a strange twist. As ingenious as Precision Manufacturing was in adapting to competition and changing markets, the company eventually fell prey to smaller, cost-cutting specialty shops that gradually won its market share. There came a time when Precision Manufacturing's owners looked around for a new market—and found nothing. Even selling out was not an option, because of the soft manufacturing market.

In this time of adversity, the mother of invention came to the fore. One owner reasoned that since the shop's facility was its greatest—if only—asset, why couldn't the company lease this asset to fledgling businesses developing new technologies, in exchange for a small interest in these companies? Precision Manufacturing could be a development cradle for entrepreneurial companies that had big ideas but little capital and required basic machining, electrical, and hydraulic capabilities.

Precision Manufacturing shared its idea with the government's local small business development center. Word of mouth—and the government's interest in new technology—did the rest.

"We were amazed at the response," says co-owner Steve Gillon. "Our first joint venture was with a small company that repaired airplane anticollision lights and stereo earphones. Our next venture was repairing anti-icing panels on commercial aircraft. And our third was developing a down-hole method of dissolving the paraffin on low-pressure oil wells."

One of the most versatile—and overlooked—areas of manufacturing is producing metal brackets for the government. Metal brackets are like "invisible" springs: They are used everywhere, but no one thinks about them until they break. Imagine the possibilities. Brackets are used in airplanes, ships, tanks—on everything that connects with anything. One contracting officer who is constantly hustling to find bracket suppliers refers to brackets as "the missing link between high-tech components and the basic structure."

Attending a small business seminar at a repair and overhaul facility, I was amazed to learn that approximately half of the government's "hard-to-get" items were brackets. Even when the government provided drawings and technical orders for finish treating and painting, as well as sample brackets, it was still difficult to locate small businesses that could manufacture a quality item in a timely manner.

Says one metal fabrication company owner, "I discovered I could manufacture brackets as an overload item during slow cycles in my commercial business. Although most of our orders are for limited quantities, there are enough large orders to make it worth my while." Another manufacturer said that he employs retired personnel part-time to produce small orders.

ANALYZE YOUR LABOR SKILLS

"Brain Over Brawn"

We all know someone who was put out to pasture before he or she was ready to eat grass. "The company called it an early retirement, but it was really a forced retirement," says Jim Kowalski, a Detroit concrete worker whose company "urged" him to retire after thirty years. "My body may have been the worse for wear, but I still had my mind. It was a matter of brain over brawn," he quips.

Kowalski could have settled for early retirement, but he didn't.

He set his mind on starting his own business. He realized that every government construction project requires concrete testing to ensure strength and durability. He also knew that despite the contract requirement, getting the workers to actually do the concrete testing is difficult, because there is never enough time or interest: The next truck is always backing up to unload, since everyone is paid by the volume poured. Consequently, testing suffers.

With no capital investment, Kowalski began a concrete testing service that was an extension of Michigan's commercial laboratories. During initial pours, he visited construction sites and took random samples of the concrete.

Because Kowalski had worked in the concrete business all his life, he already knew the truck dispatchers, who told him which government and commercial jobs were active and when the initial pours were scheduled. He also knew the state and city inspection officers, the current city and county contractors, and the tests required.

Contractors soon realized that when Kowalski did the test it would be done correctly and economically. The government labs got the tests in a timely manner, and Michigan's state commercial lab got the business that could have gone somewhere else. "It was so obvious," he says. "I just couldn't believe no one had thought of it before."

One could learn a lot from Kowalski, and from the company that let him go. Don't just analyze your labor force in terms of numbers and age; scrutinize your employees' individual skills. Are there specialized skills that have gone unnoticed—skills that could be tapped for government business, perhaps?

An architectural firm I worked with discovered untapped skills when it was threatened with being put out to pasture by its competitors. Competition in Los Angeles was keen, and it seemed that the same "high-profile" firms were getting all the new jobs. The partners realized they needed something special to market—something other than fickle popularity.

"We were using our computer-aided design drafting [CADD] system to draw plans for buildings," owner Ernest Moody says, "when a customer approached us about redoing plans for a major remodeling project. My first response was 'But we only draw plans for *new* buildings,' but on further examination, I realized there was a lot of money at stake. We took the job of updating the existing drawings, and it opened up an entire new specialty for our firm."

The architects at Moody's firm were soon sold on their new business and on the new application for their CADD system and skills—so much so, in fact, that they called me in to investigate the federal market. What I discovered has changed the scope of their business, and it could change the scope of yours: The government can no longer afford to ignore America's crumbling infrastructure, yet it can't afford to replace old structures with new ones. It must look to new technologies, products, and labor skills to repair old, rotting infrastructures.

It will take an estimated $3.3 trillion over the next twenty years to repair our deteriorating highways, railroads, airports, bridges, and educational facilities, to name a few. (See exhibit 2-1, "America Crumbles," and appendix 6 on contracting procedures for construction and architecture-engineering services.) What resulted for the architectural firm were some government contracts for the redesign of older buildings utilizing their CADD system.

===================== **EXHIBIT 2-1** =====================

AMERICA CRUMBLES

CAN SMALL BUSINESSES PATCH TOGETHER THE PIECES?

One of the biggest opportunities for small businesses in government procurement is the repair and rebuilding of America's crumbling infrastructure. A recent study conducted by the Associated General Contractors revealed that infrastructure improvements would cost $3.3 trillion over the next few years, including everything from new construction to highway and building repairs. All this comes at a time when the government is pushing for "privatization" of their programs. This translates to contracting out more and more work.

Even considering the federal budget-cutting trend, the Public Works Committee claims that we can't afford *not* to spend money for improvements *now*. According to committee members, the yellow light is flashing, and if we don't spend the money now we will face much larger costs later.

What are the priorities? In a qualitative report card released by the National Council on Public Works Improvement, the handling of hazardous wastes was given the highest priority. Other priorities include repair and construction of roads and bridges, mass transit systems, waste water treatment plants, and solid waste facilities.

Since our crumbling infrastructure spreads from coast to coast and border to border, there's bound to be some work in your market area—probably even in your backyard. This means a tremendous amount of subcontracting for local labor, materials, and support services, even if large contractors receive the prime contracts. Businesses that provide services and products in such areas as janitorial work, customized remodeling, floor space planning, furniture rental, window washing, roof patching—and yes, even managerial or consultant services—should all take a careful look at their local government agencies and contact them to become listed as a qualified source of products or services. (See appendix 6 on how to compete for construction and architecture-engineering contracts.) Start planning now!

One of the best authorities on infrastructure needs is the National Council on Public Works Improvement, established under Public Law 98-501 in October 1984. Small businesses might want to review the council's first report, *The Nation's Public Works—Defining the Issues* (see bibliography), as well as studies on infrastructure categorical needs released in May 1987.

ANALYZE YOUR MARKET AREA

"Don't Fence Me In."

After analyzing your product, your production facilities, your equipment, and your labor, you may want to take another look at your local market. Maybe there are some needs that you—with your newfound knowledge about your company—can meet.

One of the factors to consider is the location of your competition. If your government market is local and your competition is out of state (or only out of town), chances are you have a competitive advantage. Many business set-asides specify a mileage restriction. For example, most contract proposals to convert archived architectural drawings to computer files with CADD systems are restricted to small businesses located within one hundred miles of the drawing files.

A small business development center recently inquired if I knew of a local business that could provide a bar-code labeling service to label packages for shipping, since the local government contracting volume had increased enough to support a bar-code supplier. During my prospecting, I located a small computer consulting firm that was interested in adding bar coding to its business. When it realized that there was no local bar-code labeling service, and that government business was just the tip of the iceberg, it added new staff and formed a new subsidiary to develop the business.

Another company, an electric utility firm, combined its production methods with a unique waste product to challenge a competitor located halfway across the world, tapping both commercial *and* government markets. For years, electric utility companies have converted energy to electricity, only to exhaust 50 percent of that energy into the atmosphere in the form of steam. Incredibly, half of all the energy they consume is discharged as a waste product! During a natural gas shortage, the electric company decided to use this "waste" steam to take advantage of government incentives. The company realized that retailers bought flowers from overseas, and fruits and vegetables from the West Coast and Mexico. So the utility company built greenhouses, and heated them with steam "waste" heat normally exhausted through the cooling towers. It was a simple system: The company ran a closed-loop hot water system underground, then cooled it through heat exchangers in the greenhouses. When I visited the complex, the greenhouses were selling everything they could grow.

Another area that the Department of Commerce and the Department of Energy explored during the government energy conversion program was the growing and harvesting of catfish in the southern United States. They discovered that hot water could be diverted from cooling towers to fish ponds where catfish are harvested for local consumption. Formerly, catfish were being imported from Brazil where the water is always warm.

One of the biggest complaints of government contracting personnel and of small business development personnel is that they have
problems locating local people who are willing to learn to do business with the government.

"I can't tell you the number of times I've gone out knocking on
doors," confides one SBA business development official, "and even
then, small businesses turn me down. It just leaves that much more
business on the table for aggressive companies that are willing to do
business with the government."

You certainly don't have to limit yourself to local business. Perhaps the most striking example I have seen of "business knows no
borders" occurred when I was inspecting weighing scales during
the installation of a federal-highway truck-weighing station near
the border between North Dakota and Canada. One day all the
project's subcontractors got together for coffee at the local café. I
discovered that the electric lineman was from south Texas, the scale
installer from Oklahoma, and the culvert digger from New Mexico.
All had competed for and won government contracts—and all were
from out of state. "Why didn't any North Dakota subcontractors
win contracts?" I mused. The project was not major, and if the local
construction companies had bid, I am sure that the cost would have
been less than the cost of bringing in and maintaining an outside
crew.

The myth that a small business is confined to doing business in a
local area is no longer true. Even overseas markets are opening
up—especially to small businesses. Not only does the government
offer incentives, in some cases it actually offers funding, too. For
years the government has subsidized overseas development programs, offering opportunities for both service companies and manufacturers. Consider agricultural development programs in Third
World countries. The American Industrial Development Agency
(AID) is pouring millions of dollars into the development of small
industries in Central and South America to make the countries
more self-sufficient. Besides needing products and services, these
programs also need qualified consultants.

Last year I attended a meeting of several government organizations responsible for assisting in the development and expansion of
small businesses. I listened to a woman plead for the names of small
businesses with owners willing to expand overseas. Because of small

business apathy, her agency was in danger of losing federal and state funds to help such businesses develop and implement an overseas marketing program.

ANALYZE YOUR REPUTATION

"Establish a Reputation the Old-fashioned Way?"

Have you ever wondered how the government decides among several competing bids when the price is the same? No, it's not the good ol' boy network that decides who will win the contract. It's reputation.

I'd like to say you *always* establish a good reputation "the old-fashioned way"—you earn it. "But," you'll counter, "there are lots of small companies with sterling reputations that do not win contracts."

"I learned the hard way that you not only need a good reputation, you need a *visible* good reputation," says the owner of a painting shop. "I trusted that my work would speak for itself." He didn't win the first few contracts he bid on because he had to learn how to make the government aware of his quality.

Your performance history is the single most important consideration in establishing your company's good reputation. Performance not only includes meeting and beating a production or service *schedule*; it also means establishing and maintaining a superior-*quality* product or service. "But," you say, "I can't begin to build a performance history until I'm awarded a contract. Can I?"

True, most small companies cannot afford expensive public relations campaigns, but it is important that you take some time to analyze and establish your company's good reputation in the marketplace.

When was the last time you participated in a trade show, organized a committee for your trade or professional organization, published an article in a trade or professional publication, gave a speech about your company, or saw your company's name in print?

Start, of course, with timely performance and superlative quality. Remember, word of mouth is still one of the most important gauges of reputation, especially if you're doing business locally. But don't stop there.

There are several excellent professional organizations to which both government and industrial personnel belong. The American Society of Engineers, for example, offers opportunities to share new ideas, technologies, equipment capabilities, and computer interfaces.

If your company has developed a new manufacturing process or a new technology, you should contact your professional society and offer to give a speech and slide presentation. While you're at it, contact your local newspaper's or business magazine's business editors. They might want to cover the event. More important, send the government procurement buyer a *written* invitation to the event.

When your company upgrades its capabilities, opens new facilities, wins contracts, and signs important agreements, write a succinct, objective news release describing the what-where-who-when-why details of your accomplishment. (See exhibit 2-2 for a sample press release.) Send the press release to your government

---

EXHIBIT 2-2

Building Your Company's Reputation
BEGIN WITH A NEWS RELEASE

The following is an actual news release that was sent to various procurement agencies announcing a new product. A similar version was sent to local and national news media contacts, as well as potential commercial markets.

This press release is not a sales solicitation and will not substitute for standard bidding procedures detailed in subsequent chapters of this book. Nonetheless, it is one way you can establish the reputation of your company in the marketplace. After sending this press release, the company followed up with written and personal contacts.

News Release

For Release: Immediately

Contact: Deborah Bendler or Joyce Gideon
Wallis Gideon Wallis, Inc. Public Relations/Editorial Marketing

P.O. Box 700418
Tulsa, OK 74170
(For information call 918-747-2882. For ordering call 1-800-433-3947)

U.S. Surgeon General's Report on AIDS
Is Released on Videotape

Washington, D.C., Oct. 28, 1987—The official Surgeon General's Report on Acquired Immune Deficiency Syndrome (AIDS) is now available for the general public in videotape format through FutureVision, a Tulsa, Oklahoma–based video company.

"AIDS . . . What You Need to Know" is a 43-minute videotape of the official report written by U.S. Surgeon General C. Everett Koop. The videotape includes definitive information about AIDS transmission, risk, and prevention, and has been endorsed by several bipartisan political figures, including Vice-President George Bush and Senator Edward M. Kennedy.

"In preparing this report, I consulted with the best medical and scientific experts this country can offer," said Koop. "I met with leaders of organizations concerned with health, education, and other aspects of our society to gain their views of the problems associated with AIDS. The information in this report is current and timely. . . ."

According to Koop's report, by the end of 1991 an estimated 270,000 cases of AIDS will have occurred, with 179,000 deaths within the decade. In the year 1991, an estimated 145,000 patients with AIDS will need health and supportive services at a total cost of between $8 billion and $16 billion.

"AIDS is preventable," said Koop. "It is the responsibility of every citizen to be informed about AIDS and to exercise the appropriate preventive measures. This report will tell you how."

The videotape—in VHS, Beta, or 3/4-inch formats—is also available in Spanish and for the hearing-impaired from FutureVision, P.O. Box 801, Tulsa, Oklahoma 74101.

buyers, the business editors of your local paper and business publications, television stations, and even professional trade journals. If anyone subsequently publishes your story, also send the article to your government buyer with a note that you would be pleased to provide him or her with further information.

Don't forget that the government also has several publications that your buyers read. Sometimes these publications are tailored to a professional organization, and sometimes they are tailored to a specific technology.

Participating in trade shows is another way to demonstrate your product or service. Again, be sure to send your targeted government buyer(s) written notice that you will be participating in the show and would appreciate the opportunity to display your capabilities. Some shows schedule evening hours for special clients and the public. You might provide your buyers with special passes—but only if they are free. *Never, ever offer a buyer anything that has a market value*; this is absolutely illegal.

Obviously, once you win a contract you must work to maintain and prove your good reputation. Just remember that it's never too soon to analyze, build, and, yes, even *promote* your reputation.

Armed with a new sense of who *you* are, you're ready to learn who the *government* is. While there are many similarities between a commercial customer and a federal customer, there are also some major differences that will affect your decision whether to do business with the government. These differences involve the extra costs—and risks—of doing business with Uncle Sam. And these costs must be carefully weighed against your potential profits.

If you are an astute businessperson, you will want to consider carefully the next three chapters. "To bid or not to bid?" is no easy question. But by the end of chapter 5, you will be confident you've made a good decision—whatever it may be.

3

To Bid or Not to Bid?

Daily I receive calls from clients asking a variety of questions:

"My competitor just sent the government a bid for a $40,000 contract. Can I compete with him . . . *immediately?*"

"If I don't get some government contracts, my company will go out of business by next year! What should I do?"

"I keep bidding but I never win a contract. What am I doing wrong?"

If any of these questions sound familiar, this chapter is for you. Just like you, these small business owners share one thing in common: an immediate need to get on the government procurement bandwagon. Often driven by a failing market or a downturn in the economy, these otherwise successful businesspeople often throw caution to the wind to land a government contract.

Or perhaps you've been immobilized by the myths outlined in chapter 1. You've avoided the market altogether because you were convinced government procurement was too risky. This chapter is also for you. In one way, you're just like the business owner who wants to do business with the government—yesterday. Neither of you really understands the federal market. One of you throws caution to the wind, and the other lets caution take the wind out of your sails.

As alien, complex, and risky as the government market may seem at first, there is a commonsense strategy to determine whether you should make the commitment to pursue the federal market.

Let's begin with what you already know—your commercial market. Like any good manager wanting to expand your market, you look at such factors as risk, profit, competition, and investment. So let's see how these factors affect the government market. Having completed this analysis, you will be able to determine whether government business will complement or conflict with your commercial business.

LOADED QUESTION #1: CAN YOU AFFORD TO DO BUSINESS UNCLE SAM'S WAY?

It's difficult enough to estimate the costs of market expansion in a commercial market. For starters, there's product development, market research, and labor and production expansion, to name a few. When you do business with the government there are additional costs, not to mention the importance of analyzing these costs as they relate to your commercial business. Let me explain.

One day Doug Drown called me in a panic. He had just completed the financial analysis on his first government contract and his cost accountant had discovered some "hidden" costs. He had also discovered that during the time he was working on his government contract his commercial sales had fallen 5 percent.

He implored me, "Before I bid on my next federal contract, I need your help to develop a checklist of extra costs."

It turned out that developing a checklist for Doug Drown was straightforward, because he had focused his market on contracts of more than $25,000 for a single product having specific and consistent production, materials, and labor requirements. Since Doug had been through the process, he already knew the contract requirements and cost categories. But what about you as you enter the government procurement market for the first time?

If you're bidding on contracts of $25,000 or less, your investment may be considerably less than if you're bidding on a larger contract. Your investment also depends on the type of product or service you produce. Meeting government quality control specifications may cost more if you're producing a critical airplane part than if you're producing curtain rods, for example.

Regardless of the product or service you produce, you will need to consider two general categories: the administrative costs of doing business with Uncle Sam and the extra costs of producing the product or service, including materials, labor, and shipping.

Let's look at the administrative costs first. There are five cost categories that you will want to consider.

Expense #1: Penetrating the Government Market

Most small businesses enter government procurement from the inside out: Someone in the company is drafted to tackle the government market *in addition to* his or her regular job responsibilities. Such was the case with Doug Drown's company. Usually what happens is that the draftee discovers that he or she is devoting more and more time to government procurement. If the truth were known, at times the draftee is devoting more time to government procurement than to the regular job.

Unfortunately, it is very difficult to isolate the time and, therefore, the cost of finding your government market, getting on the bidders' lists, and preparing your bid. There are, however, some guidelines. If you are a novice do-it-yourselfer, you can estimate that it will take you six months (including government response time) to identify and penetrate your market. This includes ordering, studying, and filling out government forms to get on your targeted agency's bidders' list. (See appendix 1 for samples of procurement forms.) And it will take an additional week of full-time effort, which may be spread over a month, just to submit your bid proposal.

I advise companies entering the procurement market for the first time to document carefully the time spent on each of these activities. I recommend to my clients that they log their time in file folders labeled by specific activity, such as "Government Agency Identification," "Generation of Qualification Forms," "Review of Agency Market Potential," "Preparation of Bid Estimate," and "Review of Quality Control." These file folders can be used to file copies of the forms and correspondence. I also suggest that they use word-processed standardized forms and letters to correspond with the government, to reduce the time spent on repetitive activities. (See about bid preparation in chapter 8.)

Expense #2: Making Your Accounting System Accountable

Depending on the types of government contracts you bid on and the sophistication of your accounting system, another cost you may incur is for the reorganization and documentation of your company's accounting system. Regardless of the amount of your contract or government accounting requirements, you will want to segregate your commercial accounts from your government accounts in order to track the profitability of each. For any negotiated or audited contract, your accounting system must segregate and verify all direct and indirect costs incurred by the government contract. This includes everything from man-hours (verified by time cards or sheets) to overhead charges allocated to the government contract. (See chapter 7 for a discussion of accounting systems.)

Also, specific contract accounting information will protect you in the unlikely case the government terminates your contract. "But my accounting information is private," argued the owner of a large interior design and decorating firm. He quickly changed his mind when I pointed out that, should the government terminate his contract, it would be the only way he could be reimbursed for his cost and realize a reasonable profit.

Expense #3: Establishing a Quality Control Program

Of all the administrative costs you will incur in doing business with the federal government, the cost of establishing a quality control program is by far the most variable. Depending on the size of the contract and the item or service you are supplying, the cost could range from the negligible amount incurred in preparing a notarized letter to the considerable amount incurred in preparing a quality assurance program.

When you are bidding on contracts of $25,000 or less for a product or service where materials and workmanship are not critical, the government may require only that you sign a letter certifying that your product or service will meet commercial standards and that you will replace or "make good" any defective product or service.

But what if you are producing a product that is critical to life support? In that case, you would need a documented quality control procedure for monitoring the quality of your entire production process. All these requirements will be spelled out explicitly in your bid agreement.

In either case, the government expects to communicate with your quality control official. Many companies starting out in government contracting discover that their quality control personnel already utilize quality control procedures that are very similar to government requirements. The major difference is that the government requires a structured system of written documentation and record keeping. This system will improve quality throughout your company: from refining the ordering and receiving of materials, to promoting the quality of work at each step in the production process, to eliminating waste of materials, equipment, time, and man-hour expenses. (See chapter 6 for a detailed discussion of setting up a quality control system.)

It's easy to see that a well-structured and documented system can often become a boon rather than an expense. Most of the companies I've worked with discovered that a government-designed quality control program was a tremendous asset to their commercial business. Typically, once the program is in place, the company's production costs decrease for such items as scrap metal, reject parts, wasted production manpower for rework, and replacement costs for damaged shipments. More than 75 percent of the companies I've worked with on government quality control eventually included government quality controls in their routine commercial business.

Expense #4: Preparing for Your Preaward Survey

If the dollar amount of your contract is more than $25,000, the government *might* conduct a preaward survey before it awards a contract. This involves a review of facilities, capabilities, production equipment, labor skills, and insurance coverage. If you already have a good record-keeping system, the cost of preparing for this review will be minimal. For example, the government expects that your materials quotations and the delivery schedule for these materials will be in writing. Additionally, the inspectors expect that your personnel files will verify qualifications and certifications. For service contracts, the government may also require liability insurance. In that instance, an insurance quotation from your agent should be adequate. Finally, if you are bidding on a contract larger than your normal business volume and you do not have the liquid cash to cover the project, you may need a letter from your banker or other financial institution to verify short-term operating financing requirements. (See chapter 7 for a detailed discussion of preaward survey procedures.)

Expense #5: Administering Your Contract

From the moment you accept a federal contract, the government will expect to communicate with at least two government contract persons within your company. In addition to a quality control inspector, you will need a government contract administrator. While you may already have an employee who is or can easily become qualified in contract administration—perhaps in addition to his or her regular job—you need to consider the extra time required to meet government administrative requirements.

Once again, the time required for government contract administration is governed by the amount of your contract and the complexity of the product or service you are supplying. For small purchase orders, contract administration should not be any more complicated than for your commercial contracts. For contracts exceeding $25,000, however, you should figure in the time it will take to prepare monthly progress and periodic status reports disclosing any problems and the corresponding corrective actions. One way to estimate the extra time is to figure a 10 to 25 percent increase in administration time that you normally spend on commercial contracts for *every* federal inspector and government contract administrator who is assigned to your government contract. This includes the time it takes to interact personally with these inspectors, as well as to review and respond to government correspondence. (See about contract administration in chapter 9.)

LOADED QUESTION #2: CAN YOU AFFORD THE ADDED PRODUCTION, LABOR, AND INVENTORY COSTS?

When calculating your bid, you must consider the added labor, production, and inventory costs. After you carefully analyze your solicitation (see chapter 8), you should establish some good criteria for the amount you are willing to invest in expanding your labor force and production capabilities.

Establishing bid/no-bid criteria should protect you from unnecessary risks. Keep in mind that there is more than one way to approach expansion costs in the areas of production and labor. For example, one common fear small businesses confront in doing business with the federal government for the first time is the specter of boom-and-bust personnel layoffs and the accompanying expenses, such as compensation and unemployment insurance. Since the federal government has no customer loyalty, you can never be assured that you will win every contract you bid on, thus maintaining a consistent labor force. But can you honestly say that this risk is any greater than for your commercial market? Obviously, your safest strategy is to bid in multiple markets with multiple products, including both the government and commercial marketplace. With this approach, you'll improve the odds of your continued success.

There are also ways to avoid cyclical manpower problems. You can contract for quality assurance and administrative personnel until you determine whether to hire them full time. (See exhibit 3-1: "Should You Procure a Procurement Specialist?") You can also subcontract from other small businesses for personnel that can be terminated when the contract is fulfilled. Obviously, you face the risk of discontinuity of labor procedures, but you avoid financial obligations for facility expansion, retirement benefits, insurance premiums, and severance pay.

EXHIBIT 3-1

Should You Procure a Procurement Specialist?

If you plan to compete for contracts of $25,000 or less, you may not want to employ government specialists, except maybe for initial and periodic consultations. But if you plan to compete consistently for contracts of more than $25,000, you might be wise to hire procurement specialists to manage your government procurement business and coordinate federal business with commercial business.

There are potential problems, however, no matter how you decide to manage procurement duties. Companies that assign a manager procurement duties in addition to the regular job may jeopardize both the commercial and government business if the manager is spread too thin.

The other side of the coin is the problem of overspecialization. If you hire a procurement manager to deal *exclusively* with government issues such as contract management, quality assurance, packaging, marketing, and procurement accounting, you may sacrifice coordination and communication with your commercial managers.

Odd as it may seem, hiring specialists may cost you more in the long run—especially in the area of quality control—because specialists tend to overcompensate on quality and compliance. You must make sure that specialists don't unwittingly place the government's interests above your best business interests.

A company that decided to manufacture noncritical aircraft parts for the air force was pleased with the initial results of hiring a retired government inspector to manage quality assurance. A year later, however, a review disclosed severe cost overruns as a result of exceeding government production specifications. Since quality assurance is such a critical area, which affects both your profit and your ability to perform on a contract, my best advice is to develop a documented procedure so that everyone understands how and why quality is maintained. (See chapter 6 on quality control systems.)

If you are a manufacturing firm, the government typically will expect to communicate frequently with your "government contracts administrator" and "quality control assurance inspector." Obviously, your government procurement specialist(s) may perform additional duties, but make sure that when the government wants to talk about contract administration or quality control, the specialist is there to listen—and respond.

The most dramatic cost differences between the commercial and federal markets are the specialized government requirements for shipping, packaging, labeling, record keeping, lead time, and staging (storage) areas. For example, the government often requires a contractor to package and ship odd-quantity amounts uncommon in commercial markets, complicating customary packaging and inventory control systems.

Also keep in mind that the long lead times typical of so many government contracts can be a disaster in disguise. One company supplying fasteners for specialized equipment based its bid on materiel costs at the time of the contract award. As you may guess, those costs increased during the time it took to complete the contract. What looked profitable initially proved to be a break-even venture.

One of the most commonly overlooked considerations when trying to calculate bids involves staging areas, which are actually floor space requirements. These staging areas may include both the floor space needed for government inspections and the storage space for accumulating large shipments to take advantage of bulk shipping rates. While most managers accurately calculate expansion needs for the production of larger orders, many fail to realize that the finished goods can tie up valuable space until government inspectors arrive. During a preaward survey, one company bidding on a $400,000 government contract to manufacture gears for tanks discovered that it had inadequate space to store semi-truckload shipments of the gears. Luckily, the company was able to rent a warehouse from the company next door.

The government is also beginning to decrease its inventories. This may mean that you will need to store products for a longer period of time, thus complicating your normal inventory procedures. (See exhibit 3-2: "Pay-As-You-Go Procurement.")

================== **EXHIBIT 3-2** ==================

Pay-as-You-Go Procurement

Uncle Sam has discovered the benefits of innovative financing. That's old news if you consider our budget deficit. But in terms of government procurement, that's new news—and possibly good news for the small business owner like yourself.

As federal budget reductions continue, the government is looking to more innovative off-balance-sheet financing for services and supplies. How will this affect the small business person?

More lease items. More and more the government will avoid capital outlays for equipment and personnel by leasing more equipment, facilities, and—yes—even manpower.

Soldiers of fortune, come out of hiding? Let's not get too extreme. Nonetheless, government agencies are already subcontracting many labor-intensive services that formerly were assigned to in-house or on-base personnel.

The trend will probably be most visible in the leasing of high-tech equipment that rapidly becomes obsolete. Take computers and software. Consider, for example, leasing computers to the government on a short-term basis, then upgrading them, refurbishing them, and selling them on the secondary computer market. Of course, a computer-leasing company can claim depreciation during the transactions.

Vendor storage/direct issue. The government is emptying out its storehouses. Computer-relayed orders and overnight drop shipments make fast deliveries more reliable and less expensive than maintaining long-term inventory. The feds are even discovering "catalog shopping" or special "catalog contracts" as a viable method of obtaining supplies. For example, the postal service may order supplies directly from a paper supply warehouse for delivery to a storage site for immediate distribution. Sometimes the government may actually allow the contractor to use or lease government facilities for storage.

From bulk to bits. Just like the customer at a grocery store who breaks up a six-pack to purchase three sodas, the government is discovering the advantage of paying only for what it uses while retaining the financial advantages of bulk buying. The use of catalog orders for vendor storage and direct issue is somewhat like using a candy or newspaper vending machine, except that product acquisition is controlled by a computerized ordering process. The next step in the process will be for small businesses to place their stock directly at the agency's central issue point. The business would have to bear the inventory cost until the items were issued and paid for. Periodically the vendor would inventory the products to validate computer inventory reports.

Sound futuristic? Not really. Small business entrepreneurs are already profiting from such innovative approaches for providing government financing and managing the distribution of their goods and services.

Another major consideration is your investment in time. Under the best circumstances, it takes an individual approximately six months to find a market and get on all of the targeted agencies' bidders' lists. And if you manufacture a complex or critical product, it probably will take another six months to establish government-approved quality assurance procedures. This includes not only the individual's time but also government response time. Finally, it takes about two years to establish your company firmly with the government as a qualified government contractor that delivers a quality product in a timely manner. If you don't plan on this time, then you're fooling yourself and perhaps setting yourself up for disappointment and failure. This process can be expedited, but it takes an intensive effort of—and investment in—qualified personnel who are experienced in government systems.

LOADED QUESTION #3: CAN YOU EARN A REASONABLE PROFIT?

If you've ever bid on or won a government contract, you undoubtedly realize that effective estimating and cost accounting systems are crucial if you plan to make a profit. Likewise, you probably have discovered that your profit margin on a typical government contract will be modest. But what about all those stories about the government paying astronomical prices for goods and services? Yes, some of these stories are true, but they are not representative.

Let's be realistic. The government does its homework, too. It is always looking for the best product or service at the most reasonable price. And Uncle Sam doesn't care if you lost your shirt on the last contract. *Federal Acquisition Regulations (FAR)* specify that "losses on another contract are not to affect current negotiations on a newer contract."

Obviously, the bottom-line question is, is the profit worth the investment? The answer to this question must always relate to how the investment will affect your commercial business. If acquiring federal business is a matter of using your existing assets or expanding them *marginally* to produce additional goods for the government, so that your new sales complement your existing operations, then your decision to do business with the government is probably a responsible one. For example, can't you expand your vertical space utilization instead of building a new building? Or, rather than hiring new employees, can't you revamp your labor shifts through training and in-house promotion?

LOADED QUESTION #4: DO YOU UNDERSTAND THE CONTRACT?

Besides the risk of additional investment, you should also understand the contractual risks you could face. The government expects timely delivery of a quality product as spelled out in your procurement solicitation and contract. If for any reason you cannot deliver, there is a good chance the government will buy the product from someone else on an expedited basis—and charge you the difference between your contract price and what the government has to pay your competitor.

You also may face a postdelivery liability. If after delivery of your product the government determines that your product does not meet usage specifications, you may have to pay to have it returned for rework. And you'll pay to redeliver it to the government. The odds of this happening are very small, but be aware that there are risks in doing business with Uncle Sam. Yet don't you face the same risks in doing business commercially?

Surprisingly, most small businesses tend to overcompensate on quality and compliance when dealing with the federal government. Also, there are government regulations that entitle you to "cost recovery" should the government want changes in a product or service after the contract has been signed. Did you realize that it is possible for a contracting company to make more profit on government change orders than on original contracts? I advise my clients to send a formal form letter whenever a government inspector or engineer informally suggests changes. The letter should politely request that within ten days of the informal suggestion, the government send a written change order formalizing the changes discussed. This protects the manufacturer from the risk of noncompliance and establishes a basis for recovering costs from government changes.

LOADED QUESTION #5: CAN YOU OFFSET SEASONAL AND ECONOMIC BUSINESS CYCLES?

Many small business owners look upon government contracts as opportunities to improve business when things are slow. The folly of this reasoning is that, for the most part, the government does business 365 days a year. It consumes products every second of every day. Consequently, you must establish yourself and build your credibility as a reliable and responsive vendor on a full-time basis. You cannot expect the government to buy your product just when your other markets go flat. Remember, it takes at least six months to get on a bidders' list and receive a contract. So if you wait for an economic swing before tapping the market, you will be out of business before the government volume increases to support you.

There is one exception to this rule: If you sell seasonal items or services, you may be able to develop a seasonal strategy. A company in Omaha, Nebraska, discovered a new market niche in precisely this way. This company had already contracted for snow and trash removal from state highways during the winter. It didn't take much imagination for the owner to figure out that with a minimal investment it could also contract for summer grass mowing, raking, baling, and disposal.

Also, be aware that the Federal government forecasts purchases for two years in advance and then stockpiles products until it needs them. For example, if you are going to sell snow chains for government cars to the General Services Administration (GSA), you will need to submit a bid in the spring quarter, and manufacture and deliver the chains in the late summer. That way, the GSA can distribute the chains in the late summer and early fall for winter use. By being aware of government procurement cycles, you can collect from the government in the late summer, when your commercial sales for snow chains are trifling. You begin the marketing cycle for the quarter after the need, so that the product will be in the government's hands—and the money in your hands—at the time of need.

Case Study: A Time to Bid . . .

One of the most cautious companies I've ever dealt with was a manufacturer of fiber-optic communications equipment. While it didn't deliberately avoid government business, the company was satisfied with its comfortable $5 million of annual business.

Then one day a newly hired sales manager attended a seminar on government procurement for small businesses. Inspired by the seminar, he contacted an army contracting officer to see whether he would be interested in the company's product. Within a week, an army communications engineer appeared at the plant to talk about the company product. The sales manager was delighted at the thought of the commission on a potential $10-million sale, and reported to the president what he had generated.

At first the president responded negatively. He had heard all kinds of horror stories about the government "reorganizing" companies, and he wasn't about to "invest thousands and thousands of dollars to do business the government's way," he told the sales manager.

Not wanting to relinquish what promised to be the largest commission he had ever earned, the sales manager asked the president if he would hire a consultant to spell out what the investment, risk, and return investment would be. When the president agreed, the sales manager called me. I requested a tour of the facilities, an introduction to the production supervisors and quality inspector, and a meeting with the accounting supervisor.

What I found was a company ripe for doing business with the government. The first thing I discovered was that the production and quality section supervisors had come from companies that regularly did business with the government. Unbeknown to the president, these supervisors had already adopted most of the military's quality requirements in their operating instructions. Since these procedures contributed to an efficient operation, they hadn't thought it necessary to call them to the president's attention.

My meeting with the accounting supervisor was just as profitable. After I had outlined what the government required, the accounting supervisor assured me that the company time cards and most of the accounting system also met the government's requirements. The company was already doing piecework for a commercial airline on a negotiated contract that was audited for accountability at least once a year.

After I had completed my evaluation, I sat down with a resistant management to try to convince them that they could actually "contract to win." I began my discussion with a list of everything they were doing right.

"We know we're a good company," the president interrupted. "What we want to know is, how much is this going to cost us?"

At this point I presented a list of items that would require capital investment:

1. Preparing the bid and administering the contract
2. Reorganizing the facility's storage area to increase warehousing capacity
3. Ordering more materials
4. Training and expanding the labor force
5. Preparing for a government preaward survey
6. Documenting the quality control system
7. Revising the cost-accounting system to separate overhead charges applying to government work from overhead charges applying to commercial work
8. Customizing shipping procedures

To make a long story short, the company quickly realized that its return on investment would be well worth the capital outlay. The result? The company bid on a government contract and realized a good profit.

Case Study: . . . And a Time to Fold

Now that you've been stripped of the old paralyzing myths of why you shouldn't do business with the federal government, let me tell you about the company that decided *not* to do business with the government and never looked back.

It does happen. There are times when it is not to the small business's benefit to expand or bid on government business. Often these businesses have everything paid for and can project a secure future with infrequent technological breakthroughs.

Such was the case of an organic greenhouse operation that supplied salad-bar items to several restaurants and grocery stores in three adjacent towns and along a nearby interstate highway.

One day the manager of this six-person operation called me. He had the opportunity to provide produce to the commissary and clubs at a local army post. The contract could double his market. The company had the land and money to build the additional facilities, and there were sufficient numbers of unemployed people in the area to supply the labor. It sounded like the perfect setup to expand a commercial market to include government procurement.

The next afternoon I visited the operation. It was a rainy day, but all the cloud cover in the world couldn't disguise the idyllic setting—and the idyllic nature of the business. As I walked into the greenhouse I saw a group of middle-aged people enjoying a game of dominoes. For a moment I thought I had mistakenly wandered into a neighborhood social gathering.

Instead, I learned that these three couples were the owners, and that they had taken early retirement from other jobs to launch their greenhouse operation. Their new business had evolved after their children had left home and they found themselves with too much land and too much garden produce to consume or give away. They thought they had the perfect business and the perfect life. They had no debt, they sold everything they could produce in their current operation, and their day usually ended in midafternoon—just in time for a game of dominoes. No one was getting rich, but everyone was comfortable.

As I pored over the drawings, plans, and dollar figures they had compiled in preparation for our meeting, I just had to ask why, considering their contentment and their financial security, they were even considering expansion into the government market. Did they really want to take on the problems of labor supervision and training, hurried last-minute calls for more vegetables at the base, and the possibility of losing the contract after investing in an expansion? Their answer was an unqualified "No!"

I did, however, recommend that they work with the state agricultural university to provide commercial testing of new plant development and production methods. For a small investment they could benefit from the testing results and keep abreast of the latest horticultural trends.

The last time I stopped by for a visit, they were still in business . . . and still playing dominoes every afternoon.

Chances are you're not in the extraordinary position of the fiber optics company that was actually solicited for government business. No one has been knocking on your door lately. Nor are you in the enviable position of the organic greenhouse company that really didn't need government business. After all, you probably don't even know if there is a viable government market for your product or service, right?

The next two chapters will demystify the biggest puzzle in government procurement: how to find, analyze, and penetrate government markets. Chapters 4 and 5 will decode the map that leads to your *best* markets.

4

Finding Your Market

My weekend-farmer friend worked an eight-to-five job during the week so that he could support his true passion on the weekend: growing things. I realized Mark Woodworth was serious about his avocation when he bought a 160-acre farm and moved his family to the outskirts of the city. His plan, he announced one day, was to work his day job for five more years, until he could launch his own business as a tree and shrubbery wholesaler for local nurseries and landscapers.

"Why wait that long?" I asked. "Why not sell to the government?" Mark's look of disbelief turned to a smile of enlightenment. "After all," I pointed out, "your farm is only a couple hundred miles from three military posts in desperate need of landscaping."

The next day Mark called the small business advocates at the three state bases. To make a long story short, he discovered that the bases were interested in more than trees and shrubbery. They also needed rosebushes and ground cover—items they were purchasing at a premium price from out of state.

Within two years Mark had expanded his tree and shrubbery business to include ground cover, rosebushes, and perennials. Besides supplying nurseries, he landed two good local government contracts and even initiated a contract with the bases' outdoor shops that sold directly to base personnel.

In the meantime, Mark registered on the bidders' list of a state government purchasing agency. He subsequently won a contract to supply flower beds for the state capital complex, 150 miles away.

As a small business owner, you may have overlooked your potential government or prime contractor customers. Federal, state, and city governments are three such doorstep customers, and these omnipresent markets have voracious appetites. The trick to capturing these customers is first analyzing how the government buys and then finding the market for *your* product or service.

While no market boasts as much published market information as the federal government, it is this large volume of faceless purchasing information that often befuddles the businessperson who is used to dealing with the customer down the street. Besides, the customer down the street speaks English, as opposed to that foreign procurement language characterized by codes, acronyms, and references.

To complicate matters, there is no one centralized government buying agency or source for procurement information. Some agencies buy for themselves, and some execute contracts for other agencies. With more than 2,000 federal purchasing agencies, 1,200 prime contractors, and 4,000 procurement regulations, there's a lot of territory to cover to find the market(s) for your product or service. (See appendix 3 for a summary of government procurement activity and appendix 4 for a discussion of prime contracting opportunities.)

Deciding where to look for business can be exasperating. At times there seem to be no rational reasons for who purchases what where. Luckily, the government provides a number of publications, as well as personal contact opportunities, to help you identify your market. The key is knowing where to look first, and how to narrow your search strategically until you've found your perfect market(s).

Finding your government market is somewhat like running a maze. It helps to have an "aerial view" of the territory, so that you can avoid running in circles or into dead ends. This chapter provides a view of the entire map: It explains how the government buys and where it advertises. Once you get your bearings, I will show you how to read the map—a map written in code. And by the end of chapter 5 you will be able to crack that code of government acronyms and jargon to find the best market for your product or service—wherever it may be. During your journey, remember that information on ordering any publication I refer to is located in the bibliography.

HOW THE GOVERNMENT BUYS

"About the time I think I understand all the regulations of selling my product to the government, I discover another exception or contradiction," says Fred Kiribira, owner of a chemical manufacturing company.

I've heard this complaint repeatedly, and my answer contains good news and bad news. The good news is that the 4,000 regulations, "condensed" into a 1,500-page publication called *Federal Acquisition Regulations (FAR)*, assure fair and reasonable prices for the government, as well as fair and reasonable consideration for competing small businesses. These regulations also assure that your small business can compete fairly with large businesses. (See exhibit 4-1 for a description of *FAR* and appendix 7 for a summary of *FAR* topics.)

──────────────── **EXHIBIT 4-1** ────────────────

Consolidating Procurement Practices: A FAR Cry from Easy

Everything you've ever wanted to know about the regulations governing federal acquisitions is contained in one 1,500-page, 53-chapter volume, together with its supplements and appendixes, called the *Federal Acquisition Regulations—FAR*, for short. But there is nothing short about these regulations, which went into effect on April 1, 1984.

FAR was designed to unify all federal procurement practices, forms, and regulations, which previously varied among agencies. Just how easy is *FAR* to use?

Regulations by Reference, Supplements by the Pound

To save on printing costs, agencies issue solicitations or bid packages that reference (cite) regulatory clauses, rather than reproducing them in full. Solicitations incorporate whole pages of government regulations with the use of a single code number. For example, "*FAR* 52.219–8" implements *FAR*

19.704 and 19.708 (B), which state that a prime that wins a large-dollar contract must provide a six-element plan for subcontracting a percentage of its prime contract to various types of small and small disadvantaged businesses.

FAR also allows each major federal agency to issue additional supplements and to have its own "clause books" containing regulations unique to that agency. Some of these supplements may modify *FAR* regulations. Obviously, you'll need to check both *FAR* and agency supplements prior to bidding, to avoid any contracting surprises. (See *Federal Acquisition Regulations* in the bibliography for ordering information. See appendix 7 for a summary of *FAR* topics.)

And they call this consolidation!

The bad news is that these regulations will continue to change so long as Congress is charged with passing procurement legislation and approving funds for government operations. When you consider that the first law regulating federal procurement was passed in 1797, and that by 1979 these regulations had grown to approximately 4,200 pages, it is no wonder that *FAR* has been called a "farce." Although the government revised and condensed *FAR* to 1,500 pages in 1984, the publication is still not easy to use. In particular, you should be aware that the regulations governing procurement actions of $25,000 and over are considerably different from actions of less than $25,000. These differences are reflected even in the way the government advertises for its product and service needs.

Purchases for Any Dollar Amount: *U.S. Government Purchasing and Sales Directory*

No matter what the purchase amount, the single best source for finding your government market is the *U.S. Government Purchasing and Sales Directory*, published by the Small Business Administration. This directory:

- Lists commodities and services purchased by three federal supply groups, including: (1) major military purchasing offices, (2) local military installations, and (3) major federal civilian purchasing offices

- Cross-references the names of specific purchasing agencies to their addresses so that you can send for information and begin the process of registering on their bidders' lists to become qualified to bid on contracts
- Indexes the federal agencies that engage in major research and development activities
- Provides supplemental information on preparing proposals and brochures
- Contains a guide to government specifications
- Furnishes information on government property sales
- Includes copies of useful government forms

To determine which agencies buy your product or service, consult the directory's alphabetical listing of items purchased by the military (parts 2 and 3) or civilian (part 4) agencies. If you cannot find a category that relates to your product or service, try looking under a broader, related classification. (See also appendix 8: "How to Prepare an Unsolicited Proposal.")

When you locate your product or service in the alphabetical listing, record the code numbers appearing after it. These codes identify the purchasing offices that buy your product or service. You can look up these numbers in the directory's numerical index at the end of each chapter to get the names and addresses of the purchasing agencies.

For example, under the alphabetical listing of products and services purchased by major civilian purchasing offices (part 4 of the *Sales Directory*) appears the listing "Dynamite," followed by the code numbers "440, 475." If you look up 440 in the numerical section listing major civilian purchasing offices, you will find "General Services Administration" (followed by a general description of what the agency buys) and an address list, by region, of all General Services Administration offices. The entry for 475 gives the address of a specific procurement office: "Chief, Procurement Division, Panama Canal Company, 4400 Dauphine Street, New Orleans, LA 70140."

Purchases Under $25,000

Approximately 98 percent of all government procurement activity falls in the $25,000-or-below range. To award contracts between $1,000 and $25,000, the government is required to obtain only three quotations (provided that they are reasonable, based on past pricing information). And for purchases less than $1,000, the government needs only one qualified quotation. To assure fairness, the government selects who will receive a solicitation by using a rotation system, as well as by sending solicitations to bidders that request them. Even after you register your name on an agency's bidders' list, however, it could be a long time before your name comes up on the rotating list.

So often I've heard small businesspeople lament, "I sent in my forms to get on the bidders' list and I haven't heard anything." Many small companies become frustrated with the whole process of applying for the bidders' list and waiting to hear from the government. They cannot see the logic in sending in all the forms and registering on bidders' lists, when all they are interested in is local government contracts for less than $25,000. So what should they do in the meantime?

Take Action: Make Personal Contact with the Procurement Officer. If you're concentrating on local business under $25,000, penetrating your market may be much easier than you think. Since the government is not required to advertise procurement actions of less than $25,000, perusing a government publication that advertises procurements, like the *Commerce Business Daily*, would be a waste of time. For you, personal contact with local procurement officers may be the only way to unearth this business.

"I only wanted to provide custom draperies for local customers, and all those government publications just confused me," says Karen Ludwig, a Chicago drapery maker. "So I let my fingers do the walking and started telephoning nearby federal installations. I made several phone calls before I found one procurement officer who needed my services. From then on I developed my contacts by word of mouth. Procurement officers would give me leads by asking, 'Why don't you call so-and-so at such-and-such buying office?' "

Like Ludwig, you may want to confine your small business to *local* customers and contracts under $25,000. Or perhaps you want to enter the federal market gradually, by testing the waters with a very small contract. A well-placed telephone call may result in some great finds—markets often overlooked by those seeking larger, less localized markets. (See exhibit 4-2: "Ringing Up Business on the Telephone.")

══════════════════════ **EXHIBIT 4-2** ══════════════════════

Ringing Up Business on the Telephone

OR, "HELLO, YOU DON'T KNOW ME BUT . . ."

If you're interested in finding local procurement actions under $25,000, you have three alternatives: (1) research government publications such as the *U.S. Government Purchasing and Sales Directory*; (2) visit local offices of federal agencies to study public postings; and (3) telephone local agencies and ask if they purchase your product or service.

Even if you research your product in government publications, chances are you will eventually telephone or visit a local purchasing officer or assistant at some point in the procurement process. Knowing whom to talk to and what to say will not only save you time, but will also create an impression of credibility for your company.

Purchasing officers offer the following tips for making that important first contact:

• *"Do your homework first."* Contracting officers complain that too many people make calls cold. They suggest, whenever possible, contacting your local Small Business Administration's *small business advocate* (SBA) and telling him or her what your product or service is. In turn, the small business advocate will tell you which local agencies are buying your product or service and the *name* of the person you should contact.

• *"Ask to speak to the procurement agent by name."* One contracting officer told us she was tired of hearing "Hello, I wanna talk to the man who buys supplies for your outfit." It's bad enough to be addressed anonymously, but it so happened this particular purchasing officer was female.

• *"Don't waste time."* A small business advocate told me he gets an average of fifty calls a day. He adds, "Most of the people asking about products and services waste time by not being prepared." Purchasing agents and small business advocates appreciate, and are impressed by, individuals who know the National Stock Number or Federal Stock Number (see exhibit 4-4) for their product or service. An expedient telephone introduction might sound like this: "Hello, my name is Doug Rees, and I'm a bidder in federal classification code 78. The Small Business Administration told me your agency purchases my product [or service]. Do you have a moment to answer a few brief questions, or would you prefer that I make an appointment to see you?"

• *"A checklist of questions might include . . ."* According to one contracting officer, a company that is really interested in procurement activity will probably ask:

1. How often and in what quantity does the agency purchase the product or service?
2. Is there a procurement forecast and procurement history available? (See chapter 5.)
3. Approximately what amount does the agency spend on the product or service each year?
4. What is the name of the company currently providing the product or service? Where is it located?
5. Does the agency purchase the product or service for any other federal agencies? If so, how often, in what quantities, and how much, annually?
6. How may I obtain the specifications, drawings, performance, and delivery requirements (if applicable)?

• *"Don't forget the reason you called."* If you're interested in winning a contract, don't forget the most important request: to get on the bidders' list for your product or service. If you haven't requested a Standard Form 129 from your Small Business Administration, with which to register for the agency's list of qualified bidders, ask the purchasing officer to send you one. Don't forget to ask for any other supplemental forms that are required to complete the application process. (See appendix 1 for samples of forms.) Indicate that you will follow up with another phone call to make sure the officer received your Standard Form 129.

And, of course, thank the officer!

Check Public Postings. Another way to find a local market is to check the public postings at your targeted purchasing agency or Small Business Association. In fact, procurement offices are required to display publicly all solicitations exceeding $10,000 and to provide at least ten days for the submission of bids or offers. You don't need an appointment to check the bid board at your targeted agency. If you find a solicitation you are interested in, you can even ask for a copy to study. Be sure to ask if you can see a sample of the product being procured and any applicable production drawings and specifications.

Attend Seminars. Upcoming bid information, product samples, specifications, and drawings are sometimes available at seminars sponsored by your local Small Business Administration or government agency.

One Tucson-based engineering company president attended an SBA seminar where a small business advocate passed around a printed circuit board. The government was purchasing the board from a prime contractor that did not do repairs, so every time a board malfunctioned the government had to buy a new one. The government realized it could save a lot of money if the boards could be repaired. It just so happened that the Tucson engineering company had the skilled personnel to make the repairs. If the company president had not attended the seminar, chances are he would never have learned about this opportunity—a contract he eventually landed.

Study Government and Trade Publications. Regularly checking appropriate government and trade publications for market information can be just as important as attending the right seminar at the right time. For example, there are several government publications that identify small business market niches for specialized, often-overlooked product/service areas. I've discovered that few people know that some departments have gone so far as to publish "competition hit lists" for products and services that offer special opportunities for small businesses. The *Competition Catalog,* published by the Defense Industrial Supply Center, and *Competition: Hit List,* published by the Defense General Supply Center, are two excellent lists of products for which the government would like to see more competitive pricing. These publications contain not only product lists, but also pictures, past pricing, competitor listings, and even forecasted buying information.

Sometimes excellent leads are even buried in press releases. One computer maintenance company owner won a contract at his local military base after he read in a press release in a computer trade paper that the base was increasing its use of outside computer maintenance contractors because of personnel layoffs.

If you're interested in doing business with the navy, you *need* to send for the *Navy Ships Parts Control Center Buy Requirements Listing* for specialized information on how to do business with this government branch.

Purchases of $25,000 and Over

Of all procurement actions, those for $25,000 and over are most visibly publicized. In fact, with ten exceptions (see exhibit 4-3), all procurement actions of $25,000 or more must be published in a daily tabloid, the *Commerce Business Daily* (*CBD*), for you—and the rest of the world—to see.

======= **EXHIBIT 4-3** =======

Who's Who That's Not Listed

COMMERCE BUSINESS DAILY ADVERTISING EXCEPTIONS

All procurement actions of $25,000 or more are solicited by the government from qualified bidders' lists (see chapters 4 and 6), and are publicized in the Department of Commerce's daily publication *Commerce Business Daily,* except for the following:

1. Products or services classified for national security reasons
2. Perishable subsistence items (such as food)
3. Certain utility services
4. Items or services required within fifteen days
5. Products or services placed under existing contracts as ongoing purchase orders.
6. Products made by other government agencies
7. Personal professional services that are highly specialized
8. Services from educational institutions
9. Products made only from foreign sources or foreign buy directed
10. Products or services not to be given advance publicity, as determined by the Small Business Administration

---

Available at your local Small Business Administration office or by subscription, the *CBD* is the government's primary publication listing want ads for specific products and services the government needs. In fact, the *CBD* is the only source (other than personal contacts) for identifying service markets. You will probably be most interested in these five sections:

U.S. Government Procurements (services)

U.S. Government Procurements (supplies, equipment, and materials)

Contract Awards (services, supplies, equipment, and materials)

Research and Development Sources Sought

Special Notices

To use the *CBD,* you must know your product's commodity code or, in the case of services, the *CBD*'s special letter code (see appendix 9 for codes). Using these product or service codes, you can look up the classified ads in the *CBD.*

"U.S. Government Procurements" Sections. Now that you've identified your product/service codes, you are finally ready to look up some real procurement opportunities in the "U.S. Government Procurements" sections. A typical synopsis includes:

- A listing and short description of the product or service
- The name and address of the agency purchasing the item or service
- The deadline for proposals or bids
- The phone number to request specifications
- The product/service solicitation number

The following is an example of a product synopsis in the *CBD*'s product procurements section:

87 Agricultural Supplies
Directorate of Contr, Bldg 198, Ft. Leavenworth, KS 66027–5031
   1 87—TREES AND SHRUBS DABT19–88–B–0005. BOD, o/a 7 Jan 88. Contact, Debbie Smith, 913/684-2483, Contr Officer, Deanna L. Mckee. Reqmts contr FOB Ft. Leavenworth, KS. IFB to be issued o/a 10 Dec 87. See Note 13. (322).

Just how do you translate all these codes? Let's take it step by step:

1. The number *87* is the federal supply group classification number, which is the first two digits of the National Stock Number (NSN)—a nine- to thirteen-digit number assigned to every item in the government's inventory (see exhibit 4-4). Following the NSN is its corresponding classification name: "Agricultural Supplies."

=============== **EXHIBIT 4-4** ===============

Decoding Your National Stock Number

THIRTEEN DIGITS THAT COUNT

Just when you've finally memorized your SIC code, the feds tell you they do business the new-fashioned way: "Take a number, please." Not just any number will do. You'd better take the right number, the correct thirteen-digit National Stock Number (NSN), or you may get solicited to contract for a product or service you've never heard of.

Because procurement information is so extensive, the government uses National Stock Numbers (NSN) or Federal Stock Numbers (FSN—Department of Defense) to identify the specific products and services it purchases. To submit bids for government contracts, you must find the correct NSN or FSN for your product.

You can obtain the first four digits of your NSN or FSN when you obtain your targeted agency's Alphabetical/Numerical Cross-Reference Listing. This four-digit number is called the Federal Stock Code (FSC). Find your service or product in the alphabetical listing and look under the column "FSC." To get the remaining nine digits of your FSN or NSN, you must examine a buying agency's detailed buy list.

Why thirteen digits? From left to right, each digit in your NSN represents a category, subcategory, subsubcategory, and so forth. These digits represent the following categories:

- First two digits: (01–99) These two digits are called Federal Supply Groups (FSG).
- First four digits: The first four digits are called the National Stock Code (NSN) or, in the case of the Department of Defense, the Federal Stock Code (FSC). They include the first two digits (FSG) plus the third and fourth digits.
- Remaining digits: These digits identify specific items within an FSC, which can range from five to nine more digits.

---

2. The synopsis begins with the title and address of the purchasing agent/agency.

3. The *1* means "the procurement item is 100 percent set-aside for small business concerns." (See the legend on the last page of the CBD for other codes.)

4. The *87* is the NSN supply classification (repeated).

5. *TREES AND SHRUBS* is the general category of the products being procured.

6. *DABT19–88–B–0005* is the solicitation number. The first six characters, *DABT19*, identify the contracting office (Fort Leavenworth, Kansas); *88* is the solicitation's issuance year; *B* means an "invitation for bids" (for the solicitation method used in sealed bidding, see chapter 8); and *0005* is the sequential number assigned to this solicitation.

7. *BOD, O/A 7 Jan 88* means that the bid opening date (the date bids will be requested) will be on or about January 7, 1988.

8. *Contact Debbie Smith, 913-684-2483* means that if you have any further questions about the product, such as the kind and number of trees and shrubs, you should telephone Debbie Smith, who is the end user of the plants. (Don't forget to refer to the *CBD* by date and page number when you contact her.)

9. *Contr Officer Deanna L. Mckee* means that Deanna L. Mckee is the contracting officer.

10. *Reqmts contr FOB Ft. Leavenworth, KS* means that the contract requires that the trees and shrubs be shipped freight paid to Fort Leavenworth.

11. *IFB to be issued o/a 10 Dec 87* means that invitations for bids will be mailed on or about December 10, 1987.

12. *See Note 13* refers to a note or additional information that appears on the last few pages of every Thursday's edition of the CBD. In this case, Note 13 means that the small business set-aside is limited to businesses with annual sales or receipts not exceeding $3.5 million for the preceding three fiscal years.

13. The number *322* means that this synopsis was published on the 322nd day of 1987.

"Contract Awards" Section. If you think a prime contractor might want your product or service, or if you'd like to keep abreast of your competition, you will probably want to check *CBD*'s "Contract Awards" section.

This section reveals information about recent government purchases and provides valuable information about your market. For example, an independent San Diego subcontractor, Keith Jeslow, peruses this section to find work during slow seasons. While reading the contracts awards section, Keith learned that a prime contractor on the San Diego Navy Base received a $379,000 contract for road repair. Keith wrote to the prime to apply for work as a subcontractor. He subsequently received over $10,000 of work.

"Research and Development Sources Sought" Section. Firms with research and development capabilities will want to check *CBD*'s "Research and Development Sources Sought" section. This section offers an inside look at the government's present and future technological needs: "radon gas detectors," "real-time asbestos testing," and "green camouflaging pigment," for example. In some cases the solicitation states that the agency has no funding for research, but wants to know who is doing research work in a particular area. Later, when the government obtains funding, the bidders' list will include those companies that shared their information with the agency asking for data.

"Special Notices" Section. Periodically the government publishes special notices that affect government procurement. For instance, in the August 12, 1987, issue of CBD the government announced Public Law 99-399. This law establishes a 10 percent goal for American minority contractors and an additional 10 percent goal for American small business contractors for embassy design and construction projects. Always glance at this section to keep abreast of timely developments in government procurement.

PROBING THE PRIME CONTRACTOR MARKET

While there are several ways to approach government markets, the path to the primes is less defined. We've already seen how reading the *CBD*'s "Contract Awards" section will uncover information regarding recent prime contract awards. But this information is obviously after the fact. Similarly, the *Sales Directory* has no information on this $40-billion subcontracting market.

Unfortunately, most small businesses learn of subcontracting opportunities by word of mouth or personal contact, or through after-the-fact synopses in the *CBD*.

There are, however, two publications that might help you. The *Government Production Prime Contractors Directory* provides an alphabetical and address index of all prime government contractors. The monthly publication *Small Business Preferential Subcontract Opportunities* goes much further in identifying markets for small business. This publication summarizes all the contracts that contain clauses requiring the primes to subcontract to small businesses.

Since prime contractors are not government agencies but large, commercial businesses doing business with the government, your approach to this market will be less formal than your entry into the federal market. This does not mean there isn't a protocol for dealing with the primes.

If you learn of a subcontracting opportunity, you will want to contact a prime contractor in writing, providing information about your company. (See appendix 4 for specifics on probing the prime markets.)

Many businesspeople are overwhelmed by the massive amount of market information available. "I couldn't see the forest for the trees," complained a New Orleans developer of accounting software. "After studying the *U.S. Government Purchasing and Sales Directory,* I had no problem identifying who bought software. But I couldn't figure out which agencies would want my *particular* software."

A Knoxville, Tennessee, training consultant protested, "I found a huge list of agencies that might be interested in my services, but I didn't know where to go from there. I couldn't fathom sending out five hundred form letters soliciting business."

Considering the time it takes to survey general markets, it is not surprising that many small business owners give up—oftentimes at the threshold of discovering specific market(s) for their products or services.

Don't give up! By the end of the next chapter you'll be exclaiming "Eureka!" instead of "I'm sorry I asked!"

5

Following Up with Your Purchasing Agency

You are now approaching a crossroads in the journey to target the ideal market(s) for your products or services. For many companies this crossroads is the biggest test in the pilgrimage through the bureaucratic jungle. You've conquered the fear of doing business with the government, you've analyzed your company's product and market, and you've identified those government agencies that *may* be interested in your product.

But so far the government doesn't even know who you are. So where do you go from here? Forward, of course! The best, most profitable information is yet to come. In this chapter I'll show you the strategy for targeting and following up with the best market(s) for your product or service. You'll learn how to get on these agencies' coveted bidders' lists. And you'll uncover some valuable secrets about these agencies' past and future buys, including who your competition is and how much the agency paid for past purchases. With this valuable information in hand, you can position your product or service competitively in the federal marketplace. (See exhibit 5-1 for a checklist of steps explained in chapters 4 and 5.)

EXHIBIT 5-1

Markers in the Market Maze

The following checklist outlines a step-by-step process for making your way through the procurement market maze. It will keep you on track and map out a sequential strategy for targeting your best market(s):

1. *Determine who's buying what.* Check advertised and *unadvertised* market information to determine which agencies are buying what products and services. Study the *U.S. Government Purchasing and Sales Directory* and the *Commerce Business Daily.* For local procurement business, telephone or visit purchasing agencies to check bid boards (solicitation postings). Attend Small Business Administration seminars and professional trade shows, and read newspapers and business and professional publications.

2. *Request an Alphabetical/Numerical Cross-Reference Listing.* Send for an Alphabetical/Numerical Cross-Reference Listing from one of your targeted purchasing agencies to obtain your product's or service's NSN and addresses of other agencies that might purchase your product or service.

3. *Complete a Standard Form 129.* Fill out a Standard Form 129 (SF 129) for each targeted agency to register for its bidders' list. When you send in your SF 129, also request an agency buy list containing a complete coded list of the items the agency buys.

4. *Complete the buy list for your targeted agency.* When you receive your coded buy list, check off all the items or services you are interested in bidding on. Return your buy list to register officially for inclusion on the agency's bidders' list.

5. *Study future and past market information.* Even before you submit your SF 129 and buy list, you may want to request a copy of the agency's Procurement History Extraction by Federal Stock Number (PHE), the Stock Number Advanced Procurement Planning List (SNAPPL), and Automated Item Description Extraction (AIDE). Study past and future market information to determine your market's stability and competition.

6. *Analyze production drawings and specifications.* If applicable, order production drawings from the buying agency or the Small Business Administration. If specifications appearing on the production drawings are referenced, order *Military Specifications,* Naval Publication and Forms Center (see bibliography).

7. *Respond to all solicitations.* If you receive a solicitation and are not interested in bidding, inform the agency in writing that

you are not interested in submitting a proposal at this time but would like to be retained on the bidders' list.

8. *Register for PASS.* When an agency or a prime contractor cannot find enough qualified bidders on its own bidders' list, it may search the interagency PASS (Procurement Automated Source System) list. You can register with PASS by submitting form SBA 1167, available at your local Small Business Administration office.

TARGETING AGENCIES AND REGISTERING ON THEIR BIDDERS' LISTS

The *Commerce Business Daily* and the *U.S. Government Purchasing and Sales Directory* have provided you with the addresses of the government departments that might purchase your particular product or service. Now you are ready to investigate which *specific* agencies are purchasing your product(s) or service(s) so that you can register on their bidders' lists to receive solicitations.

For example, one Cleveland night-light manufacturer used the *Sales Directory* to find the names and addresses of fourteen General Services Administration agencies that purchased lamps. But this manufacturer produced only *night* lights. He still needed to know whether there was a market for night lights, and, if so, what particular agencies purchased them.

At this point, he needed to write or phone each of the fourteen agencies and request three items: the agency's Alphabetical/Numerical Cross-Reference Listing, the buy list, and a Standard Form 129 (Solicitation Mailing List Application).

The Alphabetical/Numerical Cross-Reference Listing is a map-sized pamphlet that alphabetically lists general products and services that the purchasing agency buys, with corresponding four-digit Federal Stock Code (FSC) numbers. The pamphlet also cross-references the FSC four-digit number to the corresponding procurement centers' codes and addresses.

Using the FSC, he could now locate his general category—lamps—on each agency's buy list. The buy list provided an itemized stock class numerical listing of *all* the products/services his targeted agency purchases for his particular FSC. This unabridged agency buy list is sometimes called the Procurement Source Class and Suffix List.

When the manufacturer looked up his product by FSC number on the buy list, he found an unabridged list of specific products organized by National Stock Number (NSN) up to thirteen digits long. He then checkmarked the item he was interested in providing—"night lights." Next, he wrote down his product's thirteen-digit NSN for later reference and for ordering historic and future market information (see next section below).

Finally, he filled out his SF 129 and returned it—with his completed buy list—to each buying agency. (See exhibit 5-2: "Solicitation Mailing List Application.") He realized that since his product's category was varied and complex, he would have to submit his buy list with his SF 129 before the buying agency would register him on its bidders' list. A week later, he called the agency and confirmed that he was officially registered on its bidders' list.

EXHIBIT 5-2

Solicitation Mailing List Application

STANDARD FORM 129

You may know who your markets are, but do they know who *you* are? Probably not—unless you are on the agency's bidders' list.

The Importance of SF 129

Since there is no centralized procurement office, *you must submit a separate Standard Form 129 to every procurement office with which you want to do business.* You can respond to an ad in the *Commerce Business Daily* (CBD), request a copy of the solicitation, submit a bid, and win a contract without submitting an SF 129. *But my advice is to submit an SF 129* (1) *if you are interested in long-term markets* and (2) *if you are interested in procurement actions for less than $25,000,* which account for 98 percent of all government procurement actions that are not advertised in the CBD. Also, if you happen to overlook a want ad in the CBD, you could still receive an invitation to bid or a request for a proposal if your name is registered through SF 129.

Complete and Return Your SF 129

The bidders' list application (Standard Form 129) is available almost everywhere that has anything to do with government procurement: at your Small Business Administration, by request from your local buying agency, and at a prime contractor's small business office.

Filling out SF 129 is relatively simple if you follow the instructions on the back of the form. To save time on multiple applications, fill out a master copy of the SF 129, leaving the agency, date, and signature blocks blank. Photocopy the master copy and then fill in the specialized information for each agency.

In many cases an agency will send you its "customized" version of the SF 129, including supplemental pages and special instructions on filling out your product information.

Sometimes the small business advocate will enter your company's name on the bidders' list on your initial submission of the SF 129, and sometimes he or she will test your seriousness by sending you a computerized listing of the agency's buy list (also called the Procurement Source Class and Suffix List) of everything the agency purchases. If you receive the buy list, check the individual items you can supply and return the entire listing. If you do not return your checked list, you may *not* be entered on the bidders' list, since the agency will not know what you are qualified to supply.

Follow Up

If you submit an SF 129 and are not solicited within two or three months, follow up with a phone call to your small business advocate. Ask if your SF 129 arrived, if you are on the bidders' list, and if any procurements have been made recently. Respond to any solicitations you receive as a result of submitting your SF 129. If you don't respond, the procurement office *must* remove you from the bidders' list. If you do not want to submit a bid or proposal, notify the contracting officer by postcard that you are unable to submit a bid or proposal at this time but you wish to be retained on the bidders' list for future procurements.

WHO IS YOUR COMPETITION?

If you had the chance to find out who your competitors were and how they bid in the past, wouldn't you do so? Wouldn't you welcome the opportunity to gaze into a crystal ball to foresee what the government is buying for the next one to two years?

Of course! Surprisingly, few people take advantage of this opportunity. No, it isn't because the information is expensive. It's free and readily available from most agencies. But most people don't realize it. Others don't take the time or effort to request and study the information.

Even before you send in your SF 129 and buy list, and certainly before you develop the price for a proposal or bid, you will want to request additional market information from your targeted agency. The first publication you should request is the Stock Number Advanced Procurement Planning List (SNAPPL) and a corresponding printout, the Automated Item Description Extraction (AIDE). Similar to a crystal ball, SNAPPL is a one- or two-year projection of government purchases and their estimated costs. This publication will help you determine the type and quantity of each product and service each government agency intends to buy for the next one or two fiscal years. AIDE is a computer extraction summarizing specific characteristics of the item. If SNAPPL describes a forecasted buy for metal cylinders, for example, you will probably want to know the size and function of the cylinders. AIDE translates the NSN numbers into five or six lines of product information, starting with the stock number, name ("noun") of the item, part number(s), next higher assembly that the part fits on, dimensions of the item, a brief description of its functions and materials, and the code numbers for any applicable manufacturing drawings.

Remember, agencies are under no obligation to buy any of the items listed in SNAPPL, or they may alter the quantity forecasted, depending on the field usage. Likewise, the price per unit is also only an estimate, and costs will change according to the actual market bids.

The second publication that provides crucial market information is the Procurement History Extraction (or Record) (PHE or PHR). The PHE includes information on past contract purchases, including the quantity the government bought, how much it paid, and who won the contract.

Since SNAPPL and PHE cover all products and services, when you request these publications you must specify your product's or service's National Stock Number (NSN).

How One Manufacturer Used SNAPPL and PHE

Now that you know what kind of information SNAPPL and PHE provide, let's see how one company used the information for market analysis.

Steve Drickey, a Denver metal shaping manufacturer, was interested in producing oxygen cylinders for the government and wanted to study forecasted and historical market information. Using his product's NSN, he ordered SNAPPL (and the corresponding AIDE listing) as well as the PHE from his targeted agency.

When he received SNAPPL he uncovered the following extracted information based on the second underlined item in each numbered column on table 5-1.

A. NSN (column 1): *1660005152575*. This is the National Stock Number for the cylinder named in column 2. The manufacturer obtained this number from the agency's buy list, which he received after he submitted his SF 129.

B. Noun (column 2): *Cylinder*. The "noun" is the name of the item. To determine the cylinder's characteristics and specifications, the manufacturer will need to consult the corresponding AIDE printout.

C. Mfg. Code (column 3): *19062*. This manufacturer's code number is *either* the CAGE (Commercial and Government Entity) number identifying the vendor that last supplied the item or the CAGE number identifying the manufacturer that provided the most current manufacturing drawings. (See exhibit 5-3: "Are You an Entity?")

TABLE 5-1.

STOCK NUMBER ADVANCED PROCUREMENT PLANNING LIST

Column:	1	2	3	4	5	6	7	8
					1988			
	NSN	Noun	Mfg. Code	Part Number	FY89 Quantity	FY89 Value	FY90 Quantity	FY90 Value
Items:								
1.	16600051 50855	DIAPHRAGM	59364	3163370–1	417	4,128	329	3,528
2.	16600051 52575	CYLINDER	19062	MS21227–1	1,122	165,000	1,904	280,000
3.	16600052 15935	DIAPHRAGM	59364	96354–5	970	1,969	1,200	1,320
4.	16600052 25887	SHAFT	59364	96265–1	35	5,711	27	4,428

=========================== **EXHIBIT 5-3** ===========================

Are You an Entity?

THE IMPORTANCE OF CAGE NUMBERS

If you've done any market research involving past procurements or future projections, you've probably encountered numbers that identify your competitors. Called the *manufacturer's code* in the Stock Number Advanced Procurement Planning List, or *CTR ID* (contractor's identification) in the Procurement History Extraction (or Record), these Commercial and Government Entity (CAGE) numbers are your keys to developing your competitive strategy.

But, as with anything in the government, the CAGE number is not as simple as 1-2-3. You must look in the Defense Logistics Agency's handbook *HB-8*, to identify the name behind the number. (See bibliography.) If you know only the name of the company and want to know its CAGE number, then you will need the alphabetically organized *HB-4*. (See bibliography)

If you don't have a commercial CAGE number, and you're serious about doing business with the government, then you must complete and mail Department of Defense Form 2051. (See appendix 1.)

D. Part Number (column 4): *MS21227-1*. This is a code number assigned to the product and supplements the NSN. Since part numbers are continually revised to reflect the most current modifications, you should order manufacturing drawings by part number from the small business specialist at the buying agency. This will ensure that you have the most current drawing. (See exhibit 5-4: "Do You Have the Latest Requirements?")

E. FY89 Quantity (column 5): *1,122*. This agency predicts a purchase of 1,122 cylinders for fiscal year 1989.

F. FY89 Value (column 6): *165,000*. Based on past purchase price, this agency predicts it will pay $165,000 for 1,122 cylinders in 1989.

================= **EXHIBIT 5-4** =================

Do You Have the Latest Requirements?

While the Procurement History Extraction (or Record), Stock Number Advanced Procurement Planning List, and Automated Item Description Extraction *summarize* product specifications and list part numbers, you may still need to order production drawings and detailed specifications to determine whether you will want to bid.

You can order the *most current* manufacturing drawings from the buying agency or Small Business Administration *by part number*. Part numbers are extensions of National Stock Numbers (NSN). Manufacturing drawings provide three views of the product, data on dimensions and materials, and a list of the most current revisions.

The manufacturing drawings will reference specifications (by number), which you can order from the Specifications and Standards Center. (See bibliography: *Department of Defense, Index of Specifications and Standards.*) Specifications may provide information about the manufacturing process required to produce a product and a more detailed description of a product's material composition.

Whereas part numbers may appear to be yet another detour in making your way through a numerical bureaucracy, they actually serve two purposes: First, they allow a further breakdown of an NSN (or FSN) component into subparts, so that the government can repair individual components, rather than replace a larger, more expensive assembly. Second, each company that manufactures a part is assigned a different number for the same part, so that the government can trace any item back to its supplier.

In 1970, as a supervisor of one of the Air Logistics Center's Procurement Engineering Sections, I soon discovered the benefit of part numbers, both for the government and for small businesses. I was assigned the task of saving the agency money by reducing the government's procurement purchases from single sources for buys costing more than $100,000.

One of the single-source items I received for review was an

aircraft fire-detection system. Using the NSN, I retrieved the original system design drawings from the data system. These drawings listed three different part numbers supplied by three different vendors. Using CAGE numbers, I found the names of these three subcontractors in the government handbook *HB-8*. (See exhibit 5-3 on how to trace CAGE numbers.) I checked the Procurement History Record and discovered that none of these manufacturers was our current vendor.

I wrote to all three vendors, asking for qualifying proof that they could manufacture or assemble the fire-detection system. All three responded. Two were currently producing the entire system for navy contracts, and the third was producing the items for our current sole source vendor, which was reselling them to us at a 50 percent markup!

To make a long story short, we solicited all three subcontractors and reduced our expected expenditures by 67 percent on future purchases.

G. FY90 Quantity (column 7): *1,904*. The agency predicts a purchase of 1,904 cylinders for fiscal year 1990.

H. FY90 Value (column 8): *$280,000*. The agency predicts it will pay $280,000 for 1,904 cylinders in fiscal year 1990.

Steve Drickey was surprised to glean so much information from only eight columns. Nonetheless, he still knew very little about the product itself. Using his NSN as his guide, he turned to the AIDE printout. AIDE told him that the oxygen cylinder was 200 cubic inches, capable of holding 400 psi (pounds per square inch), 9.0 inches long and 5.75 inches in diameter, and made from 1/8-inch steel. He also discovered that the government was using the cylinder in nine different airplanes, many of which were newly manufactured. This information suggested a market both large and stable for years to come.

Procurement History Extraction by Federal Stock Number.
So far, so good. Confident in the stability of the future market, Steve was ready to examine past purchases: how many were ordered, who won the contracts, and how much the government paid. Now he

turned to the second piece of the puzzle: the Procurement History Extraction by Federal Stock Number (PHE). He quickly found his product's NSN and uncovered twenty-two columns of historical information—ten years at a glance!

Let's take a brief look at the most critical columns in PHE, highlighting the first <u>underlined</u> item listed under each column:

A. Stock Number (column 1): 1660005152575. Just like the information in SNAPPL, all the information in PHE is indexed by the National Stock Number (NSN).

B. PIIN Contract Number (column 2): F3460183c3363000000. PIIN stands for "Procurement Instrument Identification Number." Specifically, the first six characters are the code that identifies the buying agency (also used in the *Commerce Business Daily*); the next two digits, *83*, designate the year of the contract award for this listing (1983); the remaining digits are sequential numbers assigned by the government to keep track of contracts throughout the year.

C. CLIN (column 3): 0001AB. CLIN stands for "Contract Line Item Number." This number tells manufacturers where in the original contract they can find the quantity and dollar information for their product or service.

D. Dt of Award (column 4): 83086. This column designates the date of the award for this listing by the last two digits of the year— 83 (1983)—and the day of the year—086 (based on 365 days in the year).

E. U (column 5): unit of measure for the product, or "each" (ea). Other common units of measure include DZ (dozen), TN (ton), and LT (miscellaneous lot).

F. Contract L/I Qty (column 6): 5. The original line item (L/I) of the contract for this purchase reveals that this agency purchased a quantity (Qty) of five.

G. L/I Price (column 7): 1,993.27. According to the contract, the total line-item purchase price for all four cylinders was $1,993.27.

H. CTR ID (column 22): 99062. This number is the contractor's identification number (CAGE code). To determine the name of the company, Steve could look up this CAGE number in government

TABLE 5-2.
PROCUREMENT HISTORY EXTRACTION (OR RECORD) (PHE OR PHR)

Column:	1	2	3	4	5	6	7	8–21	22	23
Item:	Stock Number	PIIN Contract Number	CLIN	Dt of Award	U/I	Contract L/I Qty	L/I Price	....	CTR ID	(Added for Explanation) Avg. Price (col 7÷6)
1.	1660005152575	F3460183C3363000000	0001AB	83086	ea	5	1,993.27		99062	398.65
2.	1660005152575	F3460183C3363000000	0001AC	83086	ea	21	8,371.73		99062	398.65
3.	1660005152575	F3460183C1288000000	0001AB	83175	ea	222	19,713.60		99062	88.80
4.	"	"		83275		259	21,007.49		99062	81.11
5.	"	"		84051		403	32,147.31		99062	79.77
6.	"	"		84204		401	34,044.90		99062	84.90
7.	"	"		85049		568	54,272.40		99062	95.55
8.	"	"		85294		594	62,696.70		99062	105.55
9.	"	"		86266		722	83,326.02		99062	115.41
10.	"	"		87083		207	25,529.31		99062	123.33
11.	"	"		87223		822	99,552.42		99062	121.11
12.	"	"		87355		420	50,866.20		99062	121.11
13.	"	"		88103		906	109,725.66		99062	121.11
14.	"	"		88207		930	112,632.30		99062	121.11
	Adding the forecasted SNAPPL trend for the next two years			89		1,122	165,000.00			147.06
				90		1,904	280,000.00			147.06

handbook HB-8. (See exhibit 5-3 for explanation of CAGE numbers, and see bibliography for HB-8.)

I. Avg. Price (column 23): 398.65. (Steve added this figure to the original computer printout.) To determine the price paid for each cylinder, Steve divided column 7 (total price) by column 6 (number of cylinders). The price paid for *each* cylinder was $398.65.

Steve gained valuable information by studying all the SNAPPL and PHE entries for this item. First, he discovered that the forecasted number of buys (SNAPPL) for fiscal years 1989 (1,122) and 1990 (1,904) were slightly less than the PHE totals for 1987 (1,449) and 1988 (1,836). Nonetheless, the quantity was still high enough to warrant sending for the manufacturing drawings and production specifications. (See exhibit 5-4 for ordering information.) Besides, this SNAPPL printout reviewed only one agency's requirements. There were several other buying agencies to investigate.

Second, he learned from PHE that one company (#99062) had dominated the market since 1983 and its prices were fairly consistent, regardless of whether it made 200 or 900 cylinders in a given production run.

Because PHE information provided details on a series of buys spread over many years, Steve could also get a quick idea of the price elasticity (the ratio of price to the volume produced) by plotting the data from table 5-2 onto table 5-3:

The vertical or *y* axis reflects the cost per item, calculated by dividing column 7 (line-item price—table 5-2) by column 6 (line-item quantity). The horizontal or *x* axis plots column 6, or the volume of each order. In our example, the horizontal line of price per unit is virtually the same for the past six buys over three years, despite a variance from 207 cylinders purchased on the 83rd day of 1987 to 930 cylinders purchased on the 207th day of 1988. The actual buys are represented by the *A*'s on the chart.

Steve expected to find a definitive curve reflecting a decrease in price as production volume increased—but he didn't. Instead, he discovered that the supplier was not giving the government volume discounts. This meant that Steve could easily compete, even on large orders. Encouraged by his findings, Steve sent for the cylinder production drawings from the agency's small business specialist. He wanted to develop a detailed cost estimate to see if he could undercut the PHE published prices by 10 percent or more.

TABLE 5-3

GENERIC COST VS. VOLUME CURVE

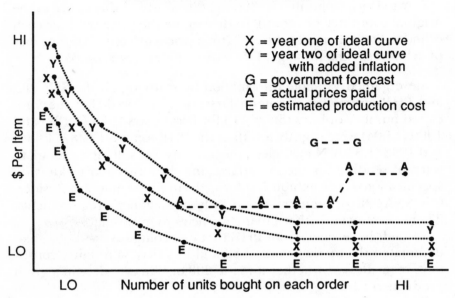

After studying the drawings and accompanying specifications, Steve plotted his estimated production costs (*E*) on the graph. He then compared his estimated production costs (*E*) to the number of actual buys (*A*). After figuring in his production, contract preparation, and administration costs, he concluded that he could underbid his competitor on the larger orders.

Now Steve began to formulate his strategy. On the first round, he would underbid his competitor only slightly—taking as much profit as the market would allow. As his competitor woke up to the new competition, Steve predicted the bidding would force the prices down further. "It took some time and effort," Steve told me afterward, "but the market information I got from SNAPPL and PHE gave me the confidence and the strategy to compete in the procurement market—and win!"

EXPANDING YOUR HORIZONS: PASS REGISTRATION

If you want to expand your procurement activity beyond the procurement agencies, you may want to register with the Procurement

Automated Source System (PASS). Operated by the Small Business Administration, PASS is used by federal agencies and prime contractors to solicit additional bidders when their own bidders' list is too limited. You can get a one-page PASS registration form (see SBA 1167 in appendix 1) from your local Small Business Administration office. However, consider PASS as an extension—*not a substitute*—for the Standard Form 129 registration for specific bidders' lists.

CASE STUDY: SEARCHING FOR MR. GOOD MARKET

Perhaps the best way to explain how the investigative procurement process works is to relate the success story of Floridia Manufacturing, a wire cable manufacturing company I worked with in Albuquerque, New Mexico. Owner Connie Floridia's first task was to identify the federal purchasing centers that would be interested in her wire cable.

First, I helped her review the SBA's *U.S. Government Purchasing and Sales Directory*—the alphabetical listing of products and services purchased by the three federal supply groups. Since the major military purchasing offices have the largest budgets, Floridia decided to target her initial inquiries to those purchasing centers.

Under the index for "Major Military Purchasing Offices" we found three applicable categories: "Wire and wire rope assemblies," "Fittings for rope, cable, and chain," and "Wire, nonelectrical, iron and steel." The purchasing centers listed were "A–32 (Army, St. Louis, MO), A–45 (Rock Island, IL), N–6 (Navy, Washington D.C.), D–5 (Defense Industrial Supply Center, Philadelphia, PA)," and so forth. (The addresses and contacts appeared in a separate table.) Out of the twenty-six purchasing centers listed in the *Sales Directory,* she found that twenty-one bought one or more of these three referenced commodity categories.

Floridia completed the basic information about her company on a copy of the Standard Form 129 (SF129), the bidders' list application, which she found in the back of the *Sales Directory*. After completing the basic information, she made twenty-one copies—one for each purchasing center. Then, on each form, she filled in the name of the particular buying agency, signed her name, and attached a cover letter requesting the purchasing center's Alphabetical/ Numerical Cross-Reference Listing and buy list (Procurement Source Class and Suffix List).

Floridia's first response came from Tinker Air Force Base in Oklahoma City. Looking at the Tinker alphabetical/numerical cross-reference pamphlet, she discovered that "wire rope assembly" was not listed. A bit perplexed, she browsed through the alphabetically organized pamphlet and found "Wire, Nonelectrical, Iron and Steel" with a Federal Stock Class number of 9505, and "Wire, Nonelectrical, Nonferrous Base Metal," FSC 9525. Looking further, she finally located a listing for "Chain and Wire Rope," FSC 4010.

When Floridia looked up 4010 on Tinker's detailed Source Class and Suffix List, she found that Tinker buys the following subcategories:

4010   Chain and Wire Rope

401001   Cable, Steel, Spooled, Aircraft Target Towing

401002   Wire Rope, Steel

401003   Wire Strand, Steel

401097   Chain and Wire Rope Not Listed Above

The instructions attached to Tinker's Source Class and Suffix List said to check off, on the numerical listing, the stock numbers Floridia Manufacturing wished to bid on. After completing this, she copied the buy list and returned the original to the Tinker purchasing center. This registered Floridia Manufacturing on Tinker's bidders' list.

After completing all this work, however, Floridia still didn't have a clue about the size of the market for which she was registering. So I recommended that she order the Stock Numbered Advanced Procurement Planning List (SNAPPL) from each of the twenty-one agencies, to examine the government's forecasted buys, and the Procurement History Extraction (PHE) to examine past buys. When both arrived, we used the NSNs selected from Tinker's buying list to locate the government's forecasted buys. Comparing the history (PHE) with the forecasted activity (SNAPPL), we determined that most agencies were forecasting consistently large buys for the next two years. This indicated a stable market.

Floridia still needed more information before she could develop a price estimate. So she examined the PHE contract line-item data to learn the quantity and total cost of individual orders. Simple division gave her the price per item for differing contract amounts.

Plotting the cost per item on the y axis and the quantities on an x axis (as in table 5-3), she graphed different contract dates as points (each year plotted in a different color). This gave Floridia the insider's information to price orders of any size.

Her next step was to identify the successful bidders by CAGE numbers, using the Defense Logistics Agency's *HB–4* and *HB–8* handbooks. (See exhibit 5-3 for identification procedure.) As it turned out, two companies consistently won the contract when the volume was more than $25,000. After some discussion, we concluded that these companies probably did not bid on purchase orders for less than $25,000, because they were not advertised in the *Commerce Business Daily*. So we decided to avoid the competition by first bidding on contracts for less than $25,000. This would also qualify Floridia Manufacturing to bid on the larger contracts and maybe—just maybe—capture that market, too.

Now we were hungry for more information on materials, specifications, and production drawings. So Floridia asked Tinker's small business advocate for the AIDE listings of the stock number items she was interested in. Using the FSN and the part numbers from SNAPPL, she requested the production drawings from Tinker's small business advocate. The production drawings referred to product specifications by numbers, which she used to order the specifications from the Specifications and Standards Center in Philadelphia, Pennsylvania. (See bibliography: Specifications and Standards Center.) After studying the drawings and specifications, Floridia was certain that her production process would be acceptable.

With the forecasted buying plans, production drawings, and material and production specifications in hand, Floridia could develop timely price estimates for solicitations as she received them.

While this research was for only one of twenty-one possible markets, she realized that the remaining market development projections would be much faster. By computerizing much of the repetitive work (graphs and correspondence) on her personal computer, she would save hundreds of hours of market research time.

If you follow the same steps as Floridia Manufacturing, you will sense a growing momentum in your journey through the bureaucratic jungle.

"The first time through is the most difficult," Connie Floridia advises. "The second time is much easier. And by the third time, your journey will seem routine. Chances are, your competitors don't even know all this information exists. In the meantime, you'll profit from being on the inside track."

Armed with this strategic information, you can now decide if you want to pursue the federal market. But before you receive your first solicitation, there are a few more things you will need to know to increase your chances of winning that contract. They're what the next three chapters will explore.

6

Setting Up a Quality Control System

Ask John Q. Public what "Made in America" means and the response may be a disillusioned snicker. Ask a Q (government quality inspector) what it means and you'll probably get a lecture on the importance of quality control.

It takes only one grim reminder to show us that quality control *must* be a top priority in doing business with the government. It takes only one failed bolt to send an airplane engine crashing to the ground. It takes only one failed O-ring to kill seven astronauts and jeopardize our space shuttle program.

Of course, *you* probably don't produce a product or service critical to life. Even so, you will be held accountable for quality, as specified in your contract. And whereas human lives may not be at stake, your future business with the government could be.

So even though these cases are exceptional, they do illustrate one thing: The government doesn't allow you to try, try, try again. Take the case of the toilet paper supplier who hasn't gotten a second chance since his product didn't hold up. Dubbed "marine" paper because *it wouldn't take anything off of anybody,* the paper left the procurement officer far from amused. And the contractor's reputation came precariously close to bottoming out.

Unfortunately, such highly publicized cases often cause small companies to shy away from doing business with the government. Maybe you, too, have used the quality-control-bottleneck argument to avoid the federal market. Ironically, you may already be doing superior work for large manufacturers. No doubt you take pride in maintaining quality standards and service. So why are you afraid of meeting government quality standards—standards that are spelled out in writing?

Let's take the mystique out of government inspection requirements: *The small business that is quality conscious should not be intimidated by government quality control standards.* Once you understand how your quality procedures can be adapted to government requirements, and see how government standards can even improve your commercial business, you will wonder why you've feared the Q for so long.

THE ABCs OF QUALITY CONTROL

Before you make any assumptions about the complexity and extent of the government's quality control requirements, be aware that the type of product or service will determine the quality control requirements, and your performance record will determine the extent to which your adherence to these requirements will be scrutinized. These requirements are spelled out in your contract as *referenced* FAR clauses, with product requirements detailed more extensively on production drawings.

Depending on the product or service you supply, the government has six different quality assurance categories, ranging from "commercial standards" for items of comparatively simple design and use to "MIL-Q [military quality] standards" for items critical to life support and/or critical performance. The classification depends on the intended application of the item or service. In some cases, a mechanically complex item may require less quality inspection than a simple one.

A Denver car tire manufacturer was amazed that the government required only a letter certifying that the tires would meet commercial requirements of "form, fit, and function." Form requirements amounted to little more than a notation that the new tires would replace the old tires, fit was summarized by the required dimensions, and function requirements were measured by time, tread wear, and freedom from defects.

On the other hand, a San Diego bracket manufacturer—who contracted to supply the navy with bulkhead brackets for vibrating equipment—was required to undertake a multitude of tests: on raw materials, contour, vibration, absorption, positioning of drilled holes, as well as equipment and other testing.

Although each solicitation lists individual quality system requirements by FAR clauses, there are seven standard elements that are included in most government-approved quality control systems:*

- *Organization.* Assigning specific authority and responsibility for each production phase of the process
- *Quality planning.* Developing written instructions with realistic "defect prevention" processes for analyzing manufacturing processes for possible quality trouble spots, for setting acceptance/rejection standards, for controlling accepted/rejected products, and for using failure information and customer complaints to improve product quality
- *Product specification control.* Making sure everyone has the latest technical data for producing, inspecting, and shipping the product
- *Supplier quality control.* Inspecting purchased raw materials, parts, and subassemblies to make sure that your suppliers observe your quality requirements and technical specifications
- *Measurement and test equipment control.* Setting up a system to ensure that equipment is accurately and regularly calibrated to established standards
- *Nonconforming material control.* Spotting defects as early in production as possible and keeping defective items from reaching customers
- *Records and reports.* Setting up a recording system to track all steps of the production process, inspection, and shipping cycle to identify problem areas

Perhaps the most important commandment to keep in mind is that *you are responsible for quality control*—not the government. Government inspection or a waiver of inspection does not cancel your responsibility for product defects—even latent defects that can be discovered months after inspection. The government maintains that *quality cannot be inspected in*—*it must be built in.* (See exhibit 6-1 for other inspection requirements.)

* Adapted from the Small Business Administration's handout, "Setting Up a Quality Control System," Management Aid Number 2812.

===================== **EXHIBIT 6-1** =====================

Standard or Special Inspection Requirements?

Depending on the product and its intended use, quality inspection requirements may range from simple to complex. All of the systems that require inspections beyond form, fit, and function will include the following requirements:

Standard Inspection Requirements

• All raw materials are subject to government inspection and testing.

• The government may reject and/or require correction for defective supplies or for supplies that don't conform to contract requirements. Correction or replacement will be at the supplier's expense. If the correction or replacement causes late deliveries, then the government may terminate the contract for default or change the financial terms of the contract:

1. The contractor must furnish reasonable facilities and assistance for government inspectors. If the government fails to inspect or reject supplies, the contractor is not relieved of his or her responsibilities, nor is the government liable.

2. Government inspection does not relieve the contractor of responsibility for latent defects, fraud, or gross mistakes that amount to fraud.

3. The contractor must provide and maintain a documented inspection system acceptable to the government—including documentation for special materials called for in the contract. The contractor must maintain complete records of all inspections for the period called for by the contract.

4. For items with critical technical requirements, inspection may be in-process as well as final end-item inspection. Critical items may also call for more detailed contract clauses defining acceptable inspection systems. When this requirement appears in the contract, a government quality assurance representative will evaluate the contractor's inspection system in accordance with the guidelines provided in DOD handbook *H–51* (see bibliography).

The price you pay to develop a superlative quality control program, however, will likely pay off. If you are designing or documenting a quality control program or revamping an old one, you should begin by setting some definite economic and performance goals. One government contractor set—and met—a goal of 90 percent decrease in product rejects. This resulted in a 40 percent decrease in overall production reject costs. By revamping its quality control program, this aerospace contractor realized savings in four areas affecting rejected parts and materials:

Raw materials	30 percent
Subcontracting work	25 percent
Purchase parts for subassemblies	15 percent
Bulk supplies, hardware, bench stock	30 percent

GETTING FROM ABC TO XYZ: THE SYSTEMS APPROACH

One day a mold casting manufacturer called me to complain, "I'm only halfway through reading my solicitation's quality control requirements, and I'm ready to throw in the towel. I don't even have a written quality control plan, let alone a gauge calibration program. Where do I go from here?"

"Don't worry," I assured him. "Even though you haven't documented your quality control procedures, it's obvious that you are conscientious. It's just a question of organizing and documenting your procedures using a systems approach."

"I've heard about the 'systems approach,'" he said, "but I'm not sure I know how it works."

I went on to explain that he needed a systematic quality program that would support all of the government's quality requirements.

Anticipating his next question, I explained that a quality program could include everything from documenting the quality of incoming raw materials to packaging and shipping. It also includes a system for reviewing and taking corrective action to resolve problems occurring within the system.

Finally, I explained, a quality manual documents your entire quality system. For example, if you sell canned ham to the commissaries, your quality manual might document the receiving and testing of the ham, processing times and temperatures, food wrapping and sealing procedures, and the shipping procedures.

Let's take a look at how a typical quality control system and quality control manual could be organized using a systems approach. (See appendix 10 for a sample quality manual outline.)

Scope and Job Responsibilities: A Team Effort

Before you begin documenting your quality procedures, you will need to formulate the scope and designate job responsibilities for your quality control program. A statement of scope or purpose should reveal why quality control is important and mention all the major areas of quality control responsibility. Although it may seem self-evident, stating why you need a good, well- documented quality control system is the first step in improving your existing system. It is also important that everyone in the company understand and support quality control.

"I realized that a good quality control program would need the support of labor as well as management," says Bob Hannay, a Boston manufacturer of coiled springs. "So we worked as a team. We not only revised our quality control program, we improved it dramatically."

By using a team approach Hannay discovered that one quality responsibility was not clearly designated: product specification control. Updated production drawings and manufacturing specifications were not being routed correctly or expediently. After clarifying who was responsible for specification control, new drawings and specifications were routed first from engineering to production, rather than to management.

Materials: Ordering, Receiving, Storage, and Inspection

The *contractor* is responsible for ensuring that any materials used to manufacture a product or provide a service meet quality requirements. This includes any materials supplied by subcontractors. Remember the problem with the faulty bolt that resulted in the engine falling off the airplane? More than one company has avoided corporate liability and certain bankruptcy by proving that the material they processed was "certified" material from their "qualified" suppliers.

Even when the government supplies the raw materials for a manufacturing process, the contractor is responsible for inspecting these materials if their characteristics are "critical" to product quality. Occasionally a government supply vendor will send a manufacturer poor-quality materials. Only if the manufacturer is able to document and prove that the received material is defective will he or she be eligible for cost reimbursements.

Besides production procedures, a good quality manual will clarify procedures for everything from filling out purchase orders to receiving and storing raw materials to shipping finished goods. (Again, see appendix 10.)

The importance of detailed procedures was dramatized when I was responsible for buying electrical control cables for the government. Although the initial testing confirmed that the first cables were good, within a week the cables failed to conduct the required current.

The reason became evident when the incoming inspector discovered a problem with storage. The supplies were stored under the first outlet duct of the air conditioning system, then moved to the warm production floor in front of the back doors of the plant. When the thin wires were moved from a cool to a warm environment, moisture from the warm air condensed and set up an oxidation resistance. Since the cables were stored for three to five days before they were encased in molded rubber, the metal strips deteriorated.

As this example illustrates, you may save a great deal of money by carefully designing procedures, taking care to document everything—before, during, and after production. Pay particular attention to any certifications for critical materials. The certification annotation must be received with the materials, and a copy must be retained with the materials throughout the production process, to be verified by inspectors at each work station.

"I was constantly searching for a cheaper supplier when I should have been looking for a more reliable supplier," says M. J. Watts, a Los Angeles furniture manufacturer. Like Watts, who learned her lesson from the Japanese, you may discover that it makes sense to concentrate your time and money on working with a limited number of suppliers to maintain higher quality. The Japanese try to develop a "lifetime qualified supplier," whereas Americans constantly search for multiple, cheaper sources. So the Japanese have to debug the quality system only once—and Americans do it repeatedly. You might accomplish a major part of your quality control savings goal by expecting zero defects and working with your suppliers to resolve quality problems so that you can attain that goal.

Production: Inspection and Testing

Your quality system should also document all the work throughout the production process. Unless the process is continuous and requires no testing before completion, the material should be tracked with a "shop travel card" that details each required step of the process, including inspections.

At each inspection point the inspector should certify with a personalized stamp that the desired characteristics have been checked and the product meets specifications on the production drawings. The personalized stamp ensures that any defects can be traced back to the inspector who missed the discrepancy.

On-Site Testing. Depending on your contract requirements, you may need to document on-site assembly inspections, functional inspections, and final testing for your product. This could involve in-process and finished product (end-item) inspections with immediate feedback so that personnel can evaluate their work. Conducting detailed testing should decrease rejects and waste. And once a buying agency sees that your testing system is a good one, it probably will require less testing and less supervision.

Says one manufacturer with a long-term contract to produce cellular automobile phones for the GSA, "The government inspector oversaw inspection on every item during my first contract. But once he realized that my process was stable and producing a good product, he inspected less and less. By my third contract, he only inspected the first and last items."

Some items, especially those with electrical components, may require only functional testing at the end of the production process. Nicknamed "the smoke test," this procedure may involve little more than turning on the unit. If the unit doesn't smoke and still works after fifteen to twenty minutes, it will usually work for the duration of its warranty.

A Minneapolis, Minnesota, small engine manufacturer was surprised to learn that he had to design and document only one good quality inspection system to comply with every agency's requirements. "I developed my inspection system to meet the highest-quality application—engines to drive electrical generators. Now I sell to four different government agencies. My engines are used for boats, air blowers, water pumps—you name it!" (See exhibit 6-2 for a description of the inspection process.)

===================== **EXHIBIT 6-2** =====================

Inspector Widget

Inspection procedures don't have to bottleneck production. Let's follow Inspector Widget, a government quality assurance inspector, on his visit through a small-engine manufacturing plant.

As the day begins, we find Inspector Widget checking the materials and subassemblies at the receiving dock area. The incoming parts require little more than a cursory inspection, as the inspector concentrates most of his effort on verifying material certifications against a copy of the purchase order specifications.

The inspector then walks the two production lines to oversee assembly procedures. He pays particular attention to new employees, reiterating what characteristics he is inspecting and how the employee can check and flag potential problems.

The inspector proceeds to the final assembly area, where the experienced workers are "buttoning up" the final assembly. Overhead is a sign, the plant slogan, which reads: "Once is enough." The slogan reminds the employees that poor work means more work for them.

The final assembly workers perform their own inspections as they exchange pleasantries with the inspector. One worker motions the inspector over to examine the paint job on some of the engines. The employees obviously have easy access to the inspector.

The inspector then goes into the test booth where employees run the engines. Most of the engines are run only long enough to get hot. Then they are purged of all fluids, touched up, packed, and stacked for final shipment. The inspector pulls out one engine, and it starts on the first pull. Then he sends it to another testing area, where it will be attached to an electrical generator to test for voltage and current output for an extended period to verify performance consistency.

Off-Site Testing. Occasionally the government will require off-site testing on your first manufactured product at a government or government-approved testing lab. Called a "first-article" test, this evaluation is performed either after the contract is awarded or, in some instances, as a prerequisite for a contract award to register a complex or critical product on a Qualified Producer List. First-article testing is ordered if you are a first-time government contractor, if you are producing a newly designed product, or if you have manufactured a product that failed in the field. Other companies producing critical raw materials may have them tested at a commercial lab. The certified findings may help them get on the Qualified Products List, prequalifying them to receive future solicitations. (See exhibit 6-3 on prequalification procedures.)

═══════════════ **EXHIBIT 6-3** ═══════════════

Becoming Prequalified: Requirements for an Insider's Market

If you manufacture or want to manufacture a product that requires critically accurate performance and reliability, you will probably need to "prequalify" your product before you can become registered on the Qualified Bidders' List. To prequalify, a contractor's product must pass special requirements for testing or quality assurance before a contract is awarded.

Prequalification is required especially for solicitations for electronic components, computers, airplanes, and submarines. These solicitations are often listed under the *Commerce Business Daily*'s "Additional Sources Sought" section. You may also explore this potential insider's market by requesting an agency's Qualified Products List. If your product appears on the list, ask about the agency's prequalification procedures.

The *FAR* requires that government agencies actively encourage increased competition from small businesses, so the buying agency should gladly provide you with information. In some cases, the government will even bear the cost of testing and certification.

Destination Testing. The government may also inspect your product at the delivery destination. Spelled out in the contract, this option usually requires a warranty that certifies form, fit, and function. Additionally, a "latent defect clause" in your contract may stipulate an interval for which the contractor guarantees product quality. This allows government inspectors to inspect a shipment quickly by random sampling. Any latent defects can then be corrected within the latency period—within a year, for example.

Equipment Testing. Besides product testing, the government may require inspection of your production equipment. This is especially true for precision equipment. The adage "your results are only as good as your equipment" clearly was demonstrated when I worked with a manufacturer of aircraft wing panels who had to scrap an entire production run because the panel holes did not match the wing frame holes. After a detailed search the manufacturer discovered that his template's holes (a pattern used to drill the panel holes) were all a fraction of an inch elongated due to wear.

Packaging, Identification, and Shipping

Perhaps the most costly government quality control requirements involve product packaging, identification, and shipping. These requirements are dictated largely by the government's intended use of the product, as well as shipping and storage conditions. These variables are often quite different from commercial markets. If you are shipping metal washers to a military field repair unit, for example, don't be surprised if you are required to ship them in sealed heavy-duty bags, each containing only two or three washers.

Similarly, shipping and storage conditions may also vary from the norm. This is why the government may require the use of technologically advanced packaging materials such as bubble plastic, egg crate foam, and poured shaped Styrofoam. Although these new technologies have decreased freight damages and made shipping easier, they have not necessarily made it less expensive. Be forewarned that quality levels in these areas tend to be specialized and stringent.

Another new technology affecting both labeling and shipping is bar coding, whereby products are labeled and tracked using bar codes that can be scanned optically by computers. This way, a product's contents and location can be easily tracked as it makes its way through various distribution points.

Discrepancy Review System

Even though your quality control program strives for efficiency and zero defects, occasionally you may fall short of your goal. In fact, when you document a new or revised quality control program, you may uncover several production problems of which you were unaware. All the better. This means your quality control program is working.

Now the real work begins. Besides providing for the prevention and expedient detection of problems, your quality program also should provide a grass-roots system for correcting any problems or discrepancies.

The government is particularly concerned that all your personnel be quality conscious and have direct access to top management to report any quality failures and suggestions. The government must verify that those responsible for quality decisions are not influenced by conflicting production quotas and profit goals.

The airplane wing panel manufacturer who discovered the faulty templates had a chance to test and revamp both his inspection system and his discrepancy review system after he had to scrap the ill-fitting panels. When he finally identified the problem, he realized that it was threefold:

1. Because his quality system did not provide timely inspection of his production equipment, the holes in the templates used to drill the panels were allowed to become elongated. This resulted in panel holes that did not fit the airplane wings.
2. Because he did not have a system for employees to report suspected quality problems the moment they occurred, production

continued—even though workers farther down the production line detected the problem.

3. And because he didn't have an adequate corrective action plan— an extra template in stock, for example—he wasted valuable production time replacing the worn template.

MIND YOUR P'S AND Q'S

If you've ever wondered where the phrase "mind your *p*'s and *q*'s" came from, ask the Q's. The Q's are government quality inspectors, and they will tell you the P's are their counterparts: the government production specialists responsible for making sure you meet your contract deadlines. Like peas in a pod, the two go together.

The Q's might tell you that, given a choice between quality and timeliness, quality should win. What they mean is that delivering the product or service on time is not always as important as delivering a *quality* item or service.

But I'm sure you're not taking any chances. You've got a quality product, and you can make a timely delivery. So now you're saying, "Bring on the feds—both the P's and the Q's!" But you're getting ahead of yourself. First you've got to land that contract. For some of you that will mean passing the P and Q inspection: the preaward survey. If you've designed a good quality control system, you're already halfway there. The next chapter will be an easy one for you.

7

The Preaward Survey

"Since I only sell a few vehicle parts to the government, I'll never have to worry about a preaward survey," insisted Ted Wormeli, owner of Seismic Vehicles, Inc.

Ted smiled as he recalled his famous last words—spoken before the army showed interest in his patented seismic device for monitoring low-frequency radio waves. Wormeli used his instrument to locate oil-rich geological formations by bouncing radio waves off geological strata. Now the army wanted his device for "experimental reasons."

After imparting my "never say never" admonitions, I helped him begin preparing for one of the most feared and least understood government procedures: the preaward survey. If he passed it, Wormeli could land a multimillion-dollar contract.

Like Wormeli, you may think that because you haven't competed for contracts of more than $25,000 or produced a product or service critical to life support, you will never have to face a preaward survey. But why limit your horizons to $25,000 contracts? Besides, just understanding what occurs during a preaward survey may give you the confidence to bid on a million-dollar deal.

PREAWARD PROTOCOL

Remember that the government awards contracts on the basis of responsibility, responsiveness, and price. In other words, it doesn't only matter that you're the lowest bidder; you must also prove that you're a responsible and responsive contractor.

The government has more than enough grim reminders that "you get what you pay for." Says one preaward official for the Defense Department, "The lowest price doesn't mean anything if I can't get parts in when I need them and they don't work when I get them." It is for this reason that *FAR* requires a preaward survey when the procuring agency does not have enough information to determine whether the prospective contractor is responsible and responsive. The government can perform a preaward when:

- The prospective contractor has never done business with the government.
- The government is significantly increasing its business with the contractor.
- The contract is for more than $25,000.
- The product or service is critical to life support.
- The contractor has been negligent on a former contract.

Before a government buying agency requests an expensive preaward survey, it will check all its "inexpensive" sources of contractor information, such as performance evaluations on previous government contracts and other internal agency computer files. (See exhibit 7-1: "They Have Their 'Sources.'") If internal sources reveal no information, then the purchasing officer asks the Defense Contract Administration Services (DCAS or DCASMA), the government agency responsible for contract administration, to evaluate one or more areas of a potential contractor's performance, production, or financial capability.

=========================== **EXHIBIT 7-1** ===========================

They Have Their "Sources"

A contracting officer will check the following sources prior to ordering an expensive preaward survey:

- A consolidated interagency list of debarred, suspended, and ineligible contractors
- The Contractor Alert List

. Agency computer records and data files, including information from knowledgeable personnel within the contracting office with whom you may have contracted

- Interagency computer records and data files of other contracting offices, audit offices, and contract administration offices that might have monitored previously awarded government contracts
- Records of government prime contractors you have worked with
- Local SBA office recommendations

The preaward survey may evaluate as many as seven different functional areas of review, including:

- General information
- Technical capability
- Production capacity
- Quality assurance
- Financial capability
- Accounting systems
- Other factors based on special requirements of the contract

Any deficient area must be corrected in time to meet the contract requirements.

If a small business fails the preaward survey, the contracting officer will refer the business to the Small Business Administration for its help in correcting the problem(s). (See below: "All Systems Go ... or ... Do Not Pass Go.")

Occasionally, the preaward survey is little more than a formality or a brief check and resolution of one problem area. For example, E-M Inc., a small Milwaukee electromechanical assemblies company, received superior ratings on its first preaward and performed superbly on several government contracts until it had two late deliveries. As the chief of production for the state's Defense Contract Administration Office, I conducted a preaward to scrutinize this production problem. When I visited the plant, I quickly discovered the problem: The company had too much business, causing bottlenecks on the production line. Not wanting to lose a good contractor, I recommended that the company owner institute a second shift. The owner agreed, and E-M went on to expand both its commercial and government business.

While E-M got by with a minimal preaward survey, your company may be examined in all seven areas. To prepare, you should know which items the government evaluates in each category. Appendix 1 includes the standard government preaward forms (SF1403/ SF1409) that contain the areas which may be evaluated. Keep in mind that while these forms provide a guideline for the preaward officials, the checklists are by no means the final word. *Don't be surprised if the preaward official requests more information. And don't hesitate to present the preaward team with other favorable information that could result in a positive recommendation—whether it asks for it or not.* On the other hand, don't be surprised if the preaward evaluator skims over the forms.

Let's prepare for the day you receive a telephone call or a letter notifying you of a pending preaward survey. Your notification will specifically identify the areas DCAS will evaluate, tell whether or not the buying office will participate, and give a date by which the preaward report must be completed. Some people panic when they receive their notification. But if you read and follow the information in this chapter, you will be confident that you're just one step closer to winning a government contract.

Technical Capabilities: Experience and Know-how

If you've never manufactured the widget that the government wants, you might assume that you can never win a contract. This assumption could cost you some lucrative business. Determining *if* you can produce an item or service is what the preaward's technical evaluation is all about, and why it is so important to your success.

The preaward technical evaluation (Standard Form 1404) evaluates the prospective contractor's technical knowledge of the solicitation, including such things as drawings, specifications, inspections, testing, and packaging. And if you've never manufactured the widget, the evaluator will want to check your past and current performance on similar or more complex items.

The preaward evaluator may also investigate the skills of the company's key management and technical personnel and/or "available" personnel. Passive Energy Engineering Company learned the importance of available personnel when it bid on a Department of Energy contract. The contract required an easy-to-understand demonstration model that could be used at public displays to explain the project.

Passive Energy was not in the model business, so it scoured the central United States for a good model maker. At first the search seemed fruitless, for model making had seemingly died out as a viable trade. Since the contract was a large one, however, the company turned its attention to hobbyists, finally locating a retiree who agreed to work for the company as a consultant for the model construction.

After evaluating the model maker's skills for the preaward, the government accepted this arrangement. The contract was subsequently awarded and completed—with an interesting twist. The model-making venture was so successful that the engineering company hired the retiree and incorporated a new business. (See exhibit 7-2 for another example of subcontracting.)

======================= **EXHIBIT 7-2** =======================

The "Cost" of Subcontracting

Your employees' capabilities and the "cost" of subcontracting often become clear when you contract with the government. IAMA Computer Software Company learned an important lesson after a preaward survey approval of its plan to hire an outside consulting firm to help complete a software development contract. The customized software was to be used for managing a special government project.

To develop the customized software for the project management, the consultants would have to understand every task of the project and the time it would take to complete the task, and then classify each worker's skills in relation to the tasks. The software program would also pinpoint missing skills and identify training or hiring needs.

After the consultants had spent weeks gathering data,

IAMA discovered that the data were improperly organized. In order to meet the contract deadline, IAMA's own staff had to work overtime revising the format—much longer than the original data gathering would have taken using IAMA's own staff.

IAMA not only learned that *who* you hire is critical, but it also learned that if it had taken the time to assess its own personnel skills, it could have done the job itself. Ironically, it took a contract to develop software for personnel evaluation for IAMA to evaluate its own personnel!

Production Capacity: On Time Every Time

Besides evaluating your technical knowledge and capabilities, the preaward team may also want to determine your company's ability to perform a contract *on time*. To do this, a government production specialist (P) will evaluate your ability to plan, control, and integrate personnel, facilities, materials, and other resources.

In the area of personnel, for example, you will need a current organizational chart that accurately reflects interaction among management, production, and inspection personnel. The P may check to see if your personnel files are updated to reflect appropriate certifications and licenses. The inspector will also want to know your method for determining the number and availability of personnel you will need and your criteria for hiring them. If you plan to hire extra personnel, do you have current résumés of available candidates organized by job category?

To evaluate your ability to plan, the P will probably want more than a list of your current contracts and a production chart chronologically plotting all your production activities. The government production specialist will expect to see a breakdown of the production capacity demands required to fulfill your current and projected *future* commercial contracts, as well as the capacity you have left over to devote to government contracts. Your pending contracts are important, since the government wants to avoid any potential bottlenecks.

If you are bidding on a product or service you have never produced, be able to document your production history on related work, such as a product requiring a similar manufacturing process, service, or use of machinery or technical skills.

Your production documentation should cover everything from written criteria for selecting subcontractors, to written and legally binding schedule commitments and quotations from suppliers and subcontractors, to records verifying your system for inventory control and purchasing.

Remember, your production plans are only as reliable as your suppliers and subcontractors. Take care to select reputable subcontractors and to document their *warranty* to meet the lead times specified in the contract. Don't be surprised when the preaward specialist wants to review the written preliminary quotations on your projected material orders and subcontracts. The inspector may even call or visit your supplier(s) or subcontractor(s) to verify these quotations.

The production specialist is very interested in your delivery performance record. If you have done business with the government before, your past will be resurrected. Keep in mind that the government's evaluation of your timeliness is based on the initial delivery date, not your ability to obtain and meet a contract extension date.

Finally, the preaward specialist might look at your plant facilities to determine whether your space, tooling, equipment, storage areas, transportation, and loading and unloading abilities will accommodate the government order.

Because of the high cost of facilities, many companies are finding innovative ways to handle cyclical government business. For example, Aerospace Investment Inc. invested in a large building expansion based on a flurry of government contracts. Then government buys suddenly decreased, and the company was left with a large building but few contracts. Rather than sell the building in a depressed market, the company arranged a long-term lease with two other multilocation government contracting companies to share the space, loading facilities, and equipment on an as-needed basis.

The arrangement worked well for several years, as each company won just enough small contracts to use the facilities for overflow work without overlap. Each company would bid on a project and provide a modified drawing of the shared facilities for the type of space it needed. The preaward team had only to verify the arrangements with the building owner.

Then the inevitable happened: Two of the three contractors received simultaneous preawards on large contracts. No matter how you sliced it, the facility was too small for both companies.

The government didn't want to lose two good contractors, and the companies didn't want to lose the largest contracts they had ever bid on. So the preaward survey team and the company owners devised a solution. Since the facility had a great deal of usable vertical space, the companies decided to expand upward by building mezzanines (floors without walls). However, the success of the plan was still dependent on the speed with which the expansion could be designed and completed.

Again, innovation came to the fore when the companies' design engineers, materials procurement personnel, and facility planners teamed up to devise a three-dimensional building design package that was generated by one company's minicomputers. The team effort paid off: The companies' plan satisfied the preaward team, and the expansion was completed in time for performance on the government contracts.

Quality Assurance: "Here Come the Q's"

If you set up a documented quality control system as outlined in chapter 6, you probably will satisfy all of the requirements of the government quality inspector (Q). As you already know, quality assurance requirements may be as simple as a written warranty of form, fit, and function—as in the case of a car tire—or as complex as multiple testing processes—as in the case of a highly critical fire-detection system for a moving vehicle. Since the elements of quality assurance vary depending on the requirements of the solicitation, you will need to study the solicitation and its referenced clauses carefully to determine which elements will be evaluated in the preaward. (See exhibit 7-3 for a quality assurance checklist.)

═══════════════ **EXHIBIT 7-3** ═══════════════

Preaward Quality Assurance Checklist

A contract's quality standard *level* (stated in section E of the contract) designates what a preaward inspector will evaluate. The following provides a description of inspections by quality levels: All (all quality levels), I (military inspection—stringent but not life-dependent), C (commercial standards), Q (highest standard—life and safety included), and As Required.

- (*All*) Understanding of technical data package
- (*All*) Understanding of packaging and marking requirements
- (*All*) Documentation of quality performance during past twelve months for similar items
- (*All*) Use of used, reconditioned, or surplus material
- (*All*) Amount of assistance required from the government
- (*All*) Number of quality assurance personnel
- (*All*) Inspection to production personnel ratio

Availability and Adequacy Of:

- (*All*) Inspection/test equipment for first article and production
- (*I, C, Q*) Calibration/metrology program
- (*I, Q*) Written procedures and instructions
- (*I, Q*) Control of engineering drawings, specifications, etc.
- (*Q*) Quality assurance/control organizational structure
- (*All*) System for determining inspection, test, and measurement requirements
- (*I, Q*) Controls for purchased materials and services
- (*I, Q*) Material control and quarantine procedures
- (*As Required*) Controls for government items
- (*All*) In-process inspection controls
- (*I, Q*) Corrective action system
- (*All*) Preservation, packaging, packing, and marking controls
- (*All*) Quality control records
- (*All*) Customer complaint investigation system
- (*As Required*) Reliability and/or maintainability program
- (*As Required*) Computer software program

Not surprisingly, quality requirements may seem an extension or variation of production requirements, since many of the same considerations will affect both quality assurance and production timeliness. Like the government production specialist, the preaward quality specialist will first examine your organizational structure and your production history. The emphasis, however, will be different. The Q will want to know, for instance, how many skilled and unskilled quality control personnel there are in each area of your plant, what their responsibilities are, and the ratio of quality personnel to production personnel. The Q will also want to see documentation indicating that your upper management regularly reviews the status and adequacy of your quality program and that your quality assurance staff can operate with the cooperation of other departments. Also expect the Q to investigate your company's quality history for the past twelve months, for identical, similar, or different items that you have produced for the government or commercial customers. If the Q doesn't have enough data, you will have to prove that you are indeed capable.

Many companies fail preawards because they overlook critical technical requirements in the solicitation. So the quality assurance inspector will want to determine whether you understand the technical data of your solicitation—including packaging and product identification requirements. If your solicitation fails to clarify specifications or materials, ask the Q during the preaward survey. For example, while most solicitations prohibit your use of used, reconditioned, or surplus materials, a few solicitations and buying agencies are "silent" about the use of these materials. Even if the solicitation and buying agency permit the use of such materials, you will need a documented system for assuring that these materials are properly tested and identical to what is required.

In addition to on-site inspections, the Q will probably expect written controls and procedures for all operations related to the supplies and services you will provide to the government. This includes your entire systems approach as documented by detailed company records and your quality control manual. The Q will pay particular attention to:

• Configuration controls to ensure that drawings and specs are current and distributed properly

- Procedures to select, inspect, and control incoming materials, vendors, and subcontractors
- A system to assure adequate product and process testing and maintenance
- Methods to control material identification, product storage, packaging, labeling, and shipping
- Plans to prevent, detect, quarantine, and correct nonconformances
- A program to correct consumer complaints on both government and commercial contracts

Financial Capability: "You Can Take It to the Bank"

FAR requires that a contractor have adequate financial resources *or the ability to attain resources* to fund a contract *to its completion.* Standard Form 1407 outlines the way in which a preaward financial analyst determines whether or not a contractor has—or can obtain—financial resources. Keep in mind that the need to obtain additional capital is not a negative factor—even if it is in the form of government progress payments to which you are entitled at various production points. (See appendix 12 for information on how to qualify for progress payments.)

The preaward financial analyst may begin by examining the company's latest certified balance sheet to determine three financial ratios:

- The ratio of current assets to current liabilities (ideally 2:1)
- The acid test of *liquid* current assets divided by current liabilities (ideally 1:1), which will indicate a company's current liquidity and debt-paying ability
- The ratio of total liabilities to net worth (the ideal ratio varies according to industry), which will indicate the owner of the company and its long-term solvency.

Although these are the three major financial ratios listed on Standard Form 1407, there are several other financial ratios and indicators that the financial analyst may compute, based on a company's balance sheet, profit-and-loss statement, and net sales and profit summaries. Obviously, it pays to have your financial records in order.

The preaward financial analysis doesn't end with an analysis of current finances. The government also needs to know the company's future cash flow, during the time of the government contract. For this evaluation, you should prepare a cash flow statement that reflects both current and future contract activity. The statement should reflect three levels: current contracts, pending contracts, and even a third level for contracts in the bidding stage. Each contract appearing at the second and third levels should be multiplied by a conservative percent of probability of receiving the award. The three levels are then added together to determine an overall projected cash flow. Using the company's profit-and-loss statement, the preaward analyst will also compare the company's net profit to net sales to determine the company's future stability.

If the prospective contractor plans to use borrowed capital to finance the costs of performing the government contract, the preaward analyst will review the contractor's financial arrangements. In most cases the government will accept only:

- A certified (unqualified) bank line of credit
- A third-party institutional credit, such as an employees' credit union *with* a cash flow analysis to prove that the third party will have the money when it is needed
- A third party corporate guarantor (another company that acts as a co-signer)
- Government financing, usually by means of progress payments at specific stages of production (see appendix 12)

All of this financial information is then compared to the contractor's cash flow chart to detail the projected monthly cash requirements for the company's government contract *and* overall operations.

Finally, the government will investigate your financial reputation and credit rating. After all, it doesn't matter how profitable you are if you don't pay your bills. Besides their own sources (see exhibit 7-1), the government might check your bank, trade creditors, and reports of commercial financial service and credit organizations, such as Dun & Bradstreet or Standard and Poor's.

The lack of proper financing is one of the leading reasons companies default on contracts, and it is also one of the leading reasons companies fail their preawards. This is particularly frustrating for small businesses that, despite their worthiness, are unable to obtain credit.

I recall the case of the woman-owned fuel distribution company that won several small government contracts to deliver fuel. Since her initial contracts were small, the owner hadn't previously needed outside financial help. Then the chance of a lifetime appeared, in the form of a multimillion-dollar contract to be the fuel distributor on an airport flight line. Since she would need capital to expand her workforce dramatically, she approached her bank for a line of credit. The bank refused because she was providing a service and had no real collateral. Without the seed capital to hire employees, she could not provide the distribution services necessary to receive the initial progress payments from the government. All she needed was one payment, but she was caught in a Catch-22.

Accounting Systems: Counting on the Unexpected

You will need an accounting system that accurately segregates all reimbursement charges if you are being considered for progress payments or a special reimbursement contract (see chapter 9 on types of contracts), or if you want to track your government contract costs in the unlikely event the government terminates your contract. Outlined in Standard Form 1408, the preaward accounting system review is conducted by the Defense Audit Agency and evaluates a contractor's ability to:

- Segregate costs to individual contracts
- Segregate costs to individual line items within individual contracts
- Determine contract costs incurred at predetermined stages during the process
- Exclude benefits or incidental expenses usually charged to commercial accounts but not allowed under FAR regulations or other contract provisions

• Segregate preproduction and production costs, since preproduction costs are generally prorated and allocated to the entire production, whereas production costs are charged directly to the item produced

If you don't see the need for an accounting system that can segregate your commercial costs from your government costs, consider the case of Wipe-Off Cleaner Company, which contracted to supply a government agency with industrial cleaning fluid for one year. After the first shipment, the company's contract was "terminated for the convenience of the government." The purchasing officer had discovered that a commercial brand-name cleaner was more effective and much less expensive. The cancellation was particularly disturbing to Wipe-Off because it had already invested considerable money in expanding its production facilities and was charging it to the government contract.

In order to be compensated for its government losses, the company needed to produce accounting records that clearly segregated government contract costs from a parallel commercial expansion. But Wipe-Off's accounting system had not segregated costs according to government requirements. When it couldn't produce the detailed cost estimates and itemized purchase orders, Wipe-Off was wiped out of reasonable compensation.

Although the government rarely cancels contracts, it behooves you always to prepare for the unexpected. The time and cost of setting up Wipe-Off's accounting system would have been far less than it forfeited. For example, the government ordered the larger bulk size, and Wipe-Off could have charged the government 90 percent of the cost of setting up the bulk-size soap-filling production line. Likewise, the equipment for bar-coding the product packages was tailored to the government's needs. The major part of that cost also could have been charged to the government, even though Wipe-Off subsequently used the equipment in its commercial work.

Other Factors: "Read the Fine Print"

Depending on "referenced clauses," often called the fine print of your government contract, preaward evaluators may inspect items not itemized on any of the standard forms. In these unique situations, a preaward survey may evaluate special factors requiring extra documentation.

Security Systems. If you are contracting to produce a classified product or service, for instance, the government will require a security system. Occasionally the government may also require a security system for patented or proprietary commercial product data that it has obtained the rights to use. If you are interested in bidding on a contract that requires extra security, contact your small business assistance office for the names of government specialists who can help you set up a security system.

Transportation. Another special factor is transportation. You might expect that the government would evaluate such things as the location of your plant and your docking capabilities. What you might *not* expect is a cost limit on what the government will allow you for subcontracting to a shipper. If your contract provides for reimbursable transportation charges, check your clauses closely. If your contract is silent about transportation reimbursement, contact your local DCAS office for a list of the qualified government shippers. In advance of the preaward, document a system that follows the solicitation requirements to the letter.

Packaging. Depending on your product, packaging can be a major concern. The government will expect you to use an approved packager. If, instead, you plan to do your own packaging, the government will want to evaluate your provisions for product preservation, packing of individual parts, box and container packing, item and box marking, and final crating.

Government Property. Occasionally the government provides a small business with such items as testing equipment, surplus government materials, or subassemblies to be added onto your product. Don't assume that your existing asset and materials control system will apply to government-furnished items. This doesn't mean that you will have to devise an elaborate control system, but it does mean that you will need a system for:

• Identifying government items
• Specifying what the government items can *and cannot* be used for

- Locating where the government property is at all times
- Indicating the condition of the property upon receipt from and return to the government

Safety, Environmental, and Energy Conservation

Other government requirements that may vary from commercial requirements include safety, environmental, and energy conservation provisions. One day I observed a government safety inspector chastise a shop supervisor for overlooking a potential hazard during the painting of a fighter plane. Even though the supervisor had observed the standard government safety requirements of electrically grounding the airplane, providing ample ventilation, and stocking adequate fire-extinguishing equipment, the plane's nose pointed into the hangar, instead of out of it. If a fire broke out in the hangar, the inspector warned, the planes could not be towed out without a tug's driving around the plane, thus losing valuable, or critical, time.

Small businesses should also consider environmental hazards and requirements for handling and disposing of hazardous wastes and by-products. One company bidding on a contract to wash military vehicles was amazed to learn that the water left after the engines were steam-cleaned had to be processed to purge the engine oil, road tar, and battery acid *before* it could be properly disposed of.

ALL SYSTEMS GO . . . OR . . . DO NOT PASS GO

If you've prepared well, you should have no problem passing your preaward evaluation. However, what if you fail in one or more areas? Does this mean you cannot win this contract? And will your failure prevent you from winning future contracts?

Certainly not! If you receive a negative evaluation in one or more areas of your preaward survey, the preaward board will review the findings to determine whether the problem(s) will prevent successful contract completion. A Tulsa, Oklahoma, fastener company was surprised to learn that it had passed a preaward survey in spite of the fact that its computer had been down during the accounting system demonstration. Given the other positive findings and the government's former positive contract experience with the company, DCAS recommended that the buying agency award the contract, stipulating that the accounting system would be monitored after the contract award. (See chapter 9 on contract administration.)

On the other hand, if the board makes a negative recommendation to the buying agency, as a small business you will get a second chance. The buying agency is required to refer you to your local Small Business Administration for help in correcting the problem discovered during the preaward survey. In turn, the SBA will review the board's negative findings and *work with you* to correct the deficiency. According to one manager of a southwestern Small Business Administration, "The SBA works with the contractor to correct the deficiency or to present evidence that, for one reason or another, may have been overlooked by the preaward evaluators."

If you correct the problem, the SBA will issue a Certificate of Competency (COC). A COC is actually a legal instrument that can reverse the negative preaward. The result could be a contract award.

The key to earning a Certificate of Competency lies in your ability to respond to and work with the SBA to provide effective information *within fifteen days.*

Says the SBA manager, "Our job is to ensure that small businesses get a fair shake in the hectic, fast-paced procurement game—where it is easier to award a contract to a proven contractor who may charge more but has successfully delivered a timely product in the past." He adds, "Many of our small businesses fail preawards because they have financial problems. We help them locate or better define where the financing is coming from so the government can be assured of fiscal responsibility."

APPEALING A NEGATIVE PREAWARD

Unfortunately, some companies that fail preawards turn their backs on federal contracting. Many companies complain that "the system is too complicated" or that "earning a Certificate of Competency is impossible and takes too much time." Others are sure that failing the preaward automatically places them on the Contractor Alert List, which excludes them from contract awards. Nothing could be further from the truth.

If you think you have no chance, consider that in 1987 one Texas Small Business Administration office resurrected more than eighty-seven awards for companies that had failed their preawards—amounting to more than $6 million in awards to small businesses!

There is a *remote* chance that you will be placed on the Contractor Alert List for failing a preaward. However, in my experience it is highly unlikely *unless* the preaward team uncovers a serious root problem that appears irresoluble. You might also be placed on the list due to poor performance on past contracts. In any case, getting on the list does not forever prohibit you from winning future contracts.

Even if you receive a poor or unfair preaward, there are methods of appeal. Gilbert Baca, a Los Angeles computer maintenance company owner, approached me at a seminar complaining about an unfair, inaccurate preaward survey.

"Our preaward production evaluator showed little understanding of what we do and what the service contract involved," Baca said. At the time of the preaward, Baca's company was successfully supplying the same computer maintenance for two other agencies—but he failed the preaward for the third agency. The contracting officer called Baca to report the negative findings, and after some discussion and subsequent investigation, the contracting officer awarded Baca the contract in spite of the negative preaward, without ever referring him to the SBA.

Since Baca had been awarded the contract, it soon became clear that his continuing concern was about being on record as having failed the preaward.

"Does the negative preaward mean my company will be placed on the Contractor Alert List or a debarred list?" Baca asked. I assured him that unless the production specialist had uncovered a serious root problem or the company had a poor performance record on other contracts, it was highly unlikely that he would be placed on the list. I told him that if it were me I'd let it ride—especially since he won the contract and hadn't received a notification that he was on the list.

But all my assurances were useless. It was a matter of principle, insisted Baca, since it was the first blemish on his record. Realizing what was at stake—how much he could gain and the goodwill he could possibly lose with DCAS—Baca asked my advice.

I told him to send letters politely refuting the negative preaward to (1) the SBA office, (2) the commander of the DCASMA office, and (3) the Defense Contractor Alert List (DCAL) monitor at the DCASMA office. I explained that all three letters should contain a brief description of his company, product, and success in performing on other government contracts. The letters should then politely and objectively refute the negative findings of the preaward and end with an invitation for each of them to visit the company for a demonstration (which would refute the negative preaward findings).

The letter to the SBA office should request a second preaward to review and document the circumstances of the negative preaward—while the information was still current. Since the buyer was awarding the contract, he would not be giving the SBA a chance to review the negative documentation officially.

The letter to the commander of the DCASMA office should say that the company did receive the award and would put special emphasis on completing it successfully. He should then request that the company's rebuttal of the negative preaward be attached to its file to refute the present negative documentation. The new documentation would then be available when the future buyers asked DCASMA for its recommendation.

Finally, the letter to the DCAL monitor should also mention the discussion with the buyer and the subsequent contract award. After pointing out why the negative information was inaccurate, Baca should request that the DCAL monitor provide any other information that Baca could review to improve his company's services.

Baca did as I advised, and although his negative preaward was not reversed, his next preaward was closely monitored by everyone involved—including the DCASMA commander. Baca was not surprised that his next preaward resulted in a positive recommendation and another contract award.

Congratulations! Now you are ready to pass the preaward—the most challenging test on your way to winning a government contract.

The moment has arrived when you can look forward to your first solicitation. But don't worry. Understanding the solicitation and the subsequent contract is a snap! You've already done most of your homework. And since you've prepared for the preaward, you should have a good understanding of many of the clauses of the solicitation.

8

Responding to Your First Solicitation

It won't arrive like the Fourth of July. There will be no fireworks or marching bands and none of the regalia so often associated with government events.

The day you receive your first solicitation could arrive as inconspicuously as a casual telephone call or as unceremoniously as a plain brown envelope placed in your mailbox. But one thing is certain: That casual phone call or plain brown envelope could change the course of your business—forever.

Another thing is also certain: The type of solicitation you receive and the response you make will vary depending on the amount and type of business you are competing for. The response you make will also mean the difference between winning and losing a government contract.

Unfortunately, there is a great deal of confusion regarding solicitation types, procedures, and the relationship of the solicitation to the contract. Do you realize, for instance, that some solicitations become legally binding contracts the moment they are signed and countersigned?

This chapter and appendix 11 explain the various types of solicitations and contracts. They map out an insider's approach to understanding and responding, so that the day your solicitation arrives you will have a strategy for winning that long-awaited contract.

119

TABLE 8-1.

REPRESENTATIVE SOLICITATION AND CONTRACT PROCEDURES[1]

Contract Value	Bidders Required	Type Solicitation	Advertisement	Solicit Form	Contract Form	Contract Types
< 1,000 (simplified procedures)	1	Verbal RFQ	Agency or local bid board	Verbal	SF 26	FFP
1,000–10,000 (simplified procedures)	3	Verbal or written RFQ	Agency bid board	SF 18	SF 26	FFP
10,000–25,000	3 or more	RFP & IFB	Agency or local bid boards	SF 18 SF 33	SF 26 SF 33	FFP[2]
> 25,000	Open	RFP & IFB	CBD, agency, or local bid boards	SF 33	SF 33	FFP[2]

[1] The procedures described here are representative. There are exceptions and special cases in every category.
[2] Besides the FFP, other contract types include firm fixed price with economic price adjustments, incentive clauses, and indefinite delivery schedules.

CONTRACT TYPES

Considering that the government purchases an astounding variety of products and services each year, it is not surprising that there are several kinds of solicitation and contract types, ranging from the "simplified" to the complex. The type of solicitation and contract you receive is governed by *FAR* regulations that will vary according to the complexity and expense of the item or service, as well as the degree of risk that the government foresees. (See exhibit 8-1 for a discussion of risk factors and table 8-1 for an outline of representative solicitation/contract procedures.)

===================== **EXHIBIT 8-1** =====================

Contracts According to Risk

There are ten major risk factors a contracting officer considers in deciding which type of solicitation/contract to issue—from the firm fixed price contract, which places most of the risk on the contractor, to the cost reimbursement contract, which places the burden of risk on the government. Before the government issues any type of contract, it will consider

1. *Price competition.* How much price competition is available based on previous purchases for the same or similar items?

2. *Price analysis.* Regardless of price competition, how much is the item or service worth based on current market price, catalog prices, or previous prices paid?

3. *Cost analysis.* Not considering price competition or price analysis, how much is the item or service worth based on actual costs of parts and labor?

4. *Type and complexity.* Is the item or service commercially available? Does it require complex specifications? Has it been procured before? If so, does the contracting history provide any insights about which contract type is most suitable? Can the contract be set aside for special business categories?

5. *Urgency.* How urgently needed is the supply or service? Is there time for competitive bids or prolonged negotiations?

6. *Performance period/length of production run.* Given the type of item or service, how long will it take to complete the contract? Are the government's interests best suited by issuing a long- or short-term contract?

7. *Technical and financial capability.* What is known about the prospective contractor's technical and financial capability(ies)?

8. *Accounting system.* Can the prospective contractor segregate government and other contract costs, as required by certain types of contracts?

9. *Previous and current contracts.* Have contractors performed successfully on past government contracts, or can prospective contractors perform successfully on current contracts—given other commercial and/or government contract commitments?

10. *Subcontracting.* Considering the prospective contractor's subcontractor(s), should the government include referenced contract clauses that pertain to a subcontractor's qualifications?

For each procurement, the government chooses a contract that will minimize its risk. These contract types will usually fall into one of seven categories:

• *Firm Fixed Price* (FFP). The most commonly awarded contract, used in over 80 percent of all procurement actions, a firm fixed price contract is awarded when specifications and prices of items and services can easily be determined. Used especially for commercial products and services, the FFP contract places the pricing risk exclusively on the contractor, regardless of varying factors that may influence what it costs to produce an item or service.

• *Firm Fixed Price with Economic Price Adjustments* (FFPEPA). Unlike the FFP, FFPEPA allows for specific price adjustments on labor and/or materials in a volatile market. For example, an FFPEPA contract for electrical cables might stipulate a firm fixed price *except* for the copper content. The price of the copper would be billed separately, based on its cost at the time the contractor purchased it. Used most often in times of high inflation, these contracts are carefully monitored on a quarterly basis as the government price indexes are published.

- *Cost Reimbursement.* The government seldom uses this contract form, because it is risky to the government by providing for the repayment of all incurred costs. Used when the cost cannot be estimated accurately, the cost reimbursement contract can be one of three types:

1. Cost with no profit. It is used for such items as research and development.
2. Cost plus incentive fee (CPIF). In this contract the government guarantees an incentive "fee" if the contractor can meet the contract deadline and a defined cost target.
3. Cost plus fixed fee (CPFF). In a CPFF, the government pays the "cost" of a project, usually in the form of hourly labor charges, as well as a "fixed fee" for "managing" the project, no matter how long it takes. (A typical CPFF contract would be one that was awarded to a company to clean up an oil spill, where the time it would take to complete the project might be hard to determine.)

- *Indefinite Delivery or Indefinite Quantities.* The government issues this contract when it is unsure of future needs. An example of an indefinite delivery contract might be the procurement of sand or salt to spread on federal highways during the winter. The government might contract for minimum quantities with *provisions* for ordering larger quantities, depending on the weather.

- *Time and Material.* When the government is unable to estimate accurately the extent and duration of the work, it might award a time and material contract. This contract is figured on the basis of a fixed hourly labor rate and/or cost of materials (including the cost of material handling). An example of a time and material contract is the removal and replacement of asbestos insulation in public buildings where the amount of work is determined by testing various types and locations of existing insulation. This contract requires careful surveillance and must be replaced with a definitive contract within 180 days or when 40 percent of the job is completed, whichever comes first.

- *General Agreements.* If the government and a company have several contracts each year, sometimes with a history of difficult negotiations, the government may use an agreement that establishes the *framework* for future contract negotiations—such as restricting the areas of negotiation. Called basic ordering agreements (BOA) or blanket purchase orders (BPA), these agreements may define a range of prices (or quantity of items) *or* a method for determining prices when exact kinds of items have not been determined.

• *Multiyear.* Multiyear contracts extend any type of contract for two to five years pending a satisfactory evaluation at the end of each year. A multiyear contract is subject to cancellation if funding is unavailable. However, it usually provides a secure long-term market for small businesses.

The following two items are clauses that may be added to the seven categories of contract types:

• *Incentive.* Gaining popularity, the incentive clauses relate profit to performance. The government issues this contract when it anticipates acquiring supplies and services at a lower cost or with improved delivery or technical performance. Contractor incentives are based on:

1. Controlling labor and materials cost
2. Obtaining specific product quality
3. Achieving or beating a target delivery date for goods or services
4. Achieving any combination of the above

• *Options.* Options are unilateral rights that may be written into *any* type of contract. The option clauses allow the government to increase contract terms (up to five years) and the quantities of the procured items or services. Option clauses are used when a requirement is certain but funding and/or consumption amounts are uncertain. An example of this type of contract might be parts used for car and truck repair where need is dependent on inspection results.

The type of contract you are offered will be designated clearly in part I of your solicitation. (See appendix 11 for a summary of solicitation/contract sections.)

ORAL AND WRITTEN RFQs: PROCUREMENTS OF $10,000 OR LESS

Many people think any government solicitation or contract involves reams of sealed legal documents written by and for the legal profession and requiring the contractor to respond with reams of proposals and documents. If this were the case, the paperwork alone would overwhelm even the government's complex machinery. For this reason, the government has simplified its buying procedures for purchases of $10,000 or less, usually reserving more complex procedures for "major" purchases of more than $10,000, where the greater expense of detailed bid evaluations will be offset by the savings. Because over 98 percent of all government solicitations are for purchases of $10,000 or less, the small business owner can reap the benefits of two types of *simplified procedures*: the oral Request for Quotation (RFQ) and, in special situations, the written RFQ.

If the purchase is for $1,000 or less, the purchasing officer is required to solicit only one contractor verbally (usually not the previous contractor), provided that the price and quality of the item or service are acceptable and the contractor can meet the delivery date. If the procurement is for more than $1,000, the purchasing officer *must solicit orally at least two*, and usually solicits three, qualified contractors. The officer usually solicits (verbally or in writing) the previous contractor plus two other contractors chosen from the qualified bidders' list, using a rotating system to avoid favoritism.

It's as simple as this. To show you how simple, let's eavesdrop on a conversation between a purchasing officer and a prospective contractor:

(Phone rings.)

"Good morning, Little John's Repair and Remodeling. May I help you?"

"Yes, this is Ima Buyer, contracting officer for Boondock Army Post. Is the owner, John Redcloud, there?"

"Speaking."

"Mr. Redcloud, Boondock needs some redwood stain, repair work, and painting completed for its community center by the fifteenth of next month. You filled out a Standard Form 129 last year as a potential supplier of wood finishes and as a contractor for building repairs and remodeling. Your name has come up on the rotation of the mechanized bidders' list."

"Oh really? Let me guess. You want me to fill out some more forms, right?"

"No, this is an *oral* solicitation. Under simplified procedure procurement guidelines we can make a single oral solicitation for certain small purchases of goods and services."

"Are you saying that you want me to make a bid?"

"Precisely. We have two opportunities for you. First, we need a quote on twenty gallons of redwood stain for outdoor furniture. Second, we need some painting and repair work done. Since we aren't sure whether the cost of our repair project will be under one thousand dollars, we are soliciting three bids."

"I follow you so far."

"Good. Are you familiar with the community center located between our parade grounds and the golf course on the east side of the base?"

"Yes."

"Well, we need to know the labor costs required to stain the furniture and repair some door handles and window sashes. If you're interested, I'll issue you a contractor's pass to visit the building and estimate the job. We need an itemized cost breakdown of both the painting and repair work. Are you interested?"

"Yes, I am. When can I visit the post?"

"Tomorrow at noon. Your pass will be at the north gate."

"Great. How do I submit my quote?"

"I was just getting to that. I'd like your quote for the paint right now, if possible. For the repair work, I'd like you to bring your itemized price quote to my office, room 222 in Building J, by 3:00 P.M. this Thursday. I'll get back to you no later than the twenty-seventh. If you're awarded the bid, we'll expect you to complete the job no later than the fifteenth of next month. Do you understand?"

"Yes, let me get my paint price list. The redwood exterior stain will be twenty dollars per gallon."

"That seems a little high. How about fifteen a gallon, delivered?"

"If you'll agree to seventeen a gallon, you've got a deal."

"That's fine. Can you deliver it tomorrow?"

"Yes. That will be great."

"Bring the stain to the engineer's office and the invoice directly to me. While you're here you can sign the purchase order agreeing to the terms."

Believe it or not, most quotations for small purchases are obtained in just this way: through a simple telephone solicitation in which the paperwork is limited to a purchase order (Optional Form 347). Even though this purchase order is signed by a government official, it is not a binding contract until *you* either sign and return it or start performance according to the terms contained in the purchase order. If you have decided you do not want to do business by the time you receive your purchase order, immediately notify the contracting officer so that the purchase order can be reissued to another contractor. It is not a good idea to make a habit of changing your mind, however, since the purchasing officer is likely to give someone else the opportunity to bid the next time. (Also see exhibit 8-2: "Bureaucracy at Breakneck Speed.")

EXHIBIT 8-2

Bureaucracy at Breakneck Speed

JUST HOW FAST CAN A CONTRACT HAPPEN?

Just when you get used to the bureaucratic wheels turning slowly, it happens: You get a call from a government official who needs something . . . yesterday.

It happened to me one Sunday morning when I was working as a chief of production for DCAS. The shrill ring of the telephone awakened me at 4:00 A.M. It was a navy procurement officer who needed some electronic equipment from one of our local vendors. I was instructed to give the order the highest priority and to ship the equipment that day.

After two phone calls—one to my transportation specialist and the other to the local vendor's contracting officer—the contracting process was well under way. I met the company's contracting officer at the front gate of the manufacturing company at 6:00 A.M. He checked the stock inventory and realized he would have to make some modifications on one equipment item, as well as "borrow" some equipment that had been produced for other federal contracts.

"Highest Priority"

Realizing there was no time for modifications, we determined that with proper technical instructions the modifications could easily be completed by the navy technicians at sea. In regard to borrowing equipment designated for other federal contracts, I assured him that the navy had the highest priority in this situation and that I would arrange for contract extensions from the other contracting officers to cover the late deliveries.

After negotiating a fair price with the plant's contracting officer, I called the navy contracting officer to report the details and get approval to finalize the verbal contract. Then I helped the plant contracting officer assemble and package the order. When we had finished, we wheeled the order to my station wagon and I was on my way to the Federal Express office, to which the transportation specialist had hand-delivered the shipping documentation.

To make a short story shorter, in eight hours we had solicited, negotiated, and delivered a contract. I realized I had a week's worth of paper work to complete, but it was worth it. I had proven that bureaucracy can function at breakneck speed— when it is important.

Although most small purchase procurements of $1,000 or less are solicited orally, there are exceptions. Five small purchase situations require the written Request for Quotation (RFQ). This written solicitation (Standard Form 18) is used when:

- The suppliers are located outside the government agency's local area
- Special technical or complex specifications are involved
- Several different items are included in a single procurement
- Obtaining oral quotations is inefficient (as in the case of classified procurements)
- The purchase is for construction work exceeding $2,000 (see appendix 6 on construction and architecture-engineering contracting procedures)

If a contracting officer sends you an RFQ, you should examine any attached specifications, review the terms, and look up and study the referenced FAR clauses. If you decide to bid, enter your best quotation, sign it, and return your RFQ by the deadline stipulated in the solicitation (see appendix 11).

If the purchasing officer selects your bid, a purchase order (Standard Form 26) will be issued. If you accept the terms of the purchase order, sign it and return it by the date indicated and/or immediately perform the contract according to the document requirements.

With the streamlined and flexible procedures offered it's not surprising that small businesses are eager to do business with the government—the simplified way.

IFBs AND RFPs: MAJOR PURCHASES OVER $10,000

If you are competing for a "major purchase" over $10,000 or a "restricted" small purchase under $10,000, the government may issue one of two written solicitations: an Invitation for Bids (IFB) or a Request for Proposal (RFP). While both of these solicitations utilize the same Standard Form 33, they are strikingly different. First of all, the IFB is always non-negotiable, while the RFP can be negotiated. Because of this difference, your response to these solicitations will be quite different.

The IFB or "Sealed Bid"

Neither the bidder nor the government is permitted to *negotiate price or terms* of the IFB, or "sealed bid." The IFB solicitation is for items or services for which the requirements and technical data are complete and clear. For example, the government would not use an IFB for a research contract to find a cure for AIDS, since there is no good estimate of the time it would take to complete the contract.

The fact that an IFB is not negotiable does not prevent you from asking questions to clarify objective information in the solicitation. On the contrary, many a flawed IFB has been exposed by contractors attempting to clarify information. You may even telephone a contracting officer to ask a question—provided it is *simple*. If, however, the question involves complex information such as clarification of technical information, you will need to put your question in writing. The contracting officer will then respond in writing. If a dispute occurs later, a *written* answer signed by the contracting officer may be your only protection.

IFB Revision, Cancellation, or Withdrawal. If the contracting officer discovers a problem with the IFB solicitation, the government can amend or cancel it. To amend a solicitation, the government issues a Standard Form 30, Amendment of Solicitation/ Modification of Contract, sometimes simultaneously extending the bidding deadline. If you receive a Standard Form 30 amendment, *you must acknowledge it,* either (1) by signing and returning Standard Form 30 with the IFB (Standard Form 33) or (2) by signing block 14 of Standard Form 33 *and* listing the modifications received. The government may also cancel an IFB by sending a "notice of cancellation" to everyone who received the IFB. Likewise, you have an opportunity to get cold feet and withdraw your bid, so long as you do so before the public opening of the bids.

IFB Prebid Conference and Response. Occasionally a contracting officer will hold a prebid conference before you submit your bid, to clarify complicated specifications and requirements in the IFB. Be sure to check section L of the solicitation for information on the time and place of a possible prebid conference, and plan to attend.

As a civilian contractor I received a prebid notification for a solicitation to remodel an open airplane hangar into an office complex. The prebid conference included a tour of the hangar and an introduction to the people who would be approving the remodeling drawings. What I learned at this preaward conference made me decide not to prepare a bid. I discovered that eight government officials would have to approve my design drawings, and each could make changes—any one of which could affect every intricate part of the complete design. Given this information, I doubted that I— or anyone else, for that matter—could complete the contract by the deadline. So I decided not to bid on the contract, informed the buyer, and asked to be considered for future bids.

After you carefully study the IFB solicitation, its referenced clauses, and any attached specifications or drawings, you should prepare your bid, following every instruction to the letter. Keep in mind that even simple errors in filling out forms—such as forgetting to sign your name—may disqualify you. And since you cannot negotiate price, take care to bid your most competitive price.

Awarding the IFB Contract. The IFB bid opening is a public event where bids are read aloud, recorded, and certified. You can even examine duplicate copies of the bids, provided you don't impede the bid opening process.

Afterward, the contracting officer will evaluate the "apparent low bidder" for responsiveness and responsibility. Although there are a number of reasons based on responsiveness (see exhibit 8-3: "Bidding Responsively"), for which a contracting officer may disqualify a bid, three of the most avoidable reasons for disqualification involve oversights or carelessness in reading and filling out the bid forms. These include

- Not acknowledging an amendment. Contractors fail to acknowledge an amendment either (1) by not signing and returning Standard Form 30 with the IFB (Standard Form 33) or (2) by not signing block 14 of Standard Form 33 *and* not listing the modifications received.
- Not having the proper company official sign the IFB. An IFB is a legal offer by the company. Therefore, it must be signed by a person who is legally empowered to bind a company to a contract.
- Not submitting the bid according to the deadline. The most common disqualification is for not returning the bid at the location and time specified in block 9 of the IFB. No excuse is accepted, unless it is the government's fault. Your bid must be postmarked at least five days prior to the bid opening date. (Use U.S. Postal Service registered or certified mail. Federal Express or a commercial carrier does not afford legal proof of receipt.)

========================== **EXHIBIT 8-3** ==========================

Bidding Responsibly and Responsively

Some contractors are surprised to learn that even though their bid was the lowest, they were still not awarded the contract. Bear in mind that cost is merely one-third of the equation: You must also be judged a *responsible* contractor whose bid is *responsive*.

Different contracts may include additional requirements of responsibility (see sections H and M of your contract). Minimal requirements of responsibility stipulate that a contractor must

- Have adequate financial resources to complete the contract or the ability to obtain them
- Be capable of complying with the required delivery or performance schedule when taking into account all other commercial and government contracts
- Have a satisfactory performance history on government and/or commercial contracts
- Have a satisfactory record of integrity
- Be "otherwise" qualified for an award under applicable laws and regulations

Being responsive requires that a contractor's bid conform to the essential requirements and specifications contained or referenced in the solicitation. In the case of an IFB, disqualification for being nonresponsive is automatic. A bid will be disqualified if it imposes conditions that modify the contract. A few of the more common reasons for disqualification include

- A nonresponsible company representative signing the bid
- Failing to state the delivery schedule in accordance with the solicitation requirements
- Failing to state a fixed price for items or materials, i.e., adding a price escalation to protect yourself from projected cost increases
- Making your bid conditional upon receiving (or not receiving) other contracts or all of the projected award when the solicitation states that partial awards may be allowed to small businesses
- Limiting or modifying any government rights stated under any contract clause

If, after checking the usual sources, the contracting officer still needs more information to determine responsibility (see exhibit 7-1 for a list of sources), a preaward survey may be ordered. If the bidder fails the preaward, the contracting officer proceeds to the next lowest bidder and the process begins again. If the bidder that failed the preaward happens to be a small business, the contracting officer must refer the company to the Small Business Administration for Certificate of Competency consideration (see chapter 7).

Whatever the results, the contracting officer formalizes the final decision by signing and returning the chosen contractor's Standard Form 33, thus forming a legally binding contract.

Although the IFB is the most rigid form of procurement, what it may lack in flexibility it makes up for in fairness. And because the evaluation factors are so specific and the results are so public, sealed bidding does not allow a contracting officer to favor one bidder over another. That's good news for the small business owner just entering the government market.

The Request for Proposal (RFP)

Since IFBs allow no negotiation and are expensive to process, it is easy to see why 85 percent of contracts for $10,000 and above make use of a solicitation that provides more flexibility. Called the Request For Proposal (RFP), this solicitation uses the same Standard Form 33 as the IFB, with different clauses and references. The RFP also follows many of the same procedures as the IFB for selection of bidders, prebid conference, solicitation amendments, cancellations, and withdrawals.

But while the IFB is used to procure items or services for which government requirements are clear and prices are easy to pinpoint, the RFP is used when the government needs additional buying information. In this sense, the RFP process provides a built-in market survey, or "comparison shopping" analysis. For example, suppose that the General Services Administration (GSA) is in the market for a commercial desktop-publishing system. The GSA can set minimum requirements, such as certain graphics-handling capabilities, but beyond that, the agency is not sure what features are available—and for what price. With an RFP, the government can consider the various software programs and weigh the options against the prices. By doing so, the agency may discover that it doesn't need a monitor that will show a full page of text for $2,000 extra, but it does need extra type styles for an additional $1,500.

The government also uses the RFP when the procurement does not easily lend itself to the non-negotiable terms and lowest-bidder criteria typical of IFBs. What if there is only one qualified bidder, as in the case of a patented item? Or what if the government needs an item or service as quickly as possible, in an emergency? Or what if the government wants to restrict competition to specific contractors, as when specialized or proven expertise is an absolute requirement, taking precedence over cost considerations? In these cases, the RFP is preferable to the IFB.

RFP Response, Evaluation, and Award. When you receive your RFP (Standard Form 33), you will notice that the form has been modified to accommodate the conditions of negotiation not found in the IFB solicitation. For starters, the type of procurement (block 4) will read "negotiated" instead of "sealed bid." *FAR* referenced clauses will also be different, as will be the requirement to submit a *proposal* to establish cost and technical ability. Unlike the IFB, which typically stresses an overall cost, an RFP solicitation may require a breakdown of all the charges contained in the composite bid. The method for evaluating the proposal (as provided in the referenced clauses) may also be more detailed, allowing the contracting officer to consider a company's technical skills and understanding or a combination of technical and cost factors.

An RFP also varies from the IFB in that a contractor may propose alternate terms and conditions—including a different contract that could prove more beneficial to the government than the original solicitation. Just remember that what you propose should follow the criteria for proposal evaluation summarized in block M of the RFP. (See exhibit 8-4 on preparing a proposal and appendix 11 for a description of RFP sections.)

Awarding the RFP Contract. Another way an RFP differs from the IFB is the way in which it is processed. Unlike the IFB, proposals submitted for RFPs are not opened in public. Instead, they are opened by the contracting officer's personnel privately. Based on their evaluations, two things may occur: Usually, without negotiat-

========= **EXHIBIT 8-4** =========

Responding to the RFP

A PROPOSAL THAT WINS THE HAND

Many a suitor has been spurned because he or she delivered an insipid or unclear marriage proposal. While a contract with the government might not be as long-lasting as a contract of marriage, the government does not want a nasty divorce. That's why it's important to pledge your troth in a well-written proposal. Here are several pointers that could help you win a contract:

1. *Study the solicitation.* Step one in preparing a good proposal is understanding the requirements of the solicitation, including all specifications and evaluation criteria. If you have questions regarding specifications, ask the contracting officer. Only the contracting officer's *written* clarification or revision is binding. Likewise, study the evaluation criteria in section M of the RFP and prepare your proposal accordingly.

2. *Provide required information.* Provide all documentation as required by part IV of the solicitation. For example, failure to provide a management proposal when it is required may cost you a contract for being "nonresponsive."

3. *Be specific.* At the core of any good proposal is a specifically worded statement of what you will accomplish: exactly what you will deliver, how much it will cost, and when you will deliver it. This statement should reveal that the offerer understands, and will provide, exactly what the contracting officer wants by the required deadline.

4. *Be forceful and informative.* Establish your expertise without being self-serving or overly technical. For example, include a professionally prepared chart or graph *if* it clarifies your written proposal or reinforces your technical understanding.

5. *Be competitive.* Price your proposal competitively. Study your market information (see chapters 4 and 5) to determine a

fair market price that will allow you a realistic profit. Although price is negotiable in the case of RFQs and RFPs, if you price your product or services too high initially, you may never get a chance to negotiate.

---

ing, the contracting officer accepts the lowest responsible proposal by signing the Standard Form 33 that the contractor has returned. On the other hand, after the officer evaluates the proposals he or she will occasionally contact all contractor(s) "within the competitive range" for further information or to begin negotiations to discuss and negotiate any aspect of the proposal. Two things contracting officers can *not* discuss are a competitor's price and a specific price an offerer must beat. They *can* say, however, that a price "seems too high."

Then the contracting officer selects an "apparent successful offerer," based on the evaluation criteria detailed in section M of the RFP. The contracting officer will then send a Standard Form 26 Award/Contract to the prospective contractor. This form confirms the latest changes to the proposal. If the changes are complex, the officer will send a contractual document with Standard Form 26. When the bidder signs Standard Form 26 and returns it to the government, a legally binding contract is established.

The government will notify all unsuccessful bidders of the number of contractors solicited and proposals received; the name and address of the bidder receiving the award; the items, quantities, and unit prices; and the *general* reason the losing bidder's proposal was not accepted. (See exhibit 8-5: "Evaluating a Contract Award.")

=================== **EXHIBIT 8-5** ===================

Evaluating a Contract Award

DEBRIEFINGS AND PROTESTS

You've just received notification that you did not win a contract. If you bid on an IFB and the contract was awarded to someone other than the lowest bidder and you were the lowest bidder, your notification will also include the reason your bid was rejected. The Freedom of Information Act stipulates that if you requested additional information at the time you submitted your bid, your notification must additionally include the name and address of the successful bidder, the contract price, and the location of the "abstract of offers," which lists all the names of your competitors that submitted bids and their numerical ranking.

If you bid on an RFP, your notification should automatically include a general description of the reason you lost the contract; the number of contractors solicited; the number of proposals received; the name and address of the offerer(s) receiving award(s); and a description of the items, quantities, and unit prices.

This is all very important information, but does not always help you determine what you might do differently to win the next contract. Or perhaps you feel you should have won the contract and would like to protest the award. So where do you go from here?

If you are an unsuccessful bidder for an RFP that was awarded on some basis *other than the lowest price*, *FAR* provides you an opportunity to be *debriefed* upon a written request. I recommend taking advantage of the opportunity, since it cannot hurt you, and you may gain knowledge that will help you win the next contract.

The purpose of a debriefing is not to protest an award or divulge information about your competitors' evaluations, but to review the strong and weak points of *your* proposal and to assure you that the selection was fair and according to regulations.

If you're still not satisfied after reviewing all this information, then you might consider filing a protest, so long as you understand the ground rules. First, in order to protest you must have a "direct economic interest" in the contract award. In other words, if you were the second choice for the award, then yes, consider filing a protest. But if you were fourth or fifth from the lowest bid, forget it. Since protest procedures (outlined in *FAR* 33.1) are very legalistic, time-consuming, and often very expensive if lawyers are involved, begin by trying to contact the *contracting officer* informally. In most cases, you will be satisfied with the officer's explanation.

If you still aren't satisfied, then proceed with the filing. This is where the second ground rule comes into play: You must file your protest with the Comptroller General of the General Accounting Office within ten calendar days of the contract award, and all your documentation must be received within twenty-four hours after the initial protest filing. The contracting officer then has twenty-five days to submit a complete report to the GAO. This report is forwarded to you, and the GAO must render a decision within ninety workdays of the protest filing date. If the contracting officer chooses not to follow the GAO's *advisory* decision, then the GAO notifies Congress.

The comptroller general decides for the protester in approximately 20 percent of all protests. Once the decision is finalized, your only other option is to challenge the decision in a federal district court or in the U.S. Claims Court.

IFB AND RFP SOLICITATION FORMAT

"I took one glance at my solicitation and called my lawyer," complained a midwestern asbestos manufacturer.

A New Jersey office supply distributor admitted, "The solicitation weighed so much I put it aside for another day. I never did get around to responding."

As hard as it is for me to believe, I have often seen businesses go to a great deal of time and expense to research government markets, only to give up when they received their first solicitation. My advice to them and to you is, don't get cold feet when you're right at the threshold of winning a government contract. Don't fall victim to solicitationitis: the inordinate fear of reading a solicitation. And above all, never ignore a solicitation. Failing to respond—even if it is to say you don't wish to bid at this time—may disqualify you from receiving any more solicitations from that agency.

With a little orientation, you can read *and understand a solicitation and a contract, since all government solicitations and contracts follow a uniform contract format.* The contract, in fact, is identical to the solicitation, except that the last three sections (K, L, M), dealing with bidding procedures, do not appear in the contract. When you've gone through the uniform contract format once, the next time will be much easier.

You made it through the maze! First you made the decision to explore the government market. You got on the bidders' list. You researched your competition and the past and future procurements of your targeted agencies. You established a good quality control system and prepared for the preaward. Then, after carefully studying your solicitation and applying your knowledge of your competition, you submitted your best bid.

Guess what happens next. One day, when you least expect it, you, too, may find a plain brown envelope in the mail. When you open it, you'll find your first government contract!

It's not quite over yet, though. You may still have to pass that preaward. And you've still got to perform on that contract. But the rest of the journey is easier. And now you can clearly see that the streets *are* paved with gold.

9

Contract Administration:
Big Brother as Partner

"You have an open market and a quality product," I reminded my client. "So why are you afraid of competing for federal contracts?"

"I'm afraid of winning the contract," Michael quipped.

I knew what he meant. He'd made this statement before. He was not afraid of competing or even performing on a contract. Michael feared "Big Brother": He was afraid of government contract *administration*. Staunchly independent, he was convinced that once he had won a contract his company would be overrun with government inspectors, meddling Big Brothers who would try to tell him how to run a business he'd been running for twenty years.

I asked, "Do you realize that if you win a contract for ten thousand dollars or less, the chances are you will never see a government contract administrator?"

"I wouldn't even bother with anything less than twenty thousand," he snapped.

"Would you agree to a couple of visits from an industrial specialist?" I asked.

"What's an industrial specialist?" he countered.

"An industrial specialist primarily checks to make sure you are performing according to schedule."

"I guess I could stand that," he admitted grudgingly.

It all comes back to the risk formula, I explained: The less risk to the government, the less the contract administration. Even high-volume, low-dollar products or services can fall under small purchase procedures. The extent and areas of contract administration are dictated by the purchasing agency's guidelines based on (1) the type of contract, (2) the results of the preaward, and (3) the contractor's performance on former procurements.

In other words, if you are a reputable small business providing a noncritical product for a contract worth less than ten thousand dollars, and final inspection occurs at the point of delivery, you will probably never see or hear from a government contract administrator. This type of contract typically will be assigned to a DCAS production clerk who will flag it for "casual" monitoring. In reality, the contract can be thirty days delinquent before any real pressure will be put on a small business contractor.

If the contract is for more than ten thousand dollars, however, the contracting officer will usually assign it to a local DCAS office for "full" or "limited" administration in the areas of production and quality.

But even if you win a contract that requires full monitoring or administration, knowing what to expect and how to relate to government officials will quell your fear of one of the most misunderstood areas of government procurement. By the end of this chapter you should see contract administration not as "Big Brother is watching you," but as a partnership between your team and the government team to *facilitate* contract performance.

POSTAWARD ORIENTATION

Depending on the complexity of the contract, the results of the preaward, and/or your experience with government contracts, the contracting officer may schedule a postaward orientation conference as the first official step in administering the contract. The purpose of the conference is to work toward a mutual understanding of all contract requirements and identify and resolve any potential problems. (See exhibit 9-1: "Preparing for the Postaward.") The postaward conference also affords the contractor an opportunity to clarify certain contract administration requirements that may not be spelled out in the contract. For example, during the postaward conference a contractor may learn when and how quality inspections will be conducted. Or, if a contractor qualifies for progress payments, he may find out the schedule and type of documentation

===================== **EXHIBIT 9-1** =====================

Preparing for the Postaward

If you have never contracted with the government before and your contract is for more than $100,000, chances are you may be asked to attend a postaward conference. Before a contracting officer schedules a postaward conference he or she will consider several factors:

- Extent and results of the preaward survey
- Importance of the product/service
- Urgency of delivery
- Procurement history of the product/service
- Type and value of the contract
- Technical complexity of the product/service
- Length of the product's production cycle
- Provisioning requirements, such as spare parts requirements
- Contractor's experience with federal contracts
- Contractor's experience with the procurement product/service
- Amount of subcontracting
- Hazard level of materials and operations

---

he needs to submit to receive payments. (See appendix 12: "Using the Government to Finance Your Contract.")

But understanding the agenda is only the first step in assuring a successful postaward orientation. Every good businessperson realizes that behind every stated agenda is a hidden agenda or protocol that can make or break a meeting. The following tips will ensure that you have a successful postaward conference:

Be prepared. Carefully review your contract and any preaward results before your postaward conference. Request a written agenda before the meeting, and if there are any items you would like to add, notify the contracting officer before the meeting. Prepare any written documentation that the contract administrators may require.

One of the first items a contract administrator will ask to see is a reconfirmation of your suppliers' material orders, to make sure that any supplies you need will still be delivered on schedule. The second item the contract administrator will probably request is a *current* production schedule.

Select conference participants carefully. Even though the agenda may stipulate limited areas for discussion, all of your key personnel should attend the conference or be available to answer questions. Include management personnel responsible for contract execution, administration, and performance; the company president or vice-president; design, production, and packaging engineers; *and* any major subcontractors. Make sure your spokespersons are responsible for their commitments, for the postaward report will specify the names of the participants responsible for future actions, as well as action target dates. If a contractor defaults on these actions, the government can use the minutes from the postaward conference to support a contract "termination by default."

Understand the rules. During the postaward conference you cannot make any contract "changes," but the meeting does provide a valuable opportunity to clarify contractual elements, sometimes resulting in "line-item modifications" to the contract. These "modifications" are usually "additions" suggested by the government or "clarifications" requested by the contractor.

Typical line-item modifications occur when a contract stipulates that a contractor provide a recommended list of replacement parts for a new product. During the postaward conference the contract administrator will review this list and negotiate the prices of the replacement parts, and subsequently he or she will add these items to the contract as additional procurements.

Bear in mind that any government clarification is not officially binding until it is written into the contract as a line-item modification. For example, a company's packaging expert asked a government engineer to explain a packaging technique inadequately explained by the contract specifications. When the government engineer explained an expensive process used for a similar contract, the company's packaging expert asked if she could use an alternative method to fulfill the contract specifications. When the engineer agreed, the company representative politely *requested that the packaging technique be put in writing as a contract modification.* The company expert knew that the engineer was not authorized to speak for the government, nor were his "suggestions" legally binding.

Be cooperative. The major goal of a postaward conference is to establish a partnership to facilitate the successful completion of the contract. A partnership requires cooperation and honesty from each participant.

I have seen some incredible feats accomplished as a result of this spirit of cooperation. At one postaward conference, a gear manufacturer disclosed that during his preaward an army engineer had presented him with drawings for a new improved gear design. His contract, however, specified and provided drawings for the old gear design—which was much cheaper to produce. He wondered which gear he should produce.

After considerable discussion and a contract modification, the manufacturer agreed to produce the new gear—without any extra compensation. His short-term profits would have been greater had he remained silent and produced exactly what the original contract specified. But his honesty probably paid off in the long term. He is still the only "qualified" manufacturer of the new gears.

CONTRACT ADMINISTRATION

"All he did was taste the food and briefly inspect the kitchen!" exclaimed a caterer after a visit from a government quality specialist. Until recently, the caterer had avoided contracting with her local Veterans' Hospital because she had heard that government inspectors were hard to satisfy.

"Nothing could be further from the truth," she admits now. "Why, the hospital patients are twice as hard to please!"

Like the caterer, many first-time government contractors are often relieved when they discover just how simple and straightforward a quality or production inspection is. And why shouldn't it be? In most cases you will schedule the visit, and your contract will stipulate exactly what the inspectors will evaluate. The industrial (production) specialist is primarily concerned with keeping you on schedule. To this end, the specialist will monitor the progression of the product or service through the production cycle, including such things as materials expediting, personnel training, and the progress of your subcontractors. (See chapter 7 for a discussion of a production specialist's areas of inspection.) The quality inspector will monitor all elements pertaining to product or service quality as stipulated in the contract.

Delivery and Payment

Not all contract administration is initiated by the government. Probably your most important concern—when you will be paid—is largely dependent on how *you* administer the payment paper trail. The government is required to pay you within thirty days from the *receipt of a proper or "qualified" invoice*—or else pay you interest. The key to prompt payment is invoicing properly and quickly.

Fast-Pay Method: Payment Before Inspection. Depending on your contract type and amount, there are two types of invoicing methods. If you are contracting under "fast-pay" simplified procedures (contracts of $10,000 and less), you may invoice *before* your product or service is inspected at its destination, by sending your shipping documentation with your invoice (Form DD 250) the moment you ship your delivery. Should your product or service not pass inspection, the government will bill you for the cost of the defective products when it discovers the defects.

Contracts Requiring Inspection Before Payment. For contracts of more than $10,000 requiring inspection at the production site or at the point of delivery, the quality inspector first must sign the DD 250 form. If the form is signed at the production site, *you* are responsible for sending the DD 250s and copies to the proper offices for payment. If the DD 250 is signed at the point of delivery, the quality inspector is responsible for forwarding the forms, which *you have addressed.*

Contracts Requiring Lab Testing. If your contract requires that a government-approved testing lab approve your first article, submit the DD 250 (and copies) to the lab with your first article. After the government-approved testing lab signs and returns them to you, send them to the proper offices for payment.

Overcoming Delays. Although these payment procedures sound straightforward, there are several ways your payment can be delayed. Most payment delays occur because the contractor fails to invoice properly using the government's DD 250 forms. (See exhibit 9-2: "Fast Pay? No Way!") Understanding how the DD 250 works is critical to contract administration. Combined with proper attachments and sent to *multiple* recipients, the DD 250 provides invoicing documentation for:

- Inspection, receipt, and acceptance of your product or service
- Packing and shipping inventory(ies)
- Notice of shipment
- Contract release for payment and removal from suspense files

---

=============== **EXHIBIT 9-2** ===============

Fast Pay? No Way!

If you think invoicing the government couldn't be much different from invoicing your commercial customers, you're in for a surprise. Even though you use the government's own invoice form, the DD 250, you can easily make mistakes that will delay your payment. In fact, there are more ways to delay payment than there are blanks on a DD 250. Following are some of the more common ways to mess up:

1. *Preparation errors.* There are twenty-three blanks on the DD 250. Each blank is important to one or more government clerks, so complete each one carefully if you want to get paid promptly. Common errors are incorrect or missing contract number (block 1), shipment number (block 2), inspection acceptance location (block 8), line-item shipment number (block 15), unit of measure (block 18), or shipped-to code (block 13).

2. *Documentation errors.* Make sure you attach the required supporting documentation—such as evidence of shipment—to your invoicing copy of the DD 250.

3. *Improper distribution of the DD 250.* Appendix I of *FAR* and your standard contract (sections A and H) stipulate where to send your multiple copies of the DD 250. The most common distribution error is sending the contract administration office a DD 250 improperly labeled "ORIGINAL INVOICE." This copy of the DD 250 is *not* an invoice; it is used to show that your contract is complete. If it is improperly marked as an invoice, it will likely be forwarded to another office and the contract will not be documented as completed. Until your contract is completed, you will not be paid.

4. *Bad timing.* You cannot send your DD 250s to their final destinations *until* you have shipped your products to their destinations. You must include the shipment number with the DD 250 invoice.

5. *Not furnishing items according to requirements.* Make sure you ship the right quantities for the right items as specified by each contract line item, and that your shipping documentation is correct. A mistake in shipment or documentation will definitely delay payment.

You should *always* use the DD 250 as your government invoice, even when it is not required under fast-pay procedures. If you submit your own company invoice, you do so at your own risk, since the government requires information that you will have to add to your invoice. The possibility of omission is simply too great. Besides, government personnel process hundreds of DD 250s daily, and they may not locate necessary data quite so quickly on your invoice in a different format.

An invoice is labeled incomplete until the DD 250 has been distributed according to *both* standard and special instructions (specified in your contract). Standard distribution includes the following:

• Send one original signed by the quality assurance inspector to the contract administration office (listed in block 10 of the DD 250). Staple the original shipping document to it. The original should be plainly stamped "ORIGINAL INVOICE" in one-inch-high red letters across the front of the page.

- Send four copies with the product shipment. If acceptance is required at the receiving end, provide stamped, addressed envelopes for distribution after quality acceptance and signing.
- Send two copies to the people who pack and ship your product(s), for their records and documentation.
- Send one copy to the purchasing office *within* twenty-four hours of shipment so that payment can be initiated. This copy must be sent in addition to the original invoice copy, *even if they go to the same office.*

When a government official is responsible for sending in the forms, *you are responsible for shepherding the process.* A polite phone call inquiring whether the DD 250s have been submitted should usually facilitate the process. Remember that the thirty-day payment process starts when the payment office *receives* the completed paperwork.

So what if you follow all the proper procedures and still receive no payment within thirty days? Call the payment office and give the payment clerk your contract number, the date you sent the DD 250s, and shipping document numbers. Then ask the clerk what you need to submit to make your invoicing complete.

SOLVING PROBLEMS

Many contractors incorrectly assume that if they fail to perform on a contract or have a serious problem, the government will automatically terminate their contracts "for reason of default." In fact, this is the government's last alternative—a costly and potentially litigious alternative that it would rather avoid. If a problem or dispute does evolve, there are a number of alternatives that the government and contractor can pursue.

Late Delivery

The most common problem or dispute is late delivery. Late delivery may even be caused by the government, as when it does not provide timely shipping instructions or complicates packing requirements by changing from a domestic to an overseas shipping destination.

Regardless of who is at fault, when you realize that there is a possibility of late delivery you should immediately contact your industrial specialist. I have seen contractors avert tragedies by admitting problems, but I have never seen a positive outcome when contractors tried to hide a major problem. If late delivery is unavoidable, the government may do nothing, terminate the contract, or amend the contract to extend delivery. However, if you are granted an extended delivery and it is your fault, you will probably have to compensate the government for processing the modification.

When I was chief of production for DCAS, I received a phone call from a manufacturer supplying the army with trash bags. He had just learned that his only raw-material supplier's plant had burned to the ground. "Will my contract be terminated?" he asked.

"Not if I can help it," I assured him. A couple of days later, DCAS had located an out-of-state vendor that could supply the raw materials in time to complete the contract on schedule.

If you approach contract administration as a partnership with the government, you should avoid contract problems and disputes altogether. Should problems occur, you'll be able to work with DCAS to solve them.

On rare occasions, however, a contract administrator will identify a *root* problem that a contractor cannot or will not resolve. If the problem is serious enough to threaten product or service quality, timely delivery, or successful contract completion, the contract management team will meet formally with the contractor in an attempt to determine the causes and find an acceptable resolution.

Depending on the results of the meeting, the contract management team may

- Recommend a corrective action plan with increased monitoring until the problem is resolved
- Place the contractor in the vigilant Contractor Improvement Program *and* on the Contractor Alert List until the problem is resolved or, in the extreme case, debar, suspend, or disqualify the contractor from doing business with the government

Disqualification, however, is not the government's goal. Besides identifying unsatisfactory contractors to other agencies through the Contractor Alert List, the Contractor Improvement Program also provides for appropriate technical expertise and the necessary level of contract administration to improve the contractor's performance. Once the problem is resolved, the government will remove the contractor's name from the Contractor Alert List, and he or she will be free to pursue other government contracts without restrictions.

But the Contractor Improvement Program is another story. Your story has a different plot: You've watched your P's and Q's, so that you successfully made it through the contract administration. Then one day you open your mail and find the shortest, sweetest correspondence you've ever received from the government since the beginning of your procurement odyssey—a check from the U.S. Treasury.

EPILOGUE

I'd be willing to bet your story doesn't end here, though. If you're as enterprising as I think you are, you'll take time to assess what you've learned on this first contract, and then you'll look ahead. There are some exciting changes on the horizon for government procurement that will involve you. So set your sights on tomorrow and turn to chapter 10.

Investing in Procurement Futures

"How does it feel to retire an 'expert' after working twenty-two years in federal procurement?" I asked my colleague at his recent retirement party.

He flashed an ironic grin and replied, "Show me someone who calls himself a procurement 'expert' and I'll show you a fool."

What my colleague knew, some of you are just discovering. It doesn't take twenty-two years working in government procurement to realize that about the time you think you've figured out the system, you discover a new wrinkle—a regulation or requirement peculiar to a particular agency. But, like my friend, what you lack in knowledge you can now make up for in resourcefulness. Now, when you approach a detour, you should know where to go or whom to ask to make your way to the federal marketplace.

What works for today's procurement traveler will also work for tomorrow's procurement trailblazer. The tools and the resources I've discussed in this book will provide you with the means to predict—and pursue—the opportunities that await you. (Also see exhibit 10-1: "Resources for Future Trends.")

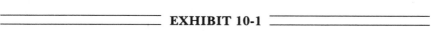

======= **EXHIBIT 10-1** =======

Resources for Future Trends

Procurement entrepreneurs find trends everywhere they look. In this respect, the whole world becomes a crystal ball and a window of opportunity. For starters, trend watchers—and trend setters—will check the following sources:

• *Newspapers.* Every day newspapers are full of opportunities that could translate into federal procurement business. Recent headlines, such as "$24 Billion in Federal Trust Reserved to Repair America's Rotting Infrastructure" and "Simulators Fastest-Growing Method of Training," could translate into some lucrative contract opportunities.

Don't think that today's news is old news. It is estimated that it takes the government at least two years to make use of new technology after it hits the market. This means you have the time to explore and develop "future" trends for future business.

• *Professional journals and organizations.* Don't stop with the newspaper! Some of the timeliest procurement information comes from more specialized publications, such as trade magazines and government publications. Professional and trade organizations are also often the first to report future market trends.

• *Educational programs.* As educational institutions embrace the era of entrepreneurship, they are offering more programs that cater to vocational and business interests—including programs to help businesses take advantage of opportunities in the federal market. State vocational schools are developing bid assistance centers to help small businesses with the procurement process. (See bibliography: *Directory of Federal and State Business Assistance Centers.*) Junior colleges and universities are teaching businesses procurement methods, and more than one school is investigating the possibility of computerized bid boards for procurements of $25,000 or less.

"Small purchase procurements are a forgotten market that can cumulatively offer economic strides for any community," attests one school official who is working to automate procurement data. The official stresses the importance of small businesses getting involved with state and private institutions to implement procurement programs. He says, "I think educational institutions have the ability to be in the vanguard of procurement-help programs—if they can enlist the help of businesses in the community."

• *Small Business Administration* (SBA). The Small Business Administration has always been an excellent resource for procurement information. (See exhibit 1-3 for a list of SBA services.) While it is known primarily as a funding source for small businesses, it is also a good source for identifying procurement opportunities.

"One day the SBA's small business advocate called to tell us about an aerospace prime contractor who wanted to subcontract circuit board repair and maintenance," reports an owner of a small electronics firm that subsequently won a contract from a prime. The SBA is involved in procurement at all levels, and it is the government's major small business advocate. So get to know your local SBA's small business advocate and provide him or her with a company brochure that clearly defines your company's capabilities. (See appendix 4 for information on primes).

• *Technological and scientific information data banks.* The government will share unclassified technological information—including information obtained in SBIR projects. Small businesses are then free to apply this information in their commercial pursuits. To request information—by specific subject—write to individual agencies according to subject type and/or the National Technical Information Service, 5285 Port Royal Road, Springfield, VA 22161 (phone: 703-487-4600).

• *Other community resources.* Don't overlook other community resources for procurement information. Your chamber of commerce is an excellent source of information on prime contracting activity, for example. And as economic development begins to focus on small business, chambers will sponsor more seminars on procurement.

Are you aware of the new resources your local library offers? If you haven't visited your library lately, you will be amazed at the variety and amount of research data available on everything from product research to market forecasts. For example, PREDICAST is an on-line computerized index of market trends and product forecasts. One inventor using PREDICAST for market research uncovered a federal law mandating computer accessibility for the handicapped. He submitted an unsolicited proposal (see appendix 8) to collect donated computers from the private sector. He would then upgrade the computers and train the handicapped in how to use them. The agency accepted his proposal and awarded him a contract.

• *Trade fairs and procurement conferences.* If your excuse for not going to procurement conferences is that you've already been to one, you're missing out on a gold mine of information and contacts. At procurement conferences more than business cards are exchanged; these conferences are a breeding ground of procurement opportunities.

Attending a procurement conference also makes you aware that small businesses are indeed the backbone of our economy and that there is power in large numbers of small businesses sharing information and cooperating on important issues. This cooperation includes some legislative efforts to ensure that small business gets its fair share of the big federal pie.

• *Department of Commerce.* Now that you've learned how to do business with the federal government, are you ready to take on the world? International procurement, that is. Using what you've learned about federal procurement, and with the help of the Department of Commerce, you will find no boundaries in your quest for markets.

If you can compete in the federal market, you can compete in international markets. In fact, the Commerce Department has a computerized "trade list" of more than 250,000 sales opportunities for American businesses. For a modest fee, the Commerce Department will also provide foreign market research on a product. Finally, for the cost of shipping your product, Department of Commerce personnel will place it in an international "made in America" trade show. Contact the Department of Commerce for details.

And what opportunities await you! To take advantage of them you don't have to ask a fortuneteller to look into a crystal ball. You can be your own fortuneteller.

There are a number of ways you can predict the trends that are changing the face of federal procurement. To see how easy it is, I'll introduce you to a few successful procurement entrepreneurs so that you can see through their crystal balls.

HARRIET MASON SEES "INFOMANIA"

Says Harriet Mason, "I knew I was in the middle of something big when I had to expand my business three times to *stay* in business . . . it was enough to make me an infomaniac!" Mason's microfiche/data entry/optical scanning business has changed three times in the last decade to keep pace with the technological advances of the computer age. "My professional organization bombarded me with market trends for the computer age. Then, when I read an article in a Department of Defense journal about the government's and prime contractors' plan to optically scan billions of pounds of paper, I knew I could stay in business *forever.*"

She is probably right. If you have been reading Department of Defense and General Service Administration publications, you know that the need for automated data is expanding procurement opportunities and even changing the way the government does business. The government is beginning to convert billions of tons of paper—regulations manuals, technical specifications, and maintenance and operations manuals—into computerized information. Information crunching is only the beginning. Also look for computers to revolutionize:

• *Movement of information and products.* The movement of government information over telephone wires (using facsimile machines), the tracking of government shipments by satellite (using transponders), new methods for materials labeling (using bar coding), and electronic libraries (database) to research information are trends affecting procurement opportunities.

• *Storage.* Besides the use of floppy and hard disk computer storage, the influx of optical-disk technology will allow mass storage of information much more cheaply and efficiently than in the past.

• *Printing.* Some centralized printing operations will be replaced by less expensive desktop publishing and computer graphics.

• *Artificial intelligence.* Look for business opportunities for programming computers and robots with reasoning ability to solve practical problems, such as methods to fight fires and land airplanes.

• *Procurement procedures.* Get ready for computerized bid boards, more computerized contract management, and "just-in-time" managed computerized inventories. Several states have already instituted computerized bid boards, allowing contractors to access solicitations by computer and modem by using their federal contractor identification numbers (CAGE). And contract administrators are already using the computers to track contract performance. Just-in-time computerized inventory control will allow the government to fill large product orders on an immediate, fast-turnover basis. Instead of maintaining large inventories, the government will use computers to inventory and order products, expecting its contractors to provide products when and where it needs them.

Ray Schowers, a computer paper manufacturer, has already responded to the just-in-time inventory trend. He recently expanded his facility to include additional storage warehouses to accommodate the government's and his commercial customers' just-in-time ordering procedures. "I got the jump on my competitors and cut out the middleman supplier," he boasts.

KEN BEASLEY SEES ASPHALT AND CONCRETE

Look into Ken Beasley's crystal ball and you will see a lot of business activity, most of it having to do with asphalt and concrete. A couple of years ago he was an unemployed subcontractor looking for work. Now Ken has landed city, county, and federal highway repair contracts.

"I read an article about the immediate need for extensive interstate highway repair. So I thought it was a good place to start for an unemployed person. I hooked my tar buggy on the back of my truck and incorporated."

You don't have to read about America's crumbling infrastructure to know about it. Have you driven into a pothole recently or across a creaking bridge? Have you walked into a federal building that needed some major repairs (if not a good demolition)? There are over $24 billion dollars in federal trust funds that should begin to hit the streets soon. Don't let opportunities fall through the cracks. (See appendix 6 for more information on construction and architecture-engineering contract opportunities.)

KATHY LITTLE SAW PRIVATIZATION

"Lots of work and no one to do it."

One day Kathy Little looked into her crystal ball and saw helicopters. Her "crystal ball" was actually a conversation she overheard at a procurement conference.

"I was sitting there thinking about how one of my four businesses could tap into the procurement market. Then I heard a base commander sitting next to me comment about his problem with helicopter repair. He didn't have enough enlisted men who could repair the base helicopters, so he was forced to use out-of-state civilian repairmen."

The last thing Little thought she needed was another business. "But how could I lose? I knew there was too much work for the enlisted men to do, and predictions were that the situation would only get worse." Now Kathy owns Fly-Well, a business specializing in small aircraft repair.

Because she attended the procurement conference, Little was able to capitalize on a trend she had heard about before: privatization of government services. She capitalized on the personnel shortages in the federal government. From the shrinking armed forces to the budget-cut dearth of management personnel, these shortages translate into procurement opportunities never before relegated to—or imagined by—the private sector.

Privatization may have started with the U.S. Postal Service, but it will not end there. The Office of Management and Budget (OMB) estimates that out of the $20-billion total of commercial goods and services that the government produces, at least $7 billion could be saved through privatization.

Surely the government has a need for your service. If you take advantage of these new opportunities, as Kathy Little did, you too might be flying high on the wings of success.

LARRY ROCK SAW IT WASN'T "GOOD ENOUGH FOR GOVERNMENT WORK"

"It's good enough for government work" is a phrase that has long plagued government procurement officials. Lately their *cause célèbre*, their resounding battle cry is: *"Before* all else fails, look to quality."

Larry Rock, technical writer and consultant, was just dotting the last *i* on a quality manual he was writing for a small manufacturing company when a government quality inspector walked in the door.

"I just read the rough draft of the quality manual you wrote. Excellent work," said the Q. "I wish all my contractors had manuals like this one." Rock got the hint. He's now writing and upgrading quality manuals for several other small companies and two prime contractors.

But you're not a technical writer, you say? You've got enough problems maintaining your own company's quality circle, toeing the "zero defects" line? That is precisely my point. Rock was so successful *because* the government is placing emphasis on quality, and this is creating opportunities for quality consultants, as well as for small businesses with progressive quality programs. If you emphasize this quality trend you will gain more than the savings on rejects. Your improved quality will translate into improved sales. Few people know that the Japanese, touted for their quality products, did not start out with quality as their primary objective—it was cost. They soon discovered that you can produce items the cheapest way when you do it right the first time. Toeing the quality line will help you in your quest for government contracts.

MARIANNE VANATTA SAW SBIR

Perhaps the quintessential opportunity is one that you make—or invent—yourself.

Marianne Vanatta had just started building Woman the Great, an industrial robot, when her professor told her about SBIR. "I looked into it and figured that I might as well turn my graduate research project into something profitable, if I could."

Small Business Innovative Research (SBIR) grants afford the opportunity to do just that. SBIR mandates that eleven government agencies must offer funding to small businesses to launch innovative research projects. (See appendix 5 for program information.)

Woman the Great now has a job in a government munitions plant, making artillery shells. She doesn't make mistakes, and even if she did, the government wouldn't have to pay worker's compensation. And her creator, Marianne Vanatta, landed a successful job right out of graduate school as a designer of automated production processes for a large automobile manufacturer.

JIM FOGLEMAN "SIMULATES" LOOKING THROUGH A CRYSTAL BALL

Jim Fogleman's small company subcontracted with a commercial aircraft company to design flight simulation programs for training pilots. One day he went to a local arcade to play a video war game.

"The more I thought about that game," Jim says, "the more I realized there were applications for simulation far beyond the pilot training programs. Why couldn't I develop programs to train soldiers and to test equipment?"

Jim and his competitors now have more federal business than they can handle. "The technology lags behind the need," says Jim. "The future for simulation programs is so vast it boggles the mind. I can only *simulate* the possibilities."

TWO ENTREPRENEURS FORESEE "SECURITY" IN THE FUTURE

The proliferation of international terrorism and espionage has created another trend in procurement markets: the need for security systems. From bulletproof vests to methods for detecting explosives, the market is *dynamite*.

Julie Yard, a manufacturer of hunting apparel, was approached by some Arkansas survivalists about making bulletproof vests. When she realized how easy it was to convert hunting vests into bulletproof vests, she began to do some market research and discovered the federal government. "My business has skyrocketed," she says.

Richard Poyner, a munitions specialist, recently responded to an SBIR presolicitation to develop a method for detonating explosives hidden in baggage before they are loaded onto airplanes. "I've had the idea a long time," he says, "and when I saw a presolicitation in an SBIR publication, I decided to try for a grant." Poyner is waiting to hear whether his proposal will be accepted. In the meantime, he is looking into international funding.

YOU DON'T NEED A CRYSTAL BALL TO SEE SPENDING CUTS

If you've been wondering when I would get around to talking about the "negative" trend of budget cuts in the federal procurement system, the time has come. But with this so-called negative trend comes a silver lining. Spending cuts mean that the government will have to procure quality items at lower cost. While this could be bad news for large companies struggling with big overhead and inefficiency caused by cumbersome layers of management, it is good news for small businesses with responsive and simple management structures. They usually can produce a higher-quality product at a lower price than their large competitors.

Spending cuts are also occurring in the ranks of the federal bureaucracy itself, especially in the area of service jobs. The Office of Management and Budget estimates that 450,000 jobs in the Defense Department alone could easily be performed by the private sector. The trend toward privatization has resulted in such recent procurements as consultants, security guards, food caterers—even travel agents in the Pentagon. After reviewing government services, agencies are discovering that they can contract out many of these services for a minimum 30 percent savings. These internal budget cuts mean more business for small businesses, not less.

It's hard *not* to get excited when you glimpse what the future holds in store. Like these procurement entrepreneurs, you too can find or make your own opportunities, blazing your own trail to the federal marketplace. So be your own fortuneteller—or rather, fortune-maker!

Appendix 1

Government Procurement Forms

The forms preceded by an asterisk are provided immediately following. The remainder of this list is provided as a quick reference for review when reading or researching procurement information. It is extremely important to *know the acronym prefix* of the form.

AFLC 53: Item Identification Marking and Shelf Life Item Provisions
AFLC 761: Screening Analysis Worksheet
AFLC 857: Request for Solicitations Sets
AFLC 2512: Engineering Instructions
AFSC 91: Order Policy Agreement for Evaluation of Unsolicited Proposals
CASB-CMF: Cost Accounting Standards Board—Cost Money for Facilities
CASB-DS–1: Cost Accounting Standards Board—Disclosure Statement and Certificate
***DD 250:** Shipping, Material Inspection and/or Receiving Report
***DD 375:** Production Progress Report
***DD 1155:** Purchase Order for Nonrepetitive Small Purchases
DD 1423: Contract Data Requirement List, Distribution of DD 375, DD 250, drws. and specs.
DD 1425: Specifications and Standards Requisition, Naval Publications and Forms
DD 1547: Weighted Guidelines Profit/Fee Objective
DD 1664: Data Item Description
DD 1861: Contract Facilities Capital and Cost of Money
***DD 2051:** Request for Assignment of a Commercial and Government Entity (CAGE) Code
DD 2345: Militarily Critical Technical Data Agreement
GSA 3088: Bidders' Mailing List Application to the General Services Administration
OF 347: Order for Supplies or Services (primarily construction)

161

PS 7429: U.S. Postal Service Bidders' Mailing List Application

PS 7429A: Postal Commodity and Geographic Location Check-Off

*SBA 1167: SBA PASS Application—Procurement Automated Source System

*SF 18: RFQ Solicitation—Small Business Set-Asides and Business Certificate

SF 21: Bid Form for Construction Contracts primarily <$25,000

SF 23: Construction Contracts, primarily <$25,000

*SF 24: Bid Bond for Construction Bidding

SF 25: Performance Bond (pending construction award)

SF 25A: Payment Bond (after construction award)

*SF 26: Award/Contract, Generally <$25,000

*SF 30: Amendment of Solicitation/Modification of Contract

*SF 33: Standardized Solicitation Offer and Award Document

SF 33A: Standard form included with SF 33, provides additional information

*SF 44: Combined: Purchase Order, Invoice, Voucher, Material Receipt— $2,500

*SF 129: Standard Form 129 for Bidders' Source List (BSL) Application

SF 196: Summary Subcontract Report

SF 252: Architect-Engineer Contract Form (being replaced by SF 33)

*SF 254: Architect-Engineer and Related Services (experience) (7 pages)

*SF 255: Architect-Engineer and Related Services for Specific Project (11 pages)

SF 294: Subcontracting Report for Individual Contracts

SF 1034: Public Voucher for Purchases and Services Other than Personal

*SF 1403: Preaward Survey, General Information

*SF 1404: Preaward Survey, Technical Capabilities

*SF 1405: Preaward Survey, Production (2-part form)

*SF 1406: Preaward Survey, Quality Assurance

*SF 1407: Preaward Survey, Financial Capability (2-part form)

*SF 1408: Preaward Survey, Accounting System

*SF 1409: Abstract of Offers (nonconstruction)

SF 1411: Contract Pricing Proposal Cover Sheet

SF 1412: Claim for Exemption from Submission of Certified Price or Price Data

SF 1417: Presolicitation Notice for Potential Construction Projects

*SF 1419: Abstract of Offers—Construction

SF 1420: Performance Evaluation for Construction Supplies and Services

SF 1421: Performance Evaluation for Construction Contracts (also EF 2459)

SF 1435: Termination—Inventory Settlement Proposal (4 pages)

SF 1436: Termination—Total Cost Settlement Proposal (4 pages)

SF 1439: Termination—Schedule of Accounting Information

SF 1442: Solicitation, Offer and Award (Construction) (being replaced by SF 33)

SF 1443: Contractor's Request for Progress Payment

Material Inspection and Receiving Report: DD 250

MATERIAL INSPECTION AND RECEIVING REPORT	1. PROC. INSTRUMENT IDEN (CONTRACT)	(ORDER) NO.	6. INVOICE NO. DATE	7. PAGE OF
				8. ACCEPTANCE POINT

2. SHIPMENT NO.	3. DATE SHIPPED	4. B/L TCN	5. DISCOUNT TERMS

9. PRIME CONTRACTOR   CODE

10. ADMINISTERED BY   CODE

11. SHIPPED FROM (IF OTHER THAN 9) CODE   F.O.B.:

12. PAYMENT WILL BE MADE BY :   CODE

13. SHIPPED TO   CODE

14. MARKED FOR   CODE

15. ITEM NO.	16. STOCK/PART NO. DESCRIPTION (INDICATE NUMBER OF SHIPPING CONTAINERS – TYPE OF CONTAINER – CONTAINER NUMBER)	17. QUANTITY SHIP/REC'D*	18. UNIT	19. UNIT PRICE	20. AMOUNT

21. PROCUREMENT QUALITY ASSURANCE

A. ORIGIN

☐PQA ☐ACCEPTANCE OF LISTED ITEMS HAS BEEN MADE BY ME OR UNDER MY SUPERVISION AND THEY CONFORM TO CONTRACT, EXCEPT AS NOTED HEREIN OR ON SUPPORTING DOCUMENTS.

DATE   SIGNATURE OF AUTH GOVT REP

TYPED NAME AND OFFICE

B. DESTINATION

☐PQA ☐ACCEPTANCE OF LISTED ITEMS HAS BEEN MADE BY ME OR UNDER MY SUPERVISION AND THEY CONFORM TO CONTRACT, EXCEPT AS NOTED HEREIN OR ON SUPPORTING DOCUMENTS.

DATE   SIGNATURE OF AUTH GOVT REP

TYPED NAME AND TITLE

22. RECEIVER'S USE

QUANTITIES SHOWN IN COLUMN 17 WERE RECEIVED IN APPARENT GOOD CONDITION AS NOTED.

DATE RECEIVED   SIGNATURE OF AUTH GOVT REP

TYPED NAME AND OFFICE

* IF QUANTITY RECEIVED BY THE GOVERNMENT IS SAME AS QUANTITY SHIPPED, INDICATE BY (√) MARK, IF DIFFERENT, ENTER ACTUAL QUANTITY RECEIVED BELOW QUANTITY SHIPPED AND ENCIRCLE.

23. CONTRACTOR USE ONLY

A. PACKING SHEET NO.	B. TYPE OF PACKAGE	C. SIZE	D. GROSS WT.	E. NET WT.	F. OUR ORDER NO. (S. O.)

G. REMARKS

H. ACCT. NO.	AMT.

DD FORM 250   PREVIOUS EDITIONS ARE OBSOLETE

CLASSIFICATION

PRODUCTION PROGRESS REPORT

REPORT PERIOD

REPORT NUMBER

Form Approved
OMB No. 22-R0309

NOTE:
If final report, so indicate by placing "F" after Report No. →

PURCHASING OFFICE AND ADDRESS

CONTRACT ADMINISTRATION OFFICE AND ADDRESS

NAME AND ADDRESS OF CONTRACTOR (City, State, ZIP Code)

PII (Contract) NUMBER

NAME AND ADDRESS OF PLANT (City, State, ZIP Code)

SECTION I - PRODUCTION DATA

CONTRACT LINE ITEM NUMBER *a*	IDENTIFICATION		TOTAL CONTRACT QUANTITY *d*	SCH	ACTUAL DLVRY.		DELIVERY FORECAST								BALANCE TO COMPLETE *o*
	FSN AND NOMENCLATURE *b*	PURCHASE REQUEST/PRON/MIPR *c*			REPORT PERIOD *e*	CUMULA-TIVE *f*	1ST *g*	2ND *h*	3RD *i*	4TH *j*	5TH *k*	6TH *l*	NEXT 3 *m*	NEXT 3 *n*	
				C											
				D											
				C											
				D											
				C											
				D											
				C											
				D											
				C											
				D											

SECTION II - DELAY FACTORS (If none, place "X" in box) → ☐

DATA (Place "X" in proper column)	YES	NO	DATA (Place "X" in proper column)	YES	NO
1. DESIGN AND ENGINEERING PROBLEMS			6. MATERIAL		
2. SPECIFICATIONS			A. REQUESTED LATE		
A. SUBMITTED LATE			B. PROCURED/SUPPLIED LATE		
B. INADEQUATE/DEFECTIVE			C. REJECTED		
C. APPROVED LATE			7. PROPERTY		
3. FACILITIES			A. ORDERED LATE		
4. SPECIAL TOOL AND TESTING EQUIPMENT			B. SUPPLIED/PROCURED LATE		
A. REQUESTED LATE			C. DEFECTIVE/REJECTED		
B. PROCURED/SUPPLIED LATE			8. PROTOTYPE MODEL		
5. PRODUCTION PROBLEMS			A. SUBMITTED LATE		
			8. REJECTED		
			9. APPROVED LATE		
			10. FINANCIAL DIFFICULTY		
			10. SUBCONTRACTOR FAILURE		
			11. CONTRACT AMENDMENTS		
			12. PRIORITY ACTIONS		
			13. NATURAL DISASTER		
			14. STRIKE		
			15. UNDETERMINED/OTHER		

16. TYPED NAME AND TITLE OF CONTRACTOR'S REPRESENTATIVE

17. SIGNATURE

18. DATE

19. TYPED NAME OF GOVERNMENT REPRESENTATIVE

20. SIGNATURE

21. DATE

DD FORM **375** 1 JUL 72   REPLACES 1 AUG 68 EDITION WHICH MAY BE USED.

CLASSIFICATION

PAGE _____ OF _____ PAGE(S)

INSTRUCTIONS FOR COMPLETION OF DD FORM 375

(Self-explanatory items are not discussed)

1. The report, when required in the contract, is to be prepared by the contractor in accordance with the dates specified in the Production Progress Reporting clause. Reports will be mailed within two working days after the report period. Reports on exceptions to the contract delivery schedule shall reflect current status and projected deliveries and shall be submitted immediately upon knowledge of the pending or actual exception and dated accordingly.

2. Classify in accordance with applicable DD Form 254.

3. DD Form 375C shall be used for remarks required.

HEADING:

REPORT PERIOD - Insert the date(s) of the period being reported.

REPORT NUMBER - Insert sequential report number as applicable to the contract.

SECTION I - PRODUCTION DATA:

COLUMN a, CONTRACT LINE ITEM NUMBER - Insert line item or subline number from the contract. Items once reported complete may be omitted in subsequent reports. Only one contract item is to be reported on each line of SECTION I.

COLUMN b, FSN AND NOMENCLATURE - Insert the Federal Stock Number from the contract in the upper space in this column and a descriptive word of nomenclature in the lower space on this line.

COLUMN c, PURCHASE REQUEST/PRON/MIPR - Insert the Purchase Request Number, Procurement Request Order Number, or the Military Interdepartmental Purchase Request Number if contained in the contract.

COLUMN e, REPORT PERIOD - Insert on line C the quantity of items scheduled by the contract for the report period. Insert on line D the quantity of items actually delivered during the report period.

COLUMN f, CUMULATIVE - Insert on line C the cumulative total of the item scheduled by the contract through the end of the report period. Insert on line D the cumulative total of the item actually delivered through the end of the report period.

COLUMN g, 1ST - Insert on line C the quantity of the item scheduled by the contract for the next report period following the period reported. Insert on line D the best estimate of the quantity of the item actually to be delivered the first period following the period reported.

COLUMN h THROUGH n - Insert on line C the quantity of the item scheduled for delivery under the contract during each of the succeeding report periods. Insert on line D the best estimate of actual deliveries to be made during each of the succeeding report periods.

COLUMN o, BALANCE TO COMPLETE - Insert on line C the balance of the contract quantity not shown in columns f through n. Insert on line D the balance of actual deliveries of the contract quantity not shown in columns f through n. The quantities in columns f through o on both line C and line D should each equal the quantity shown in the d column for the item.

SECTION II - DELAY FACTORS:

Omit all line entries in this Section if there are no actual or potential delay factors to report and place "X" in the box to the right of the words "Delay Factors." Otherwise all lines in SECTION II shall be completed. On DD Form 375C explain all delay factors indicating the urgency of the factor, the nature of the difficulty, what is being done or proposed, and what assistance, if any, is desired.

ORDER FOR SUPPLIES OR SERVICES		Form Approved OMB No. 0704-0187 Expires Jul 31, 1989	PAGE 1 OF

5. CERTIFIED FOR NATIONAL DEFENSE UNDER DMS REG 1

DO

1 CONTRACT / PURCH ORDER NO	2 DELIVERY ORDER NO	3 DATE OF ORDER	4 REQUISITION / PURCH REQUEST NO

6 ISSUED BY	CODE	7 ADMINISTERED BY (if other than 6)	CODE	8 DELIVERY FOB

☐ DEST

☐ OTHER

(See Schedule if other)

9 CONTRACTOR	CODE	FACILITY CODE	10 DELIVER TO FOB POINT BY (Date)	11 MARK IF BUSINESS IS

☐ SMALL

☐ SMALL DISADVANTAGED

☐ WOMEN-OWNED

NAME AND ADDRESS

12 DISCOUNT TERMS

13 MAIL INVOICES TO

14 SHIP TO	CODE	15 PAYMENT WILL BE MADE BY	CODE

MARK ALL PACKAGES AND PAPERS WITH CONTRACT OR ORDER NUMBER

16. TYPE OF ORDER

DELIVERY — This delivery order is issued on another Government agency or in accordance with and subject to terms and conditions of above numbered contract.

Reference your _____ furnish the following on terms specified herein

PURCHASE — ACCEPTANCE. THE CONTRACTOR HEREBY ACCEPTS THE OFFER REPRESENTED BY THE NUMBERED PURCHASE ORDER AS IT MAY PREVIOUSLY HAVE BEEN OR IS NOW MODIFIED, SUBJECT TO ALL OF THE TERMS AND CONDITIONS SET FORTH, AND AGREES TO PERFORM THE SAME

NAME OF CONTRACTOR	SIGNATURE	TYPED NAME AND TITLE	DATE SIGNED

☐ If this box is marked, supplier must sign Acceptance and return the following number of copies

17. ACCOUNTING AND APPROPRIATION DATA / LOCAL USE

18. ITEM NO.	19. SCHEDULE OF SUPPLIES / SERVICE	20. QUANTITY ORDERED / ACCEPTED*	21 UNIT	22 UNIT PRICE	23. AMOUNT

*If quantity accepted by the Government is same as quantity ordered, indicate by X. If different, enter actual quantity accepted below quantity ordered and encircle.

24. UNITED STATES OF AMERICA

BY _____ CONTRACTING / ORDERING OFFICER

25. TOTAL	
29. DIFFERENCES	

26. QUANTITY IN COLUMN 20 HAS BEEN

☐ INSPECTED ☐ RECEIVED ☐ ACCEPTED, AND CONFORMS TO THE CONTRACT EXCEPT AS NOTED

DATE	SIGNATURE OF AUTHORIZED GOVERNMENT REPRESENTATIVE

36. I certify this account is correct and proper for payment.

DATE	SIGNATURE AND TITLE OF CERTIFYING OFFICER

27 SHIP NO	28. D.O. VOUCHER NO	30 INITIALS

☐ PARTIAL ☐ FINAL

32 PAID BY

33. AMOUNT VERIFIED CORRECT FOR

31. PAYMENT

☐ COMPLETE ☐ PARTIAL ☐ FINAL

34 CHECK NUMBER

35. BILL OF LADING NO.

37. RECEIVED AT	38. RECEIVED BY	39 DATE RECEIVED	40 TOTAL CONTAINERS	41 S/R ACCOUNT NUMBER	42 S/R VOUCHER NO.

DD Form 1155, JUL 87 — Previous editions are obsolete. — **CONTRACTOR MUST SUBMIT FOUR COPIES OF INVOICE**

REQUEST FOR ASSIGNMENT OF A COMMERCIAL AND GOVERNMENT ENTITY (CAGE) CODE	NOTE: See Instructions on Reverse	Form Approved OMB No. 0704-0134

SECTION A - TO BE COMPLETED BY INITIATOR

1. NAME OF REQUESTING GOVERNMENT AGENCY/ACTIVITY

1a. STREET ADDRESS, CITY, STATE, ZIP CODE

2. TYPE OF CODE REQUESTED ("X" One)
☐ a. FSCM   ☐ b. MILSCAP

3. EXCEPTION CODES
a. CAO   b. ADP

4. OFFICE SYMBOL (Initiator)

4a. TELEPHONE NUMBER (Initiator)

4b. TYPED NAME OF INITIATOR (Last, First, Middle Initial)

4c. SIGNATURE OF INITIATOR

SECTION B - TO BE COMPLETED BY FIRM TO BE CODED

1. NAME OF FIRM (Include "Branch of", "Division of", etc.)

1a. STREET ADDRESS, CITY, STATE, ZIP CODE

1b. CAGE CODE (If previously assigned)

2. IF FIRM PREVIOUSLY OPERATED UNDER OTHER NAME(S) OR OTHER ADDRESS(ES) SPECIFY THE PREVIOUS NAME(S) AND/OR ADDRESS(ES) (Use separate sheet of paper, if necessary)

3. PARENT COMPANY AND AFFILIATED FIRMS ("X" One, and complete, as applicable)
☐ a. NONE
☐ b. CURRENTLY AFFILIATED WITH OTHER FIRMS (List name and addresses of such firms on a separate sheet of paper)
☐ c. PREVIOUSLY AFFILIATED WITH OTHER FIRMS (List name and addresses of such firms on a separate sheet of paper)

4. PRIMARY BUSINESS CATEGORY ("X" One)
☐ a. MANUFACTURER   ☐ b. DEALER/DISTRIBUTOR   ☐ c. CONSTRUCTION FIRM   ☐ d. SERVICE COMPANY
☐ e. SALES OFFICE   ☐ f. OTHER (Specify):

5. NUMBER OF EMPLOYEES

6. DISADVANTAGED SMALL BUSINESS ("X" One, if applicable)
☐ a. APPROVED BY SMALL BUSINESS ADMINISTRATION (SBA) FOR SECTION 8(a) PROGRAM
☐ b. NOT APPROVED BY SBA FOR SECTION 8(a) PROGRAM

7. WOMAN OWNED BUSINESS ("X" One)
☐ a. YES
☐ b. NO

8. STANDARD INDUSTRIAL CLASSIFICATION (SIC) CODE(S)
a. PRIMARY   b. OTHER (Specify)

9. REMARKS

THIS FORM MAY BE REPRODUCED, HOWEVER, THE SIGNATURE IN BLOCK 10a MUST BE ORIGINAL

10. TYPED NAME OF FIRM OFFICIAL (Last, First, Middle Initial)

10a. SIGNATURE OF FIRM OFFICIAL

10b. DATE (YYMMDD)

10c. TELEPHONE NUMBER

DD FORM 2051, 80 NOV   REPLACES EDITION OF 1 OCT 76 WHICH IS OBSOLETE

XXI

INSTRUCTIONS FOR COMPLETING DD FORM 2051

GENERAL NOTE FOR PERSONNEL PREPARING OR PROCESSING THIS REPORT: Coding must be as indicated in the instructions. In cases where specific coding instructions are provided, reference must be made to the Department of Defense Manual for Standard Data Elements, DoD 5000.12-M. Noncompliance with either the coding instructions contained herein or those published in referenced manual will make the organization which fails to comply responsible for required concessions in data base communication. Items marked with an asterisk (*) have been registered in the DoD Data Element Program.

SPECIFIC INSTRUCTIONS:

SECTION A - TO BE COMPLETED BY THE INITIATING GOVERNMENT ACTIVITY

Items 1 and 1 a: Self-explanatory.

Item 2: "X" the type of code being requested.

*2a - A Federal Supply Code for Manufacturers (FSCM) five position all numeric code (e.g., 12345) which is used in the Federal Catalog System to identify a certain facility at a specific location which is a possible source for the manufacture and/or design control of items cataloged by the Federal Government; or,

*2b - A MILSCAP code of five positions (e.g., 1A367). These are assigned to contractors which are nonmanufacturers or are manufacturers not qualifying for inclusion in the Federal Catalog System.

*Item 3: If applicable, enter the exception DoD Activity Address Code for the Servicing Contract Administration Office (CAO) or ADP point.

Items 4, 4a, *4b, 4c. Self-explanatory.

SECTION B - TO BE COMPLETED BY THE FIRM TO WHICH THE CODE WILL BE ASSIGNED

Items 1, 1a: Self-explanatory.

*Item 1b: If a CAGE Code (FSCM or MILSCAP) was previously assigned, enter it in this block.

Item 2: Self-explanatory.

*Item 3: If a block other than "None" is "X'd", identify the "Parent" company by a (P) beside the firm name.

*Item 4: Self-explanatory.

Item 5: Enter the number of employees. This number should include the employees of all affiliates.

*Item 6: A disadvantaged business firm is defined as a firm that is 51%, or more, owned, controlled, and operated by a person(s) who is socially and economically disadvantaged. "Controlled" is defined as actively involved in the day-to-day management of the firm.

*Item 7: A woman-owned business is defined as a firm that is 51%, or more, owned, controlled, and operated by a woman or women. "Controlled" and "Operated" are as defined in Item 6.

*Item 8: The SIC Code is a Government Index used to identify business activity and indicates the function (manufacturer, wholesaler, retailer, or service) and the line of business in which the company is engaged. If multiple SIC Codes, indicate the primary first, next important, etc.

Items 9, *10, 10a, *10b, 10c: Self-explanatory.

NOTE. When any future changes are made to the coded facility; i.e., name change, location change, business sold or operations discontinued, etc., please notify, in writing, stating the appropriate change of your facility to the address reflected below:

> Commander
> Defense Logistics Services Center
> ATTN: DLSC-CGC
> Federal Center
> Battle Creek, MI 49016

*U.S. Government Printing Office: 1981—346-879/625

Want Government Business?
This could be your PASS
to potential government contracts
or subcontracts

Fill out and
mail today!

Take a minute...
fill out this form today!

Your capabilities will be computer listed and could lead to new business opportunities for you !

Instructions

Here's what happens as soon as we receive your reply

Fill out all the applicable information, tear off this portion at the perforation, fold the two remaining halves so that your company profile is on the inside, fold the flap, moisten it, seal and mail. That's all there is to it . **PASS** pays the postage !

Your company becomes computer listed through our Procurement Automated Source System (**PASS**) and your company's capabilities are available to government agencies and major corporations when they request potential bidders for contracts and subcontracts. **YOUR COMPANY SHOULD BE THERE !**

This is a free service !

You have nothing to lose and you may have new contracts to gain ! Don't delay ... mail back this information today ! You will be notified as soon as your company is listed in **PASS** !

Tear off at perforation

Is this an updated profile form?　　Yes ☐　　No ☐

PROCUREMENT AUTOMATED SOURCE SYSTEM — COMPANY PROFILE

IDENTIFICATION　PASS is designed only for small businesses which are organized for profit and independently owned and operated

MPANY NAME _____

MAILING ADDRESS _____

CITY _____ STATE _____ ZIP _____

CONTACT PERSON _____ TITLE _____

EMPLOYER IDENTIFICATION NO. (if avail.) _____

NO. OF EMPLOYEES _____

TOTAL SALES LAST FISCAL YEAR _____

YEAR BUSINESS ESTABLISHED _____

PHONE __ __ __ — __ __ __ — __ __ __ __
　　　　　Area Code　　　Number

PASS is divided into 4 types of businesses. Please estimate the percentage of your business allocated to the following (total must equal 100%) and complete the appropriate section(s).

MANUFACTURING/SUPPLIES　%

CHECK ONE ☑

☐ MANUFACTURER　☐ DEALER　☐ WHOLESALE DISTRIBUTOR

MANUFACTURING FACILITY　SIZE _____ SQ FT

RESEARCH and DEVELOPMENT　%

No. of engineers & scientists _____
Expertise of key personnel _____

CONSTRUCTION　%

MAXIMUM CURRENT BONDING LEVEL　$___
　　　　　　　　　　　　　　　　(if applicable)

MAXIMUM OPERATING RADIUS _____ MILES
ANYWHERE IN U.S. ENTER 3999 ABOVE
ANYWHERE IN THE WORLD. ENTER 9999 ABOVE

SERVICES　%

MAXIMUM CURRENT BONDING LEVEL　$___
　　　　　　　　　　　　　　　　(if applicable)

MAXIMUM OPERATING RADIUS _____ MILES
ANYWHERE IN U.S. ENTER 3999 ABOVE
ANYWHERE IN THE WORLD. ENTER 9999 ABOVE

CAPABILITIES　(limit 32 words — avoid abbreviations)

List products and services offered and special capabilities.

_____
_____
_____
_____

OWNERSHIP　CHECK ALL APPLICABLE BOXES ☑

Company is at least
51% OWNED, CONTROLLED
and ACTIVELY MANAGED BY:

☐ VETERAN(S)
☐ CHECK IF ANY SERVICE WAS IN VIETNAM ERA (1964-1975)
☐ WOMAN/WOMEN
☐ MINORITY PERSON(S)

IF MINORITY OWNER CHECK ☑

☐ BLACK AMERICAN
☐ NATIVE AMERICAN
　American Indian.
　Eskimo, Aleut & Native
　Hawaiian)

☐ HISPANIC AMERICAN
☐ ASIAN PACIFIC AMERICAN
　(Includes Oriental)

EXPORTS　CHECK ONE BOX ☑ FOR INTERNATIONAL TRADE INTEREST

☐ ACTIVE EXPORTER　☐ INTERESTED IN EXPORTS　☐ NOT INTERESTED IN EXPORTS

SIGNATURE　Important! Signature is required

INFORMATION CONTAINED IN THIS PROFILE MAY BE DISCLOSED AT THE DISCRETION OF THE SMALL BUSINESS ADMINISTRATION

Please sign here
_____　_____　_____
　Signature of Company Officer　　　Title　　　Date

(for SBA Use)

Questions? Contact your regional or district U.S. Small Business Administration Office for answers.

FILL OUT .... SEAL .... AND MAIL TODAY! IT'S EASY!

★ GPO : 1985 0 – 480-733

SBA Form 1167 (7–85)
Prev. Editions Obsolete
OMB Approved: 3245-0024
Exp: 3-31-86

REQUEST FOR QUOTATIONS *(THIS IS NOT AN ORDER)*	The Notice of Small Business-Small Purchase Set-Aside on the reverse of this form ☐ is ☐ is not applicable.		PAGE	OF	PAGES

1. REQUEST NO.	2. DATE ISSUED	3. REQUISITION/PURCHASE REQUEST NO.	4. CERT. FOR NAT. DEF. UNDER BDSA REG. 2 AND/OR DMS REG. 1 ▶	RATING

5A. ISSUED BY

6. DELIVER BY *(Date)*

7. DELIVERY

5B. FOR INFORMATION CALL: *(Name and telephone no.)* *(No collect calls)*

☐ FOB DESTINATION ☐ OTHER *(See Schedule)*

8. TO: NAME AND ADDRESS, INCLUDING ZIP CODE

9. DESTINATION *(Consignee and address, including ZIP Code)*

10. PLEASE FURNISH QUOTATIONS TO THE ISSUING OFFICE ON OR BEFORE CLOSE OF BUSINESS *(Date)*

11. BUSINESS CLASSIFICATION *(Check appropriate boxes)*

☐ SMALL ☐ OTHER THAN SMALL ☐ DISADVANTAGED ☐ WOMEN-OWNED

IMPORTANT: This is a request for information, and quotations furnished are not offers. If you are unable to quote, please so indicate on this form and return it. This request does not commit the Government to pay any costs incurred in the preparation of the submission of this quotation or to contract for supplies or services. Supplies are of domestic origin unless otherwise indicated by quoter. Any representations and/or certifications attached to this Request for Quotations must be completed by the quoter.

12. SCHEDULE *(Include applicable Federal, State and local taxes)*

ITEM NO. (a)	SUPPLIES/SERVICES (b)	QUANTITY (c)	UNIT (d)	UNIT PRICE (e)	AMOUNT (f)

13. DISCOUNT FOR PROMPT PAYMENT ▶	10 CALENDAR DAYS %	20 CALENDAR DAYS %	30 CALENDAR DAYS %	CALENDAR DAYS %

NOTE: Reverse must also be completed by the quoter.

14. NAME AND ADDRESS OF QUOTER *(Street, city, county, State and ZIP Code)*	15. SIGNATURE OF PERSON AUTHORIZED TO SIGN QUOTATION	16. DATE OF QUOTATION
	17. NAME AND TITLE OF SIGNER *(Type or print)*	18. TELEPHONE NO. *(Include area code)*

NSN 7540-01-152-8084
PREVIOUS EDITION NOT USABLE

18-118

STANDARD FORM 18 (REV. 10-83)
Prescribed by GSA
FAR (48 CFR) 53.215-1(a)

REPRESENTATIONS, CERTIFICATIONS, AND PROVISIONS

The following representation applies when the contract is to be performed inside the United States, its territories or possessions, Puerto Rico, the Trust Territory of the Pacific Islands, or the District of Columbia.

52.219-1 SMALL BUSINESS CONCERN REPRESENTATION (Apr 84)

The quoter represents and certifies as part of its quotation that it ☐ is, ☐ is not a small business concern and that ☐ all, ☐ not all supplies to be furnished will be manufactured or produced by a small business concern in the United States, its possessions, or Puerto Rico. "Small business concern, as used in this provision, means a concern, including its affiliates, that is independently owned and operated, not dominant in the field of operation in which it is bidding on Government contracts, and qualified as a small business under the criteria and size standards in 13 CFR 121.

The following provision is applicable if required on the face of the form:

52.219-2 Notice of Small Business-Small Purchase Set-Aside (Apr 84)

Quotations under this acquisition are solicited from small business concerns only. Any acquisition resulting from this solicitation will be from a small business concern. Quotations received from concerns that are not small businesses shall not be considered and shall be rejected.

STANDARD FORM 18 BACK (REV. 10-83)

FAC 84-7   APRIL 30, 1985

PART 53—FORMS   53.301-24

OMB NO 9000-0045

BID BOND
(See Instructions on reverse)

DATE BOND EXECUTED *(Must not be later than bid opening date)*	

PRINCIPAL *(Legal name and business address)*

TYPE OF ORGANIZATION *("X" one)*

☐ INDIVIDUAL   ☐ PARTNERSHIP

☐ JOINT VENTURE   ☐ CORPORATION

STATE OF INCORPORATION

SURETY(IES) *(Name and business address)*

PENAL SUM OF BOND					BID IDENTIFICATION	
PERCENT OF BID PRICE	AMOUNT NOT TO EXCEED				BID DATE	INVITATION NO.
	MILLION(S)	THOUSAND(S)	HUNDRED(S)	CENTS		
					FOR *(Construction, Supplies or Services)*	

OBLIGATION:

We, the Principal and Surety(ies) are firmly bound to the United States of America (hereinafter called the Government) in the above penal sum. For payment of the penal sum, we bind ourselves, our heirs, executors, administrators, and successors, jointly and severally. However, where the Sureties are corporations acting as co-sureties, we, the Sureties, bind ourselves in such sum "jointly and severally" as well as "severally" only for the purpose of allowing a joint action or actions against any or all of us. For all other purposes, each Surety binds itself, jointly and severally with the Principal, for the payment of the sum shown opposite the name of the Surety. If no limit of liability is indicated, the limit of liability is the full amount of the penal sum.

CONDITIONS:

The Principal has submitted the bid identified above.

THEREFORE:

The above obligation is void if the Principal — (a) upon acceptance by the Government of the bid identified above, within the period specified therein for acceptance (sixty (60) days if no period is specified), executes the further contractual documents and gives the bond(s) required by the terms of the bid as accepted within the time specified (ten (10) days if no period is specified) after receipt of the forms by the principal; or (b) in the event of failure so to execute such further contractual documents and give such bonds, pays the Government for any cost of procuring the work which exceeds the amount of the bid.

Each Surety executing this instrument agrees that its obligation is not impaired by any extension(s) of the time for acceptance of the bid that the Principal may grant to the Government. Notice to the surety(ies) of extension(s) are waived. However, waiver of the notice applies only to extensions aggregating not more than sixty (60) calendar days in addition to the period originally allowed for acceptance of the bid.

WITNESS:

The Principal and Surety(ies) executed this bid bond and affixed their seals on the above date.

	PRINCIPAL		
Signature(s)	1. *(Seal)*	2. *(Seal)*	Corporate Seal
Name(s) & Title(s) (Typed)	1.	2.	

	INDIVIDUAL SURETIES		
Signature(s)	1. *(Seal)*	2.	*(Seal)*
Name(s) (Typed)	1.	2.	

	CORPORATE SURETY(IES)			
SURETY A	Name & Address		STATE OF INC.	LIABILITY LIMIT $
	Signature(s)	1.	2.	Corporate Seal
	Name(s) & Title(s) (Typed)	1.	2.	

NSN 7540-01-152-8059
PREVIOUS EDITION NOT USABLE

24-105

STANDARD FORM 24 (REV. 4-85)
Prescribed by GSA
FAR (48 CFR 53.228(a))

174

CORPORATE SURETY(IES) *(Continued)*					
SURETY B	Name & Address		STATE OF INC.	LIABILITY LIMIT $	Corporate Seal
	Signature(s)	1.	2.		
	Name(s) & Title(s) (Typed)	1.	2.		
SURETY C	Name & Address		STATE OF INC.	LIABILITY LIMIT $	Corporate Seal
	Signature(s)	1.	2.		
	Name(s) & Title(s) (Typed)	1.	2.		
SURETY D	Name & Address		STATE OF INC.	LIABILITY LIMIT $	Corporate Seal
	Signature(s)	1.	2.		
	Name(s) & Title(s) (Typed)	1.	2.		
SURETY E	Name & Address		STATE OF INC.	LIABILITY LIMIT $	Corporate Seal
	Signature(s)	1.	2.		
	Name(s) & Title(s) (Typed)	1.	2.		
SURETY F	Name & Address		STATE OF INC.	LIABILITY LIMIT $	Corporate Seal
	Signature(s)	1.	2.		
	Name(s) & Title(s) (Typed)	1.	2.		
SURETY G	Name & Address		STATE OF INC.	LIABILITY LIMIT $	Corporate Seal
	Signature(s)	1.	2.		
	Name(s) & Title(s) (Typed)	1.	2.		

INSTRUCTIONS

1 This form is authorized for use when a bid guaranty is required. Any deviation from this form will require the written approval of the Administrator of General Services.

2 Insert the full legal name and business address of the Principal in the space designated "Principal" on the face of the form. An authorized person shall sign the bond. Any person signing in a representative capacity (e.g., an attorney-in-fact) must furnish evidence of authority if that representative is not a member of the firm, partnership, or joint venture, or an officer of the corporation involved.

3 The bond may express penal sum as a percentage of the bid price. In these cases, the bond may state a maximum dollar limitation (e.g., 20% of the bid price but the amount not to exceed _____ dollars).

4 (a) Corporations executing the bond as sureties must appear on the Department of the Treasury's list of approved sureties and must act within the limitation listed herein. Where more than one corporate surety is involved, their names and addresses shall appear in the spaces (Surety A, Surety B, etc.) headed "CORPORATE SURETY(IES)". In the space designated "SURETY(IES)" on the face of the form, insert only the letter identification of the sureties.

(b) Where individual sureties are involved, two or more responsible persons shall execute the bond. A completed Affidavit of Individual Surety (Standard Form 28), for each individual surety, shall accompany the bond. The Government may require these sureties to furnish additional substantiating information concerning their financial capability.

5. Corporations executing the bond shall affix their corporate seals. Individuals shall execute the bond opposite the word "Corporate Seal", and shall affix an adhesive seal if executed in Maine, New Hampshire, or any other jurisdiction requiring adhesive seals.

6. Type the name and title of each person signing this bond in the space provided.

7. In its application to negotiated contracts, the terms "bid" and "bidder" shall include "proposal" and "offeror".

STANDARD FORM 24 BACK (REV 4-85)

FAC 84–5　　　　**APRIL 1, 1985**

PART 53—FORMS　　　　　　　　　　　　　　　　　　　　　　53.301–26

AWARD/CONTRACT	1. THIS CONTRACT IS A RATED ORDER UNDER DPAS (15 CFR 350)	▶	RATING	PAGE	OF	PAGES

2. CONTRACT (Proc. Inst. Ident.) NO.	3. EFFECTIVE DATE	4. REQUISITION/PURCHASE REQUEST/PROJECT NO.

5. ISSUED BY	CODE	6. ADMINISTERED BY (If other than Item 5)	CODE

7. NAME AND ADDRESS OF CONTRACTOR (No., street, city, county, State and ZIP Code)

8. DELIVERY
- [ ] FOB ORIGIN　　[ ] OTHER (See below)

9. DISCOUNT FOR PROMPT PAYMENT

10. SUBMIT INVOICES (4 copies unless otherwise specified) TO THE ADDRESS SHOWN IN　ITEM ▶

CODE　　　　　　FACILITY CODE

11. SHIP TO/MARK FOR	CODE	12. PAYMENT WILL BE MADE BY	CODE

13. AUTHORITY FOR USING OTHER THAN FULL AND OPEN COMPETITION:	14. ACCOUNTING AND APPROPRIATION DATA
[ ] 10 U.S.C. 2304(c)( )　　[ ] 41 U.S.C. 253(c)( )	

15A. ITEM NO	15B. SUPPLIES/SERVICES	15C. QUANTITY	15D. UNIT	15E. UNIT PRICE	15F. AMOUNT

15G. TOTAL AMOUNT OF CONTRACT ▶ | $

16. TABLE OF CONTENTS

(✓)	SEC	DESCRIPTION	PAGE(S)	(✓)	SEC	DESCRIPTION	PAGE(S)
		PART I — THE SCHEDULE				PART II — CONTRACT CLAUSES	
	A	SOLICITATION/CONTRACT FORM			I	CONTRACT CLAUSES	
	B	SUPPLIES OR SERVICES AND PRICES/COSTS				PART III — LIST OF DOCUMENTS, EXHIBITS AND OTHER ATTACH.	
	C	DESCRIPTION/SPECS/WORK STATEMENT			J	LIST OF ATTACHMENTS	
	D	PACKAGING AND MARKING				PART IV — REPRESENTATIONS AND INSTRUCTIONS	
	E	INSPECTION AND ACCEPTANCE			K	REPRESENTATIONS, CERTIFICATIONS AND OTHER STATEMENTS OF OFFERORS	
	F	DELIVERIES OR PERFORMANCE			L	INSTRS., CONDS., AND NOTICES TO OFFERORS	
	G	CONTRACT ADMINISTRATION DATA			M	EVALUATION FACTORS FOR AWARD	
	H	SPECIAL CONTRACT REQUIREMENTS					

CONTRACTING OFFICER WILL COMPLETE ITEM 17 OR 18 AS APPLICABLE

17. [ ] CONTRACTOR'S NEGOTIATED AGREEMENT (Contractor is required to sign this document and return _____ copies to issuing office.) Contractor agrees to furnish and deliver all items or perform all the services set forth or otherwise identified above and on any continuation sheets for the consideration stated herein. The rights and obligations of the parties to this contract shall be subject to and governed by the following documents: (a) this award/contract, (b) the solicitation, if any, and (c) such provisions, representations, certifications, and specifications, as are attached or incorporated by reference herein. (Attachments are listed herein.)

18. [ ] AWARD (Contractor is not required to sign this document.) Your offer on Solicitation Number _____ including the additions or changes made by you which additions or changes are set forth in full above, is hereby accepted as to the items listed above and on any continuation sheets. This award consummates the contract which consists of the following documents: (a) the Government's solicitation and your offer, and (b) this award/contract. No further contractual document is necessary.

19A. NAME AND TITLE OF SIGNER (Type or print)	20A. NAME OF CONTRACTING OFFICER

19B. NAME OF CONTRACTOR	19C. DATE SIGNED	20B. UNITED STATES OF AMERICA	20C. DATE SIGNED
BY _____ (Signature of person authorized to sign)		BY _____ (Signature of Contracting Officer)	

NSN 7540-01-152-8069　　　　　　　25–106　　　　　　STANDARD FORM 26 (REV. 4-85)
PREVIOUS EDITION UNUSABLE　　　　　　　　　　　　　Prescribed by GSA
　　　　　　　　　　　　　　　　　　　　　　　　　　FAR (48 CFR) 53.214(a)

AMENDMENT OF SOLICITATION/MODIFICATION OF CONTRACT	1. CONTRACT ID CODE	PAGE OF PAGES

2. AMENDMENT/MODIFICATION NO.	3. EFFECTIVE DATE	4. REQUISITION/PURCHASE REQ. NO.	5. PROJECT NO. *(If applicable)*

6. ISSUED BY CODE	7. ADMINISTERED BY *(If other than Item 6)* CODE

8. NAME AND ADDRESS OF CONTRACTOR *(No., street, county, State and ZIP Code)*

(√) 9A. AMENDMENT OF SOLICITATION NO.

9B. DATED *(SEE ITEM 11)*

10A. MODIFICATION OF CONTRACT/ORDER NO.

10B. DATED *(SEE ITEM 13)*

CODE   FACILITY CODE

11. THIS ITEM ONLY APPLIES TO AMENDMENTS OF SOLICITATIONS

☐ The above numbered solicitation is amended as set forth in Item 14. The hour and date specified for receipt of Offers ☐ is extended, ☐ is not extended.

Offers must acknowledge receipt of this amendment prior to the hour and date specified in the solicitation or as amended, by one of the following methods:

(a) By completing Items 8 and 15, and returning _____ copies of the amendment; (b) By acknowledging receipt of this amendment on each copy of the offer submitted; or (c) By separate letter or telegram which includes a reference to the solicitation and amendment numbers. FAILURE OF YOUR ACKNOWLEDGMENT TO BE RECEIVED AT THE PLACE DESIGNATED FOR THE RECEIPT OF OFFERS PRIOR TO THE HOUR AND DATE SPECIFIED MAY RESULT IN REJECTION OF YOUR OFFER. If by virtue of this amendment you desire to change an offer already submitted, such change may be made by telegram or letter, provided each telegram or letter makes reference to the solicitation and this amendment, and is received prior to the opening hour and date specified.

12. ACCOUNTING AND APPROPRIATION DATA *(If required)*

13. THIS ITEM APPLIES ONLY TO MODIFICATIONS OF CONTRACTS/ORDERS, IT MODIFIES THE CONTRACT/ORDER NO. AS DESCRIBED IN ITEM 14.

(√) A. THIS CHANGE ORDER IS ISSUED PURSUANT TO: *(Specify authority)* THE CHANGES SET FORTH IN ITEM 14 ARE MADE IN THE CONTRACT ORDER NO. IN ITEM 10A.

B. THE ABOVE NUMBERED CONTRACT/ORDER IS MODIFIED TO REFLECT THE ADMINISTRATIVE CHANGES *(such as changes in paying office, appropriation date, etc.)* SET FORTH IN ITEM 14, PURSUANT TO THE AUTHORITY OF FAR 43.103(b).

C. THIS SUPPLEMENTAL AGREEMENT IS ENTERED INTO PURSUANT TO AUTHORITY OF:

D. OTHER *(Specify type of modification and authority)*

E. IMPORTANT: Contractor ☐ is not, ☐ is required to sign this document and return _____ copies to the issuing office.

14. DESCRIPTION OF AMENDMENT/MODIFICATION *(Organized by UCF section headings, including solicitation/contract subject matter where feasible.)*

Except as provided herein, all terms and conditions of the document referenced in Item 9A or 10A, as heretofore changed, remains unchanged and in full force and effect.

15A. NAME AND TITLE OF SIGNER *(Type or print)*	16A. NAME AND TITLE OF CONTRACTING OFFICER *(Type or print)*
15B. CONTRACTOR/OFFEROR *(Signature of person authorized to sign)*	15C. DATE SIGNED	16B. UNITED STATES OF AMERICA BY _____ *(Signature of Contracting Officer)*	16C. DATE SIGNED

NSN 7540-01-152-8070
PREVIOUS EDITION UNUSABLE

30-105

STANDARD FORM 30 (REV. 10-83)
Prescribed by GSA
FAR (48 CFR) 53.243

INSTRUCTIONS

Instructions for items other than those that are self-explanatory, are as follows:

(a) Item 1 (Contract ID Code). Insert the contract type identification code that appears in the title block of the contract being modified.

(b) Item 3 (Effective date).

(1) For a solicitation amendment, change order, or administrative change, the effective date shall be the issue date of the amendment, change order, or administrative change.

(2) For a supplemental agreement, the effective date shall be the date agreed to by the contracting parties.

(3) For a modification issued as an initial or confirming notice of termination for the convenience of the Government, the effective date and the modification number of the confirming notice shall be the same as the effective date and modification number of the initial notice.

(4) For a modification converting a termination for default to a termination for the convenience of the Government, the effective date shall be the same as the effective date of the termination for default.

(5) For a modification confirming the contracting officer's determination of the amount due in settlement of a contract termination, the effective date shall be the same as the effective date of the initial decision.

(c) Item 6 (Issued By). Insert the name and address of the issuing office. If applicable, insert the appropriate issuing office code in the code block.

(d) Item 8 (Name and Address of Contractor). For modifications to a contract or order, enter the contractor's name, address, and code as shown in the original contract or order, unless changed by this or a previous modification.

(e) Items 9, (Amendment of Solicitation No.–Dated), and 10, (Modification of Contract/Order No.–Dated). Check the appropriate box and in the corresponding blanks insert the number and date of the original solicitation, contract, or order.

(f) Item 12 (Accounting and Appropriation Data). When appropriate, indicate the impact of the modification on each affected accounting classification by inserting one of the following entries:

(1) Accounting classification ....
    Net increase $ ....

(2) Accounting classification ....
    Net decrease $ ....

NOTE: If there are changes to multiple accounting classifications that cannot be placed in block 12, insert an asterisk and the words "See continuation sheet"

(g) Item 13. Check the appropriate box to indicate the type of modification. Insert in the corresponding blank the authority under which the modification is issued. Check whether or not contractor must sign this document. (See FAR 43.103.)

(h) Item 14 (Description of Amendment/Modification).

(1) Organize amendments or modifications under the appropriate Uniform Contract Format (UCF) section headings from the applicable solicitation or contract. The UCF table of contents, however, shall not be set forth in this document.

(2) Indicate the impact of the modification on the overall total contract price by inserting one of the following entries:

(i)   Total contract price increased by $ ....

(ii) Total contract price decreased by $ ....

(iii) Total contract price unchanged.

(3) State reason for modification.

(4) When removing, reinstating, or adding funds, identify the contract items and accounting classifications.

(5) When the SF 30 is used to reflect a determination by the contracting officer of the amount due in settlement of a contract terminated for the convenience of the Government, the entry in Item 14 of the modification may be limited to —

(i) A reference to the letter determination; and

(ii) A statement of the net amount determined to be due in settlement of the contract.

(6) Include subject matter or short title of solicitation/contract where feasible.

(i) Item 16B. The contracting officer's signature is not required on solicitation amendments. The contracting officer's signature is normally affixed last on supplemental agreements.

STANDARD FORM 30 BACK (REV. 10-83)

53.301-33	**FAC 84-5**	**APRIL 1, 1985**

FEDERAL ACQUISITION REGULATION (FAR)

SOLICITATION, OFFER AND AWARD	1 THIS CONTRACT IS A RATED ORDER UNDER DPAS (15 CFR 350)	RATING	PAGE OF PAGES

2. CONTRACT NO.	3. SOLICITATION NO.	4. TYPE OF SOLICITATION	5. DATE ISSUED	6. REQUISITION/PURCHASE NO.
		☐ SEALED BID (IFB) ☐ NEGOTIATED (RFP)		

7. ISSUED BY	CODE	8. ADDRESS OFFER TO (If other than Item 7)

NOTE: In sealed bid solicitations "offer" and "offeror" mean "bid" and "bidder".

SOLICITATION

9. Sealed offers in original and _____ copies for furnishing the supplies or services in the Schedule will be received at the place specified in Item 8, or if handcarried, in the depository located in _____ until _____ local time _____
(Hour) (Date)

CAUTION — LATE Submissions, Modifications, and Withdrawals See Section L. Provision No. 52.214-7 or 52.215-10 All offers are subject to all terms and conditions contained in this solicitation.

10. FOR INFORMATION CALL:	A. NAME	B TELEPHONE NO (Include area code) (NO COLLECT CALLS)

11. TABLE OF CONTENTS

(✓)	SEC.	DESCRIPTION	PAGE(S)	(✓)	SEC	DESCRIPTION	PAGE(S)
		PART I — THE SCHEDULE				**PART II — CONTRACT CLAUSES**	
	A	SOLICITATION/CONTRACT FORM			I	CONTRACT CLAUSES	
	B	SUPPLIES OR SERVICES AND PRICES/COSTS				**PART III — LIST OF DOCUMENTS, EXHIBITS AND OTHER ATTACH.**	
	C	DESCRIPTION/SPECS./WORK STATEMENT			J	LIST OF ATTACHMENTS	
	D	PACKAGING AND MARKING				**PART IV — REPRESENTATIONS AND INSTRUCTIONS**	
	E	INSPECTION AND ACCEPTANCE			K	REPRESENTATIONS, CERTIFICATIONS AND OTHER STATEMENTS OF OFFERORS	
	F	DELIVERIES OR PERFORMANCE					
	G	CONTRACT ADMINISTRATION DATA			L	INSTRS., CONDS., AND NOTICES TO OFFERORS	
	H	SPECIAL CONTRACT REQUIREMENTS			M	EVALUATION FACTORS FOR AWARD	

OFFER (Must be fully completed by offeror)

NOTE: Item 12 does not apply if the solicitation includes the provisions at 52.214-16, Minimum Bid Acceptance Period.

12 In compliance with the above, the undersigned agrees, if this offer is accepted within _____ calendar days (60 calendar days unless a different period is inserted by the offeror) from the date for receipt of offers specified above, to furnish any or all items upon which prices are offered at the price set opposite each item, delivered at the designated point(s), within the time specified in the schedule.

13. DISCOUNT FOR PROMPT PAYMENT (See Section I, Clause No. 52-232-8)	10 CALENDAR DAYS %	20 CALENDAR DAYS %	30 CALENDAR DAYS %	CALENDAR DAYS %

14. ACKNOWLEDGMENT OF AMENDMENTS (The offeror acknowledges receipt of amendments to the SOLICITATION for offerors and related documents numbered and dated	AMENDMENT NO	DATE	AMENDMENT NO	DATE

15A. NAME AND ADDRESS OF OFFEROR	CODE	FACILITY	16 NAME AND TITLE OF PERSON AUTHORIZED TO SIGN OFFER (Type or print)

15B. TELEPHONE NO. (Include area code)	15C CHECK IF REMITTANCE ADDRESS IS DIFFERENT FROM ABOVE ENTER SUCH ADDRESS IN SCHEDULE	17 SIGNATURE	18 OFFER DATE

AWARD (To be completed by Government)

19. ACCEPTED AS TO ITEMS NUMBERED	20. AMOUNT	21. ACCOUNTING AND APPROPRIATION

22. AUTHORITY FOR USING OTHER THAN FULL AND OPEN COMPETITION: ☐ 10 U.S.C. 2304(c)( ) ☐ 41 U.S.C. 253(c)( )	23 SUBMIT INVOICES TO ADDRESS SHOWN IN (4 copies unless otherwise specified)	ITEM

24. ADMINISTERED BY (If other than Item 7)	CODE	25 PAYMENT WILL BE MADE BY	CODE

26. NAME OF CONTRACTING OFFICER (Type or print)	27 UNITED STATES OF AMERICA (Signature of Contracting Officer)	28. AWARD DATE

IMPORTANT — Award will be made on this Form, or on Standard Form 26, or by other authorized official written notice.

NSN 7540-01-152-8064
PREVIOUS EDITION NOT USABLE

33-132

STANDARD FORM 33 (REV. 4-85)
Prescribed by GSA
FAR (48 CFR) 53 214(c)

U.S. GOVERNMENT

PURCHASE ORDER—INVOICE—VOUCHER

Anyone who finds this booklet, please notify:

OFFICE:

TELEPHONE NUMBER:

NSN 7540—01—152—8068
PREVIOUS EDITION USABLE
44—108

STANDARD FORM 44 (Rev. 10—83)
PRESCRIBED BY GSA
FAR (48 CFR) 53.213(e)

INSTRUCTIONS

(This form is for official Government use only)

1. Filling in the Form

(a) All copies of the form must be legible. To insure legibility, indelible pencil or ball-point pen should be used. SELLER'S NAME AND ADDRESS MUST BE PRINTED.

(b) Items ordered will be individually listed. General descriptions such as "hardware" are not acceptable. Show discount terms.

(c) Enter project reference or other identifying description in space captioned "PURPOSE." Also, enter proper accounting information, if known.

2. Distributing Copies

Copy No. 1—Give to seller for use as the invoice or as an attachment to his commercial invoice.

Copy No. 2—Give to seller for use as a record of the order.

Copy No. 3—

(1) On over-the-counter transactions where delivery has been made, complete receiving report section and forward this copy to the proper administrative office.

(2) On other than completed over-the-counter transactions, forward this copy to location specified for delivery (Upon delivery, receiving report section is to be completed and this copy then forwarded to the proper administrative office.)

Copy No. 4—Retain in the book, unless otherwise instructed.

3. When Paying Cash at Time of Purchase

(a) Enter the amount of cash paid and obtain seller's signature in the space provided in the Seller section of Copy No. 1. If seller prefers to provide a commercial cash receipt, attach it to Copy No. 1 and check the "paid in cash" block at the bottom of the form

(b) Distribution of copies when payment is by cash is the same as described above, except that Copy No. 1 is retained by Government representative when cash payment is made. Copy No. 1 is used thereafter in accordance with agency instructions pertaining to handling receipts for cash payment.

U.S. GOVERNMENT

PURCHASE ORDER—INVOICE—VOUCHER

DATE OF ORDER   ORDER NO

PRINT NAME AND ADDRESS OF SELLER *(Number, Street, City, and State)*

P
A
Y
E
E

FURNISH SUPPLIES OR SERVICES TO *(Name and address)*

SUPPLIES OR SERVICES	QUANTITY	UNIT PRICE	AMOUNT

AGENCY NAME AND BILLING ADDRESS*

P
A
Y
O

TOTAL

DISCOUNT TERMS   %   DAYS

DATE INVOICE RECEIVED

ORDERED BY *(Signature and title)*

PURPOSE AND ACCOUNTING DATA

PURCHASER—*To sign below for over-the-counter delivery of items*

RECEIVED BY

TITLE   DATE

SELLER—*Please read instructions on Copy 2*

☐ PAYMENT RECEIVED $............................ ☐ PAYMENT REQUESTED $............................

NO FURTHER INVOICE NEED BE SUBMITTED

SELLER   DATE

BY
        (Signature)

I certify that this account is correct and proper   DIFFERENCES
for payment in the amount of

$

ACCOUNT VERIFIED:

                                    CORRECT FOR

(Authorized certifying officer)   BY

PAID BY ☐ CASH DATE PAID   VOUCHER NO.

OR ....
    (Check No.)

PLEASE INCLUDE   1. SELLER'S INVOICE   STANDARD FORM 444 (Rev. 10-83)
ZIP CODE   *(See instructions on Copy 2)*   PRESCRIBED BY GSA.
                                            FAR (48 CFR) 53.213(c)

U.S. GOVERNMENT
PURCHASE ORDER—INVOICE—VOUCHER

DATE OF ORDER	ORDER NO

PRINT NAME AND ADDRESS OF SELLER (*Number, Street, City, and State*)*

P A Y E E

FURNISH SUPPLIES OR SERVICES TO (*Name and address*)*

SUPPLIES OR SERVICES	QUANTITY	UNIT PRICE	AMOUNT

AGENCY NAME AND BILLING ADDRESS*

P A Y O R

TOTAL	
DISCOUNT TERMS	
%	DAYS
DATE INVOICE RECEIVED	

ORDERED BY (*Signature and title*)

PURPOSE AND ACCOUNTING DATA

PURCHASER—To sign below for over-the-counter delivery of items

RECEIVED BY

TITLE	DATE

SELLER—Please read instructions on Copy 2

☐ PAYMENT RECEIVED $............................   ☐ PAYMENT REQUESTED $............................

NO FURTHER INVOICE NEED BE SUBMITTED

SELLER	DATE
BY	
(Signature)	

INSTRUCTIONS TO SELLER

After satisfactory identification of the Government representative presenting this purchase order, verify the itemization, including quantity, unit price, amount, total and discount sections.

This form is so designed that Copy 1 may be used as a cash payment receipt or as your invoice by completing, as appropriate, either the Payment Received or Payment Request blocks and signing the Seller Section.

If you would rather submit your own invoice, DO NOT SIGN COPY 1, but attach it unsigned to your invoice to expedite verification and processing for payment.

2. SELLER'S COPY OF ORDER   STANDARD FORM 44b (Rev. 10–83) PRESCRIBED BY GSA. FAR (48 CFR) 53.213(c)

U.S. GOVERNMENT
PURCHASE ORDER—INVOICE—VOUCHER

DATE OF ORDER	ORDER NO

PRINT NAME AND ADDRESS OF SELLER (*Number, Street, City, and State*)*

P A Y E E

FURNISH SUPPLIES OR SERVICES TO (*Name and address*)*

SUPPLIES OR SERVICES	QUANTITY	UNIT PRICE	AMOUNT

AGENCY NAME AND BILLING ADDRESS*

P A Y O R

TOTAL	
DISCOUNT TERMS	
%	DAYS
DATE INVOICE RECEIVED	

ORDERED BY (*Signature and title*)

PURPOSE AND ACCOUNTING DATA

PURCHASER—To sign below for over-the-counter delivery of items

RECEIVED BY

TITLE	DATE

SELLER—Please read instructions on Copy 2

☐ PAYMENT RECEIVED $............................   ☐ PAYMENT REQUESTED $............................

NO FURTHER INVOICE NEED BE SUBMITTED

SELLER	DATE
BY	
(Signature)	

REMARKS	DIFFERENCES	
	ACCOUNT VERIFIED	CORRECT FOR
	BY	

3. RECEIVING REPORT— ACCOUNTING COPY   STANDARD FORM 44c (Rev. 10–83) PRESCRIBED BY GSA FAR (48 CFR) 53.213(c)

FEDERAL ACQUISITION REGULATION (FAR)

SOLICITATION MAILING LIST APPLICATION

SOLICITATION MAILING LIST APPLICATION	1. TYPE OF APPLICATION ☐ INITIAL ☐ REVISION	2. DATE
		FORM APPROVED OMB NO. 3090-0009

NOTE—Please complete all items on this form. Insert N/A in items not applicable. See reverse for Instructions.

3. NAME AND ADDRESS OF FEDERAL AGENCY TO WHICH FORM IS SUBMITTED (Include ZIP code)	4. NAME AND ADDRESS OF APPLICANT (Include county and ZIP code)

5. TYPE OF ORGANIZATION (Check one)

☐ INDIVIDUAL   ☐ NON-PROFIT ORGANIZATION

☐ PARTNERSHIP   ☐ CORPORATION, INCORPORATED UNDER THE LAWS OF THE STATE OF:

6. ADDRESS TO WHICH SOLICITATIONS ARE TO BE MAILED (If different than Item 4)

7. NAMES OF OFFICERS, OWNERS, OR PARTNERS

A. PRESIDENT	B. VICE PRESIDENT	C. SECRETARY
D. TREASURER	E. OWNERS OR PARTNERS	

8. AFFILIATES OF APPLICANT (Names, locations and nature of affiliation. See definition on reverse.)

9. PERSONS AUTHORIZED TO SIGN OFFERS AND CONTRACTS IN YOUR NAME (Indicate if agent)

NAME	OFFICIAL CAPACITY	TELE. NO. (Include area code)

10. IDENTIFY EQUIPMENT, SUPPLIES, AND/OR SERVICES ON WHICH YOU DESIRE TO MAKE AN OFFER (See attached Federal agency's supplemental listing and instructions, if any)

11A. SIZE OF BUSINESS (See definitions on reverse)	11B. AVERAGE NUMBER OF EMPLOYEES (Including affiliates) FOR FOUR PRECEDING CALENDAR QUARTERS	11C. AVERAGE ANNUAL SALES OR RECEIPTS FOR PRECEDING THREE FISCAL YEARS
☐ SMALL BUSINESS (If checked, complete items 11B and 11C) ☐ OTHER THAN SMALL BUSINESS		$

12. TYPE OF OWNERSHIP (See definitions on reverse) (Not applicable for other than small businesses)	13. TYPE OF BUSINESS (See definitions on reverse)			
☐ DISADVANTAGED BUSINESS ☐ WOMAN-OWNED BUSINESS	☐ MANUFACTURER OR PRODUCER ☐ SERVICE ESTABLISHMENT	☐ REGULAR DEALER (Type 1) ☐ REGULAR DEALER (Type 2)	☐ CONSTRUCTION CONCERN ☐ RESEARCH AND DEVELOPMENT	☐ SURPLUS DEALER

14. DUNS NO. (If available)	15. HOW LONG IN PRESENT BUSINESS?

16. FLOOR SPACE (Square feet)		17. NET WORTH	
A. MANUFACTURING	B. WAREHOUSE	A. DATE	B. AMOUNT $

18. SECURITY CLEARANCE (If applicable, check highest clearance authorized)

FOR	TOP SECRET	SECRET	CONFIDENTIAL	C. NAMES OF AGENCIES WHICH GRANTED SECURITY CLEARANCES (Include dates)
A. KEY PERSONNEL				
B. PLANT ONLY				

CERTIFICATION — I certify that information supplied herein (Including all pages attached) is correct and that neither the applicant nor any person (Or concern) in any connection with the applicant as a principal or officer, so far as is known, is now debarred or otherwise declared ineligible by any agency of the Federal Government from making offers for furnishing materials, supplies, or services to the Government or any agency thereof.

19. NAME AND TITLE OF PERSON AUTHORIZED TO SIGN (Type or print)	20. SIGNATURE	21. DATE SIGNED

NSN 7540-01-152-8086
PREVIOUS EDITIONS UNUSABLE

129-106

STANDARD FORM 129 (REV. 10-83)
Prescribed by GSA
FAR (48 CFR) 53.214(c)

INSTRUCTIONS

Persons or concerns wishing to be added to a particular agency's bidder's mailing list for supplies or services shall file this properly completed and certified Solicitation Mailing List Application, together with such other lists as may be attached to this application form, with each procurement office of the Federal agency with which they desire to do business. If a Federal agency has attached a Supplemental Commodity list with instructions, complete the application as instructed. Otherwise, identify in Item 10 the equipment supplies and/or services on which you desire to bid. (Provide Federal Supply Class or Standard Industrial Classification Codes if available.) The application shall be submitted and signed by the principal as distinguished from an agent, however constituted.

After placement on the bidder's mailing list of an agency, your failure to respond (submission of bid, or notice in writing, that you are unable to bid on that particular transaction but wish to remain on the active bidder's mailing list for that particular item) to solicitations will be understood by the agency to indicate lack of interest and concurrence in the removal of your name from the purchasing activity's solicitation mailing list for the items concerned.

SIZE OF BUSINESS DEFINITIONS
(See Item 11A.)

a. Small business concern—A small business concern for the purpose of Government procurement is a concern, including its affiliates, which is independently owned and operated, is not dominant in the field of operation in which it is competing for Government contracts and can further qualify under the criteria concerning number of employees, average annual receipts, or other criteria, as prescribed by the Small Business Administration. (See Code of Federal Regulations, Title 13, Part 121, as amended, which contains detailed industry definitions and related procedures.)

b. Affiliates—Business concerns are affiliates of each other when either directly or indirectly (i) one concern controls or has the power to control the other, or (ii) a third party controls or has the power to control both. In determining whether concerns are independently owned and operated and whether or not affiliation exists, consideration is given to all appropriate factors inclu:ing common ownership, common management, and contractual relationship. (See Items 8 and 11A.)

c. Number of employees—(Item 11B) In connection with the determination of small business status, "number of employees" means the average employment of any concern, including the employees of its domestic and foreign affiliates, based on the number of persons employed on a full-time, part-time, temporary, or other basis during each of the pay periods of the preceding 12 months. If a concern has not been in existence for 12 months, "number of employees" means the average employment of such concern and its affiliates during the period that such concern has been in existence based on the number of persons employed during each of the pay periods of the period that such concern has been in business.

TYPE OF OWNERSHIP DEFINITIONS
(See Item 12.)

a. "Disadvantaged business concern"—means any business concern (1) which is at least 51 percent owned by one or more socially and economically disadvantaged individuals; or, in the case of any publicly owned business, at least 51 percent of the stock of which is owned by one or more socially and economically disadvantaged individuals; and (2) whose management and daily business operations are controlled by one or more of such individuals.

b. "Women-owned business"—means a business that is at least 51 percent owned by a woman or women who are U.S. citizens and who also control and operate the business.

TYPE OF BUSINESS DEFINITIONS
(See Item 13.)

a. Manufacturer or producer—means a person (or concern) owning, operating, or maintaining a store, warehouse, or other establishment that produces, on the premises, the materials, supplies, articles, or equipment of the general character of those listed in Item 10, or in the Federal Agency's Supplemental Commodity List, if attached.

b. Service establishment—means a concern (or person) which owns, operates, or maintains any type of business which is principally engaged in the furnishing of nonpersonal services, such as (but not limited to) repairing, cleaning, redecorating, or rental of personal property, including the furnishing of necessary repair parts or other supplies as part of the services performed.

c. Regular dealer (Type 1)—means a person (or concern) who owns, operates, or maintains a store, warehouse, or other establishment in which the materials, supplies, articles, or equipment of the general character listed in Item 10, or in the Federal Agency's Supplemental Commodity List, if attached, are bought, kept in stock, and sold to the public in the usual course of business.

d. Regular dealer (Type 2)—In the case of supplies of particular kinds (at present, petroleum, lumber and timber products, machine tools, raw cotton, green coffee, hay, grain, feed, or straw, agricultural liming materials, tea, raw or unmanufactured cotton linters and used ADPE), Regular dealer means a person (or concern) satisfying the requirements of the regulations (Code of Federal Regulations, Title 41, 50-201.101(a)(2)) as amended from time to time, prescribed by the Secretary of Labor under the Walsh-Healey Public Contracts Act (Title 41 U.S. Code 35-45). For coal dealers see Code of Federal Regulations, Title 41, 50-201.604(a).

• COMMERCE BUSINESS DAILY—The Commerce Business Daily, published by the Department of Commerce, contains information concerning proposed procurements, sales, and contract awards. For further information concerning this publication, contact your local Commerce Field Office.

STANDARD FORM 129 BACK (REV. 10-83)

STANDARD FORM (SF)

254 Architect-Engineer and Related Services Questionnaire

Form Approved
OMB No. 3090–0028

Purpose:

The policy of the Federal Government in acquiring architectural, engineering, and related professional services is to encourage firms lawfully engaged in the practice of those professions to submit annually a statement of qualifications and performance data. Standard Form 254, "Architect-Engineer and Related Services Questionnaire" is provided for that purpose. Interested A-E firms (including new, small, and/or minority firms) should complete and file SF 254's with each Federal agency and with appropriate regional or district offices for which the A-E is qualified to perform services. The agency head for each proposed project shall evaluate these qualification resumes, together with any other performance data on file or requested by the agency, in relation to the proposed project. The SF 254 may be used as a basis for selecting firms for discussions, or for screening firms preliminary to inviting submission of additional information.

Definitions:

"**Architect-engineer and related services**" are those professional services associated with research, development, design and construction, alteration, or repair of real property, as well as incidental services that members of these professions and those in their employ may logically or justifiably perform, including studies, investigations, surveys, evaluations, consultations, planning, programming, conceptual designs, plans and specifications, cost estimates, inspections, shop drawing reviews, sample recommendations, preparation of operating and maintenance manuals, and other related services.

"**Parent Company**" is that firm, company, corporation, association or conglomerate which is the major stockholder or highest tier owner of the firm completing this questionnaire; i.e. Firm A is owned by Firm B which is, in turn, a subsidiary of Corporation C. The "parent company" of Firm A is Corporation C.

"**Principals**" are those individuals in a firm who possess legal responsibility for its management. They may be owners, partners, corporate officers, associates, administrators, etc.

"**Discipline**", as used in this questionnaire, refers to the primary technological capability of individuals in the responding firm. Possession of an academic degree, professional registration, certification, or extensive experience in a particular field of practice normally reflects an individual's primary technical discipline.

"**Joint Venture**" is a collaborative undertaking by two or more firms or individuals for which the participants are both jointly and individually responsible.

"**Consultant**", as used in this questionnaire, is a highly specialized individual or firm having significant input and responsibility for certain aspects of a project and possessing unusual or unique capabilities for assuring success of the finished work.

"**Prime**" refers to that firm which may be coordinating the concerted and complementary inputs of several firms, individuals or related services to produce a completed study or facility. The "prime" would normally be

regarded as having full responsibility and liability for quality of performance by itself as well as by subcontractor professionals under its jurisdiction.

"**Branch Office**" is a satellite, or subsidiary extension, of a headquarters office of a company, regardless of any differences in name or legal structure of such a branch due to local or state laws. "Branch offices" are normally subject to the management decisions, bookkeeping, and policies of the main office.

Instructions for Filing (Numbers below correspond to numbers contained in form):

1. Type accurate and complete name of submitting firm, its address, and zip code.

   1a. Indicate whether form is being submitted in behalf of a parent firm or a branch office. (Branch office submissions should list only personnel in, and experience of, that office.)

2. Provide date the firm was established under the name shown in question 1.

3. Show date on which form is prepared. All information submitted shall be current and accurate as of this date.

4. Enter type of ownership, or legal structure, of firm (sole proprietor, partnership, corporation, joint venture, etc.)

   Check appropriate boxes indicating if firm is (a) a small business concern; (b) a small business concern owned and operated by socially and economically disadvantaged individuals; and (c) Women-owned; (See 48 CFR 19.101 and 52.219-9).

5. Branches of subsidiaries of large or parent companies, or conglomerates, should insert name and address of highest-tier owner.

   5a. If present firm is the successor to, or outgrowth of, one or more predecessor firms, show name(s) of former entity(ies) and the year(s) of their original establishment.

6. List not more than two principals from submitting firm who may be contacted by the agency receiving this form. (Different principals may be listed on forms going to another agency.) Listed principals must be empowered to speak for the firm on policy and contractual matters.

7. Beginning with the submitting office, list name, location, total number of personnel and telephone numbers for all associated or branch offices, (including any headquarters or foreign offices) which provide A-E and related services.

   7a. Show total personnel in all offices. (Should be sum of all personnel, all branches.)

8. Show total number of employees, by discipline, in submitting office. (If form is being submitted by main or headquarters office, firm should list total employees, by discipline, in all offices.) While some personnel may be qualified in several disciplines, each person should be counted only once in accord with his or her primary function. Include clerical personnel as "administrative." Write in any additional disciplines—sociologists, biologists, etc.—and number of people in each, in blank spaces.

9. Using chart (below) insert appropriate index number to indicate range of professional services fees received by submitting firm each calendar year for last five years, most recent year first. Fee summaries should be broken down to

STANDARD FORM 254 (Rev. 10-83)
PRESCRIBED BY GSA, FAR (48 CFR) 53.236-2(b)

STANDARD FORM 254 (REV. 10-83)

STANDARD
FORM (SF)

254

Architect-Engineer
and Related Services
Questionnaire

reflect the fees received each year for (a) work performed directly for the Federal Government (not including grant and loan projects) or as a sub to other professionals performing work directly for the Federal Government; (b) all other domestic work, U.S. and possessions, including Federally-assisted projects, and (c) all other foreign work.

Ranges of Professional Services Fees

INDEX		INDEX	
1.	Less than $100,000	5.	$1 million to $2 million
2.	$100,000 to $250,000	6.	$2 million to $5 million
3.	$250,000 to $500,000	7.	$5 million to $10 million
4.	$500,000 to $1 million	8.	$10 million or greater

10. Select and enter, in numerical sequence, **not more than thirty** (30) "Experience Profile Code" numbers from the listing (next page) which most accurately reflect submitting firm's demonstrated technical capabilities and project experience. **Carefully review list.** (It is recognized some profile codes may be part of other services or projects contained on list; firms are encouraged to select profile codes which best indicate type and scope of services provided on past projects.) For each code number, show total number of projects and gross fees (in thousands) received for profile projects performed by firm during past few years. If firm has one or more capabilities not included on list, insert same in blank spaces at end of list and show numbers in question 10 on the form. In such cases, the filled-in listing **must** accompany the complete SF 254 when submitted to the Federal agencies.

11. Using the "Experience Profile Code" numbers in the same sequence as entered in item 10, give details of at least one recent (within last five years) representative project for each code number, up to a **maximum** of thirty (30) separate projects, or portions of projects, for which firm was responsible. (Project examples may be used more than once to illustrate different services rendered on the same job. Example: a dining hall may be part of an auditorium or educational facility.) Firms which select less than thirty "profile codes" may list two or more project examples (to illustrate specialization) for each code number so long as total of all project examples does not exceed thirty (30). After each code number in question 11, show: (a) whether firm was "P," the prime professional, or "C," a consultant, or "JV," part of a joint venture on that particular project (New firms, in existence less than five (5) years may use the symbol "IE" to indicate "Individual Experience" as opposed to firm experience); (b) provide name and location of the specific project which typifies firm's (or individual's) performance under that code category; (c) give name and address of the owner of that project (if government agency indicate responsible office); (d) show the estimated construction cost (or other applicable cost) for that portion of the project for which the firm was primarily responsible. (Where no construction was involved, show approximate cost of firm's work); and (e) state year work on that particular project was, or will be, completed.

12. The completed SF 254 should be signed by a principal of the firm, preferably the chief executive officer.

13. Additional data, brochures, photos, etc. should not accompany this form unless specifically requested.

NEW FIRMS (not reorganized or recently-amalgamated firms) are eligible and encouraged to seek work from the Federal Government in connection with performance of projects for which they are qualified. Such firms are encouraged to complete and submit Standard Form 254 to appropriate agencies. Questions on the form dealing with personnel or experience may be answered by citing experience and capabilities of individuals in the firm, based on performance and responsibility while in the employ of others. In so doing, notation of this fact should be made on the form. In question 9, write in "N/A" to indicate "not applicable" for those years prior to firm's organization.

2

Experience Profile Code Numbers
for use with questions 10 and 11

001 Acoustics; Noise Abatement
002 Aerial Photogrammetry
003 Agricultural Development; Grain Storage; Farm Mechanization
004 Air Pollution Control
005 Airports; Navaids; Airport Lighting; Aircraft Fueling
006 Airports; Terminals & Hangars; Freight Handling
007 Arctic Facilities
008 Auditoriums & Theatres
009 Automation; Controls; Instrumentation
010 Barracks; Dormitories
011 Bridges
012 Cemeteries *(Planning & Relocation)*
013 Chemical Processing & Storage
014 Churches; Chapels
015 Codes; Standards; Ordinances
016 Cold Storage; Refrigeration; Fast Freeze
017 Commercial Buildings *(low rise)*; Shopping Centers
018 Communications Systems; TV; Microwave
019 Computer Facilities; Computer Service
020 Conservation and Resource Management
021 Construction Management
022 Corrosion Control; Cathodic Protection; Electrolysis
023 Cost Estimating
024 Dams *(Concrete; Arch)*
025 Dams *(Earth; Rock)*; Dikes; Levees
026 Desalination *(Process & Facilities)*
027 Dining Halls; Clubs; Restaurants
028 Ecological & Archeological Investigations
029 Educational Facilities; Classrooms
030 Electronics
031 Elevators; Escalators; People-Movers
032 Energy Conservation; New Energy Sources
033 Environmental Impact Studies, Assessments or Statements
034 Fallout Shelters; Blast-Resistant Design
035 Field Houses; Gyms; Stadiums
036 Fire Protection
037 Fisheries; Fish Ladders
038 Forestry & Forest Products
039 Garages; Vehicle Maintenance Facilities; Parking Decks
040 Gas Systems *(Propane; Natural, Etc.)*
041 Graphic Design

042 Harbors; Jetties; Piers; Ship Terminal Facilities
043 Heating; Ventilating; Air Conditioning
044 Health Systems Planning
045 Highrise; Air-Rights-Type Buildings
046 Highways; Streets; Airfield Paving; Parking Lots
047 Historical Preservation
048 Hospital & Medical Facilities
049 Hotels; Models
050 Housing *(Residential, Multi-Family; Apartments; Condominiums)*
051 Hydraulics & Pneumatics
052 Industrial Buildings; Manufacturing Plants
053 Industrial Processes; Quality Control
054 Industrial Waste Treatment
055 Interior Design; Space Planning
056 Irrigation; Drainage
057 Judicial and Courtroom Facilities
058 Laboratories; Medical Research Facilities
059 Landscape Architecture
060 Libraries; Museums; Galleries
061 Lighting *(Interiors; Display; Theatre, Etc.)*
062 Lighting *(Exteriors; Streets; Memorials; Athletic Fields, Etc.)*
063 Materials Handling Systems; Conveyors; Sorters
064 Metallurgy
065 Microclimatology; Tropical Engineering
066 Military Design Standards
067 Mining & Mineralogy
068 Missile Facilities *(Silos; Fuels; Transport)*
069 Modular Facilities Design; Pre-Fabricated Structures or Components
070 Naval Architecture; Off-Shore Platforms
071 Nuclear Facilities; Nuclear Shielding
072 Office Buildings; Industrial Parks
073 Oceanographic Engineering
074 Ordnance; Munitions; Special Weapons
075 Petroleum Exploration; Refining
076 Petroleum and Fuel *(Storage and Distribution)*
077 Pipelines *(Cross-Country—Liquid & Gas)*
078 Planning *(Community, Regional, Areawide and State)*
079 Planning *(Site, Installation, and Project)*
080 Plumbing & Piping Design
081 Pneumatic Structures; Air-Support Buildings
082 Postal Facilities
083 Power Generation, Transmission, Distribution
084 Prisons & Correctional Facilities
085 Product, Machine & Equipment Design

086 Radar; Sonar; Radio & Radar Telescopes
087 Railroad; Rapid Transit
088 Recreation Facilities *(Parks, Marinas, Etc.)*
089 Rehabilitation *(Buildings; Structures; Facilities)*
090 Resource Recovery; Recycling
091 Radio Frequency Systems & Shieldings
092 Rivers; Canals; Waterways; Flood Control
093 Safety Engineering; Accident Studies; OSHA Studies
094 Security Systems; Intruder & Smoke Detection
095 Seismic Designs & Studies
096 Sewage Collection, Treatment and Disposal
097 Soils & Geologic Studies; Foundations
098 Solar Energy Utilization
099 Solid Wastes; Incineration; Land Fill
100 Special Environments; Clean Rooms, Etc.
101 Structural Design; Special Structures
102 Surveying; Platting; Mapping; Flood Plain Studies
103 Swimming Pools
104 Storm Water Handling & Facilities
105 Telephone Systems *(Rural; Mobile; Intercom, Etc.)*
106 Testing & Inspection Services
107 Traffic & Transportation Engineering
108 Towers *(Self-Supporting & Guyed Systems)*
109 Tunnels & Subways
110 Urban Renewals; Community Development
111 Utilities *(Gas & Steam)*
112 Value Analysis; Life-Cycle Costing
113 Warehouses & Depots
114 Water Resources; Hydrology; Ground Water
115 Water Supply, Treatment and Distribution
116 Wind Tunnels; Research/Testing Facilities Design
117 Zoning; Land Use Studies
201 _____
202 _____
203 _____
204 _____
205 _____

STANDARD FORM 254 (REV 10-83)

3

187

STANDARD FORM (SF)

254

Architect-Engineer and Related Services Questionnaire

1. Firm Name / Business Address:

2. Year Present Firm Established:

3. Date Prepared:

4. Specify type of ownership *and* check below, if applicable.

A. Small Business
B. Small Disadvantaged Business
C. Woman-owned Business

1a. Submittal is for ☐ Parent Company ☐ Branch or Subsidiary Office

5. Name of Parent Company, if any:

5a. Former Parent Company Name(s), if any, and Year(s) Established:

6. Names of not more than Two Principals to Contact: Title / Telephone
1)
2)

7. Present Offices: City / State / Telephone / No. Personnel Each Office

7a. Total Personnel _____

8. Personnel by Discipline: (*List each person only once, by primary function.*)

____ Administrative	____ Electrical Engineers	____ Oceanographers
____ Architects	____ Estimators	____ Planners: Urban/Regional
____ Chemical Engineers	____ Geologists	____ Sanitary Engineers
____ Civil Engineers	____ Hydrologists	____ Soils Engineers
____ Construction Inspectors	____ Interior Designers	____ Specification Writers
____ Draftsmen	____ Landscape Architects	____ Structural Engineers
____ Ecologists	____ Mechanical Engineers	____ Surveyors
____ Economists	____ Mining Engineers	____ Transportation Engineers

9. Summary of Professional Services Fees Received: (Insert index number)

Last 5 Years (most recent year first)

Direct Federal contract work, including overseas   19____ 19____ 19____ 19____ 19____
All other domestic work
All other foreign work*
*Firms interested in foreign work, but without such experience, check here: ☐

Ranges of Professional Services Fees

INDEX
1. Less than $100,000
2. $100,000 to $250,000
3. $250,000 to $500,000
4. $500,000 to $1 million
5. $1 million to $2 million
6. $2 million to $5 million
7. $5 million to $10 million
8. $10 million or greater

STANDARD FORM 254 (REV. 10-83)

4

10. Profile of Firm's Project Experience, Last 5 Years

Profile Code	Number of Projects	Total Gross Fees (in thousands)	Profile Code	Number of Projects	Total Gross Fees (in thousands)	Profile Code	Number of Projects	Total Gross Fees (in thousands)
1)			11)			21)		
2)			12)			22)		
3)			13)			23)		
4)			14)			24)		
5)			15)			25)		
6)			16)			26)		
7)			17)			27)		
8)			18)			28)		
9)			19)			29)		
10)			20)			30)		

11. Project Examples, Last 5 Years

	Profile Code	"P", "C", "JV", or "IE"	Project Name and Location	Owner Name and Address	Cost of Work (in thousands)	Completion Date (Actual or Estimated)
1						
2						
3						
4						
5						
6						
7						

STANDARD FORM 254 (REV 10-83)

5

8	9	10	11	12	13	14	15	16	17	18	19

STANDARD FORM 254 (REV. 10-83)

6

20											
21											
22											
23											
24											
25											
26											
27											
28											
29											
30											

12. The foregoing is a statement of facts

Signature: _____ Typed Name and Title: _____ Date:

STANDARD FORM 254 (REV 10-83)

U.S. GOVERNMENT PRINTING OFFICE 1985-461-275/20145

7

STANDARD
FORM (SF)

255

Architect-Engineer and Related Services Questionnaire for Specific Project

Standard Form 255
General Services Administration,
Washington, D. C. 20405
Fed. Proc. Reg. (41 CFR) 1-16 . 803
Armed Svc. Proc. Reg. 18–403

Purpose:

This form is a supplement to the "Architect-Engineer and Related Services Questionnaire" (SF 254). Its purpose is to provide additional information regarding the qualifications of interested firms to undertake a specific Federal A-E project. Firms, or branch offices of firms, submitting this form should enclose (or already have on file with the appropriate office of the agency) a current (within the past year) and accurate copy of the SF 254 for that office.

The procurement official responsible for each proposed project may request submission of the SF 255 "Architect-Engineer and Related Services Question-naire for Specific Project" in accord with applicable civilian and military procurement regulations and shall evaluate such submissions, as well as related information contained on the Standard Form 254, and any other performance data on file with the agency, and shall select firms for subsequent discussions leading to contract award in conformance with Public Law 92-582. This form should only be filed by an architect-engineer or related services firm when requested to do so by the agency or by a public announcement. Responses should be as complete and accurate as possible, contain data relative to the specific project for which you wish to be considered, and should be provided, by the required due date, to the office specified in the request or public announcement.

This form will be used only for the specified project. Do not refer to this submittal in response to other requests or public announcements.

Definitions:

"Architect-engineer and related services" are those professional services associated with research, development, design and construction, alteration, or repair of real property, as well as incidental services that members of these professions and those in their employ may logically or justifiably perform, including studies, investigations, surveys, evaluations, consultations, planning, programming, conceptual designs, plans and specifications, cost estimates, inspections, shop drawing reviews, sample recommendations, preparation of operating and maintenance manuals, and other related services.

"Principals" are those individuals in a firm who possess legal responsibility for its management. They may be owners, partners, corporate officers, associates, administrators, etc.

"Discipline" as used in this questionnaire, refers to the primary technological capability of individuals in the responding firm. Possession of an academic degree, professional registration, certification, or extensive experience in a particular field of practice normally reflects an individual's primary technical discipline.

"Joint Venture" is a collaborative undertaking of two or more firms or individuals for which the participants are both jointly and individually responsible.

"Key Persons, Specialists, and Individual Consultants", as used in this questionnaire, refer to individuals who will have major project responsibility or will provide unusual or unique capabilities for the project under consideration.

Instructions for Filing (Numbers below correspond to numbers contained in form):

1. Give name and location of the project for which this form is being submitted.

2. Provide appropriate data from the *Commerce Business Daily* (CBD) identifying the particular project for which this form is being filed.

2a. Give the date of the *Commerce Business Daily* in which the project announcement appeared, or indicate "not applicable" (N/A) if the source of the announcement is other than the CBD.

2b. Indicate Agency identification or contract number as provided in the CBD announcement.

3. Show name of the individual or firm (or joint venture) which is submitting this form for the project.

3a. List the name, title, and telephone number of that principal who will serve as the point of contact. Such an individual must be empowered to speak for the firm on policy and contractual matters and should be familiar with the programs and procedures of the agency to which this form is directed.

3b. Give the address of the specific office which will have responsibility for performing the announced work.

4. Insert the number of personnel by discipline presently employed (on date of this form) at work location. While some personnel may be qualified in several disciplines, each person should be counted only once in accord with his or her primary function. Include clerical personnel as "administrative." Write in any additional disciplines — sociologists, biologists, etc.— and number of people in each, in blank spaces.

5. Answer only if this form is being submitted by a joint venture of two or more collaborating firms. Show the names and addresses of all individuals or organizations expected to be included as part of the joint venture and describe their particular areas of anticipated responsibility, (i.e., technical disciplines, administration, financial, sociological, environmental, etc.)

5a. Indicate, by checking the appropriate box, whether this particular joint venture has successfully worked together on other projects.

Each firm participating in the joint venture should have a Standard Form 254 on file with the contracting office receiving this form. Firms which do not have such forms on file should provide same immediately along with a notation

Standard Form 255 July 1975
Prescribed By GSA Fed Proc. Reg. (41 CFR) 1-16.803

255-101

192

STANDARD FORM (SF)

255

Architect-Engineer and Related Services Questionnaire for Specific Project

Standard Form 255
General Services Administration,
Washington, D. C. 20405
Fed. Proc. Reg. (41 CFR) 1-16 . 803
Armed Svc. Proc. Reg. 18-403

regarding their association with this joint venture submittal.

6. If respondent is not a joint venture, but intends to use outside (as opposed to in-house or permanently and formally affiliated) consultants or associates, he should provide names and addresses of all such individuals or firms, as well as their particular areas of technical/professional expertise, as it relates to this project. Existence of previous working relationships should be noted. If more than eight outside consultants or associates are anticipated, attach an additional sheet containing requested information.

7. Regardless of whether respondent is a joint venture or an independent firm, provide brief resumes of key personnel expected to participate on this project. Care should be taken to limit resumes to only those personnel and specialists who will have major project responsibilities. Each resume must include: (a) name of each key person and specialist and his or her title, (b) the project assignment or role which that person will be expected to fulfill in connection with this project, (c) the name of the firm or organization, if any, with whom that individual is presently associated, (d) years of relevant experience with present firm and other firms, (e) the highest academic degree achieved and the discipline covered (if more than one highest degree, such as two Ph.D.'s, list both), the year received and the particular technical/professional discipline which that individual will bring to the project, (f) if registered as an architect, engineer, surveyor, etc., show only the field of registration and the year that such registration was first acquired. If registered in several states, do not list states, and (g) a synopsis of experience, training, or other qualities which reflect individual's potential contribution to this project. Include such data as: familiarity with Government or agency procedures, similar type of work performed in the past, management abilities, familiarity with the geographic area, relevant foreign language capabilities, etc. Please limit synopsis of experience to directly relevant information.

8. List up to ten projects which demonstrate the firm's or joint venture's competence to perform work similar to that likely to be required on this project. The more recent such projects, the better. Prime consideration will be given to projects which illustrate respondent's capability for performing work similar to that being sought. Required information must include: (a) name and location of project, (b) brief description of type and extent of services provided for each project (submissions by joint ventures should indicate which member of the joint venture was the prime on that particular project and what role it played), (c) name and address of the owner of that project (if Government agency, indicate responsible office), (d) completion date (actual or estimated), (e) total construction cost of completed project, (or where no construction was involved, the approximate cost of your work) and that portion of the cost of the project for which the named firm was/is responsible.

9. List only those projects which the A-E firm or joint venture, or members of the joint venture, are currently performing under direct contract with an agency or department of the Federal Government. Exclude any grant or loan projects being financed by the Federal Government but being performed under contract to other non-Federal governmental entities. Information provided under each heading is similar to that requested in the preceding Item 8, except for (d) "Percent Complete." Indicate in this item the percentage of A-E work completed upon filing this form.

10. Through narrative discussion, show reason why the firm or joint venture submitting this questionnaire believes it is especially qualified to undertake the project. Information provided should include, but not be limited to, such data as: specialized equipment available for this work, any awards or recognition received by a firm or individuals for similar work, required security clearances, special approaches or concepts developed by the firm relevant to this project, etc. Respondents may say anything they wish in support of their qualifications. When appropriate, respondents may supplement this proposal with graphic material and photographs which best demonstrate design capabilities of the team proposed for this project.

11. Completed forms should be signed by the chief executive officer of the joint venture (thereby attesting to the concurrence and commitment of all members of the joint venture), or by the architect-engineer principal responsible for the conduct of the work in the event it is awarded to the organization submitting this form. Joint ventures selected for subsequent discussions regarding this project must make available a statement of participation signed by a principal of each member of the joint venture. ALL INFORMATION CONTAINED IN THE FORM SHOULD BE CURRENT AND FACTUAL.

Standard Form 255 July 1975
Prescribed By GSA Fed Proc. Reg. (41 CFR) 1-16.803

2

193

STANDARD FORM (SF) 255

Architect-Engineer Related Services for Specific Project

OMB Approval No. 29–RO235

1. Project Name / Location for which Firm is Filing:

2a. *Commerce Business Daily* Announcement Date, if any:

2b. Agency Identification Number, if any:

3. Firm (or Joint-Venture) Name & Address

3a. Name, Title & Telephone Number of Principal to Contact

3b. Address of office to perform work, if different from Item 3

4. Personnel by Discipline:

___ Administrative
___ Architects
___ Chemical Engineers
___ Civil Engineers
___ Construction Inspectors
___ Draftsmen
___ Ecologists
___ Economists
___ Electrical Engineers
___ Estimators
___ Geologists
___ Hydrologists
___ Interior Designers
___ Landscape Architects
___ Mechanical Engineers
___ Mining Engineers
___ Oceanographers
___ Planners: Urban/Regional
___ Sanitary Engineers
___ Soils Engineers
___ Specification Writers
___ Structural Engineers
___ Surveyors
___ Transportation Engineers
___ **Total Personnel**

5. If submittal is by Joint-Venture list participating firms and outline specific areas of responsibility (including administrative, technical and financial) for each firm: (Attach SF 254 for each if not on file with Procuring Office.)

5a. Has this Joint-Venture previously worked together? ☐ yes ☐ no

Standard Form 255 July 1975
Prescribed By GSA Fed. Proc. Reg. (41 CFR) 1-16.803

3

194

6. Outside Key Consultants/Associates Anticipated for this Project (Attach SF 254 for Consultants/Associates Listed, if not already of file with the Procuring Office)		
Name & Address	Specialty	Worked with Prime before (Yes or No)
1)		
2)		
3)		
4)		
5)		
6)		
7)		
8)		

Standard Form 255 July 1975
Prescribed By GSA Fed. Proc. Reg. (41 CFR) 1-16.803

7. Brief Resume of Key Persons, Specialists, and Individual Consultants Anticipated for this Project

a. Name & Title:

b. Project Assignment:

c. Name of Firm with which associated:

d. Years experience: With This Firm ____   With Other Firms ____

e. Education: Degree(s) / Year / Specialization

f. Active Registration: Year First Registered/Discipline

g. Other Experience and Qualifications relevant to the proposed project:

a. Name & Title:

b. Project Assignment:

c. Name of Firm with which associated:

d. Years experience: With This Firm ____   With Other Firms ____

e. Education: Degree(s) / Years / Specialization

f. Active Registration: Year First Registered/Discipline

g. Other Experience and Qualifications relevant to the proposed project:

Standard Form 255 July 1975
Prescribed By GSA Fed Proc Reg (41 CFR) 1-16.803

5

196

7. Brief Resume of Key Persons, Specialists, and Individual Consultants Anticipated for this Project

a. Name & Title:

b. Project Assignment:

c. Name of Firm with which associated:

d. Years experience: With This Firm ——   With Other Firms ——

e. Education: Degree(s) / Year / Specialization

f. Active Registration: Year First Registered/Discipline

g. Other Experience and Qualifications relevant to the proposed project:

a. Name & Title:

b. Project Assignment:

c. Name of Firm with which associated:

d. Years experience: With This Firm ——   With Other Firms ——

e. Education: Degree(s) / Years / Specialization

f. Active Registration: Year First Registered/Discipline

g. Other Experience and Qualifications relevant to the proposed project:

Standard Form 255 July 1975
Prescribed By GSA Fed Proc. Reg (41 CFR) 1-16.803

6

197

7. Brief Resume of **Key** Persons, Specialists, and Individual Consultants Anticipated for this Project

a. Name & Title:	a. Name & Title:
b. Project Assignment:	b. Project Assignment:
c. Name of Firm with which associated:	c. Name of Firm with which associated:
d. Years experience: With This Firm ___ With Other Firms ___	d. Years experience: With This Firm ___ With Other Firms ___
e. Education: Degree(s) / Year / Specialization	e. Education: Degree(s) / Years / Specialization
f. Active Registration: Year First Registered/Discipline	f. Active Registration: Year First Registered/Discipline
g. Other Experience and Qualifications relevant to the proposed project:	g. Other Experience and Qualifications relevant to the proposed project:

Standard Form 255 July 1975
Prescribed By GSA Fed Proc Reg (41 CFR) 1-16.803

7

7. Brief Resume of **Key** Persons, Specialists, and Individual Consultants Anticipated for this Project

a. Name & Title:

b. Project Assignment:

c. Name of Firm with which associated:

d. Years experience: With This Firm _____   With Other Firms _____

e. Education: Degree(s) / Year / Specialization

f. Active Registration: Year First Registered/Discipline

g. Other Experience and Qualifications relevant to the proposed project:

---

a. Name & Title:

b. Project Assignment:

c. Name of Firm with which associated:

d. Years experience: With This Firm _____   With Other Firms _____

e. Education: Degree(s) / Years / Specialization

f. Active Registration: Year First Registered/Discipline

g. Other Experience and Qualifications relevant to the proposed project:

Standard Form 255 July 1975
Prescribed By GSA Fed. Proc. Reg. (41 CFR) 1-16.803

8

8. Work by Firm or Joint Venture Members which Best Illustrates Current Qualifications Relevant to this Project (List not more than 10 Projects)

a. Project Name & Location	b. Nature of Firm's Responsibility	c. Owner's Name & Address	d. Completion Date (actual or estimated)	e. Estimated Cost (in thousands)	
				Entire Project	Work for which Firm was/is responsible
(1)					
(2)					
(3)					
(4)					
(5)					
(6)					
(7)					
(8)					
(9)					
(10)					

Standard Form 255 July 1975
Prescribed by GSA Fed. Proc. Reg. (41 CFR) 1-16.806

9

9. All work by firms or Joint Venture members **currently being performed directly for Federal agencies**

a. Project Name & Location	b. Nature of Firm's Responsibility	c. Agency (Responsible Office) Name & Address	d. Percent complete	e. Estimated Cost (In Thousands)	
				Entire Project	Work for which firm is responsible

Standard Form 255 July 1975
Prescribed By GSA Fed. Proc. Reg. (41 CFR) 1-16.803

10

10. Use this space to provide any additional information or description of resources supporting your firm's qualifications for the proposed project

11. The foregoing is a statement of facts.

Signature: _____ Typed Name and Title: _____

Date: _____

Standard Form 255 July 1975
Prescribed By GSA Fed. Proc. Reg. (41 CFR) 1-16.803

☆ U.S. GOVERNMENT PRINTING OFFICE : 1984 O - 436-623

11

202

PREAWARD SURVEY OF PROSPECTIVE CONTRACTOR (GENERAL)	1. SERIAL NO. (For surveying activity use)	FORM APPROVED OMB NO. 3090-0110

SECTION I – REQUEST *(For Completion by Contracting Office)*

2. NAME AND ADDRESS OF SURVEYING ACTIVITY	3. SOLICITATION NO.	4. TOTAL OFFERED PRICE $
	5. TYPE OF CONTRACT	
6A. NAME AND ADDRESS OF SECONDARY SURVEY ACTIVITY *(For surveying activity use)*	7. NAME AND ADDRESS PROSPECTIVE CONTRACTOR	
6B. TELEPHONE NO. *(Include autovon, Wats/FTS, if available)*		

8. WILL CONTRACTING OFFICE PARTICIPATE IN SURVEY? ☐ YES ☐ NO

9. DATE OF THIS REQUEST	10. DATE REPORT REQUIRED

11. Prospective contractor represents that it ☐ is, ☐ is not a small business concern.

12. WALSH-HEALEY CONTRACTS ACT *(Check applicable box(es))*

A. IS NOT APPLICABLE
B. IS APPLICABLE AND PROSPECTIVE CONTRACTOR REPRESENTS HIS CLASSIFICATION AS:
☐ MANUFACTURER   ☐ REGULAR DEALER
☐ OTHER *(Specify)*

13. NAME AND ADDRESS OF PARENT COMPANY *(If applicable)*	14. PLANT AND LOCATION *(If different from Item 7, above)*
15A. NAME OF REQUESTING ACTIVITY CONTRACTING OFFICER	16A. NAME AND ADDRESS OF SECONDARY REQUESTING ACTIVITY *(For surveying authority use)*
15B. SIGNATURE	
15C. TELEPHONE NO. *(Include autovon, Wats/FTS, if available)*	16B. TELEPHONE NO. *(Include autovon, Wats/FTS, if available)*

17. FIRM'S CONTACT FOR SURVEY

A. NAME AND TITLE	B. TELEPHONE NO. *(Include Area Code)*

SECTION II – DATA *(For Completion by Contracting Office)*

18A. ITEM NO.	18B. NATIONAL STOCK NUMBER (NEW) AND NOMENCLATURE		18C. TOTAL QUANTITY	18D. UNIT PRICE	18E. DELIVERY SCHEDULE				
					(a)	(b)	(c)	(d)	(e)
		SOLICITED							
		OFFERED		$					
		SOLICITED							
		OFFERED		$					
		SOLICITED							
		OFFERED		$					
		SOLICITED							
		OFFERED		$					
		SOLICITED							
		OFFERED		$					
		SOLICITED							
		OFFERED		$					
		SOLICITED							
		OFFERED		$					
		SOLICITED							
		OFFERED		$					
		SOLICITED							
		OFFERED		$					

NSN 7540-01-140-5525   1403-101   STANDARD FORM 1403 (10-83)
Prescribed by GSA
FAR (48 CFR) 53.209-1(a)

SECTION III – FACTORS TO BE INVESTIGATED

Column (a) is for request. Columns (b) and (c) are for survey results. Provide a narrative explanation substantiating each factor for which Column (b) or (c) is checked.

19. MAJOR FACTORS	CHK. (a)	SAT. (b)	UN-SAT. (c)	20. OTHER FACTORS *(Provide specific requirements in Remarks)*	CHK. (a)	SAT. (b)	UN-SAT. (c)
A. TECHNICAL CAPABILITY				A. GOVERNMENT PROPERTY CONTROL			
B. PRODUCTION CAPABILITY				B. TRANSPORTATION			
C. QUALITY ASSURANCE CAPABILITY				C. PACKAGING			
D. FINANCIAL CAPABILITY				D. SECURITY			
E. ACCOUNTING SYSTEM				E. PLANT SAFETY			
21. IS THIS A SHORT FORM PREAWARD REPORT?				F. ENVIRONMENTAL/ENERGY CONSIDERATIONS			

21. IS THIS A SHORT FORM PREAWARD REPORT?

☐ YES   ☐ NO

G. OTHER *(Specify)*

22. IS A FINANCIAL ASSISTANCE PAYMENT PROVISION IN THE SOLICITATION?

☐ YES   ☐ NO

23. REMARKS

SECTION IV – SURVEYING ACTIVITY RECOMMENDATIONS

24. RECOMMEND	25A. NAME AND TITLE OF SURVEY APPROVING OFFICIAL	25B. TELEPHONE NO.
☐ A. COMPLETE AWARD		
☐ B. PARTIAL AWARD *(Quantity_____)*	25C. SIGNATURE	25D. DATE
☐ C. NO AWARD		

STANDARD FORM 1403 BACK (10-83)

PREAWARD SURVEY OF PROSPECTIVE CONTRACTOR TECHNICAL	SERIAL NO. *(For surveying activity use)*	FORM APPROVED OMB NO. 3090-0110
	PROSPECTIVE CONTRACTOR	

Provide the following information in narrative, or attach continuation on sheets of paper if necessary, concerning key personnel.	4. FIRM HAS AND/OR UNDERSTANDS	YES	NO
1. Names, qualifications/experience and length of affiliation with prospective contractor.	a. Specifications		
2. Evaluate technical capabilities with respect to the requirements of the proposed contract or item classification.	b. Exhibits		
	c. Drawings		
3. Description of any technical capabilities which the prospective contractor lacks. *(Comment on the prospective contractor's efforts to obtain the needed technical capabilities.)*	d. Technical data requirements		
	Give explanation for any items marked "NO" in 5. Narrative.		

5. NARRATIVE

6. SURVEY MADE BY	a. SIGNATURE *(Include typed or printed name)*	b. OFFICE	c. TELEPHONE NO. *(Include area code)*
			d. DATE

NSN 7540-01-142-0133   1404-101

☆ GPO : 1983 0 – 381-526 (9036)

STANDARD FORM 1404 (10-83)
Prescribed by GSA,
FAR (48 CFR) 53.209-1(b)

PREAWARD SURVEY OF PROSPECTIVE CONTRACTOR PRODUCTION	SERIAL NO. *(For surveying activity use)*	FORM APPROVED OMB NO. **3090-0110**
	PROSPECTIVE CONTRACTOR	

SECTION I — ORGANIZATION AND MANAGEMENT DATA

Provide the following information in narrative or attach continuation on sheets of paper if necessary.

1. Describe the relationship between management, production, and inspection. Attach an organizational chart, if available.

2. Describe the prospective contractor's production control system. State whether or not it is operational.

3. Evaluate the prospective contractor's production control system in terms of (a) historical effectiveness, (b) the proposed contract, and (c) total production during performance of the proposed contract.

4. Comment on or evaluate other areas unique to this survey (include all special requests by the contracting office and any other information pertinent to the proposed contract or item classification).

5. NARRATIVE

SECTION II — PLANT FACILITIES

1. SIZE OF TRACT		4. DESCRIPTION AND TYPE OF BUILDING(S)
2. SQUARE FEET UNDER ROOF	3. NO. OF BUILD-INGS	☐ OWNED ☐ LEASED *(Give expiration date)*

5. SPACE					6. MISCELLANEOUS PLANT OBSERVATIONS		
	TYPE	SQUARE FEET	ADE-QUATE	INADE-QUATE	*(Explain any items marked "NO" on an attached sheet.)*	YES	NO
MANUFAC-TURING	a. Total manufacturing space				a. Good housekeeping maintained		
	b. Space available for offered item				b. Power and fuel supply adequate to meet production requirements		
	c. Total storage space				c. Alternate power and fuel source available		
	d. For inspection lots				d. Adequate material handling equipment available		
STORAGE	e. For shipping quantities				e. Transportation facilities available for shipping product		
	f. Space available for offered item				OTHER *(Specify)* f.		
					g.		
	g. Amount of storage that can be converted for manufacturing, if required				h.		

SECTION III — PRODUCTION EQUIPMENT

LIST MAJOR EQUIPMENT REQUIRED *(Include GFP and annotate it as such)* (a)	QUANTITY REQUIRED FOR PROPOSED CONTRACT (b)	TOTAL QTY. REQD. DUR-ING LIFE OF PROPOSED CONTRACT (c)	QUANTITY ON HAND (d)	CONDI-TION (e) G F P	QUANTITY SHORT * (Col. (c) minus (d)) (f)	SOURCE, IF NOT ON HAND (g)	VERIFIED DELIVERY DATE (h)
MANUFACTURING 1.							
SPECIAL TOOLING 2.							
SPECIAL TEST 3.							

* Coordinate shortage information for financial implications.

STANDARD FORM 1405 (10-83)
PAGE 2

SECTION IV — MATERIALS AND PURCHASED PARTS

1. PARTS/MATERIALS WITH LONGEST LEAD TIME

DESCRIPTION (a)	SOURCE (b)	VERIFIED DELIVERY DATE TO MEET PROD. (c)

2. DESCRIBE THE MATERIAL CONTROL SYSTEM, INDICATING WHETHER IT IS CURRENTLY OPERATIONAL, AND EVALUATE ITS ABILITY TO MEET THE NEEDS OF THE PROPOSED ACQUISITION.

SECTION V — SUBCONTRACTING

HOW MUCH OF THE TOTAL PROPOSED CONTRACT WILL BE SUBCONTRACTED? ▶ _____ %

DESCRIPTION OF SUBCONTRACT ITEMS (a)	SOURCE (b)	VERIFIED DELIVERY DATE TO MEET PROD. (c)

SECTION VI — PERSONNEL

TYPE OF EMPLOYEES	NO. ON BOARD	ADD. NO. REQUIRED	AVAIL. YES	AVAIL. NO	SOURCE
a. Skilled Production					
b. Unskilled Production					
c. Engineering					
d. Administrative					
e. TOT. *(Lines a, b + c)*					

1. NUMBER AND SOURCE OF EMPLOYEES

2. SHIFTS ON WHICH WORK IS TO BE PERFORMED
☐ FIRST ☐ SECOND ☐ THIRD

3. UNION AFFILIATION

AGREEMENT EXPIRATION DATE ▶

4. RELATIONSHIP WITH LABOR INDICATES PROBLEMS AFFECTING TIMELY PERFORMANCE OF PROPOSED CONTRACT *(If "Yes," explain on attached sheet)*
☐ YES ☐ NO

SECTION VII — DELIVERY PERFORMANCE RECORD

SECTION VIII – RELATED PREVIOUS PRODUCTION (Government)

PAST YEAR PRODUCTION		GOVERNMENT CONTRACT NUMBER.1/	PERFORMANCE		QUANTITY	DOLLAR VALUE ($000)
ITEM NOMENCLATURE (a)	NATIONAL STOCK NO. (NSN) (b)	(c)	ON SCHED. (d)	DELIN- QUENT (e)	(f)	(g)

1/ Identify identical items by an asterisk (*) after the Government contract number.

SECTION IX – CURRENT PRODUCTION

(Government and civilian concurrent production schedule using same equipment and/or personnel as offered item.)

ITEM(S) *(Include Government Contract No., if applicable. Identify unsatisfactory performance with asterisk (*).)*	MONTHLY SCHEDULE OF CONCURRENT DELIVERIES *(Quantity)*										
	1st	2nd	3rd	4th	5th	6th	7th	8th	9th	10th	BAL.

BEING PRODUCED — 1.

PENDING AWARD — 2.

SECTION X – RECOMMENDATION

1. RECOMMENDED

☐ a. COMPLETE AWARD   ☐ b. PARTIAL AWARD *(Quantity:* _____ *)*   ☐ c. NO AWARD

2. REMARKS *(Cite those sections of this report which substantiate the recommendations. List any other backup information in this space or on attached sheet if necessary. Identify any formal systems reviews and state results.)*

If continuation sheets attached – mark here ☐

3. SURVEY MADE BY	a. SIGNATURE AND OFFICE *(Include typed or printed name)*	b. TELEPHONE NO. *(Include area code)*	c. DATE SIGNED
4. SURVEY REVIEWING OFFICIAL	a. SIGNATURE AND OFFICE *(Include typed or printed name)*	b. TELEPHONE NO. *(Include area code)*	c. DATE REVIEWED

☆ GPO : 1983 O – 381-526 (9035)   STANDARD FORM 1405 (10-83) PAGE 4

PREAWARD SURVEY OF PROSPECTIVE CONTRACTOR QUALITY ASSURANCE	*If more space is required, continue on the back in Section IV or attach continuation sheets.*	FORM APPROVED OMB NO. **3090-0110**
		SERIAL NO. *(For surveying activity use)*

SECTION I — GENERAL

1. PROSPECTIVE CONTRACTOR	2. LOCATION

SECTION II — COMPANY AND SOLICITATION DATA

1. QUALITY ASSURANCE ORGANIZATION *(Describe briefly and attach organization chart.)*

2. QUALITY ASSURANCE OFFICIALS CONTACTED *(Names, titles, and years of quality assurance experience)*

3. QUALITY RELIABILITY, MAINTAINABILITY REQUIREMENTS WHICH APPLY ◄	MIL-I-45208	MIL-C-45662	☐ OTHER *(Specify)*
	MIL-I-45007	MIL-STD-785	
	MIL-Q-9555	MIL-STD-470	

4. IDENTICAL OR SIMILAR ITEMS HAVE BEEN ☐ PRODUCED ☐ SERVICED BY PROSPECTIVE CONTRACTOR.

SECTION III — EVALUATION CHECKLIST

STATEMENTS		YES	NO
1. AS PERTAINS TO THE CONTRACT, THESE ITEMS ARE UNDERSTOOD BY THE CONTRACTOR	a. Exhibits, technical data, drawings, specifications, and approval requirements.		
	b. Preservation, packaging, packing, and marking requirements.		
	c. OTHER *(Specify)*		
2. Records available indicate that the prospective contractor has a satisfactory quality performance record during the past twelve (12) months for similar items.			
3. Used or reconditioned material and former Government surplus material will be furnished by the prospective contractor. *(If Yes, explain in Section IV, on the back of this form.)*			
4. Prospective contractor will require unusual assistance from the Government.			
5. Did prospective contractor fulfill commitments to correct deficiencies, as proposed on previous surveys, when awarded that contract?			
6. Quality control, inspection, and test personnel.	NUMBER SKILLED · NUMBER SEMI-SKILLED		
7. Inspection to production personnel ratio.	RATIO		
The following are available and adequate. (If not applicable, show "N/A" in "Yes" column.)			
8. Inspection and test equipment, guages, and instruments for first article and production (including solicitation specified equipment).			
9. Calibration/metrology program.			
10. Written procedures and instructions for inspections, tests, process controls, and other requirements; conformance thereto; in conjunction with other planning control functions.			
11. Control of specifications, drawings, changes and modifications, work/process instructions.			
12. Quality assurance/control organizational structure.			
13. System for determining inspection, test, and measurement requirements.			
14. Controls for selecting qualified supplies and assuring the quality of purchased materials.			
15. Material control: identification, segregation, maintenance, preservation, and correction of defects.			
16. Government furnished property controls.			

NSN 7540-01-140-5527   1406-101   STANDARD FORM 1406 (10-83)
Prescribed by GSA,
FAR (48 CFR) 53.209-1(d)

SECTION III — EVALUATION CHECKLIST — STATEMENTS, Continued	YES	NO
17. In-process inspection controls.		
18. System for timely identification and correction of deficiencies to prevent recurrence.		
19. Preservation, packaging, packing, marking controls.		
20. Quality control records (such as, inspection, test, corrective actions, calibration, etc.		
21. Controls for investigation of customer complaints and correction of deficiencies.		
22. Reliability and/or maintainability program.		

SECTION IV — QUALITY ASSURANCE RECOMMENDATIONS

1. RECOMMEND ☐ AWARD ☐ NO AWARD *(Provide full substantiation for recommendation)*

If more space is needed, use plain paper. identify continued item.(s), and attach to this form.

NO. OF PAGES ATTACHED, IF ANY ☐

2. SURVEY MADE BY *(Include signature, typed/printed name, and office)*	3. TELEPHONE NO. *(Include area code)*	4. DATE SUBMITTED

5. REVIEWING/APPROVING OFFICIAL *(Include signature, typed/printed name, and office)*	6. DATE APPROVED	7. NEXT HIGHER AUTHORITY *(Code/title)*

GPO : 1983 O – 581-526 (9025)

STANDARD FORM 1406 BACK (10-83)

PREAWARD SURVEY OF PROSPECTIVE CONTRACTOR FINANCIAL CAPABILITY	If more space is needed, continue on page 3, back. Identify continued items.	SERIAL NO. (For surveying activity use)	FORM APPROVED OMB NO. 3090-0110
PROSPECTIVE CONTRACTOR		LOCATION	

SECTION I – BALANCE SHEET/PROFIT AND LOSS STATEMENT

PART A – LATEST BALANCE SHEET		PART B – LATEST PROFIT AND LOSS STATEMENT		
1. DATE	2. FILED WITH	1. CURRENT PERIOD		2. FILED WITH
		a. FROM	b. TO	

3. FINANCIAL POSITION				
a. Cash	$	3. NET SALES	a. CURRENT PERIOD	$
b. Other current assets			b. First prior fiscal year	
c. Working capital			c. Second prior fiscal year	
d. Current liabilities		4. NET PROFITS BEFORE TAXES	a. CURRENT PERIOD	$
e. Net worth			b. First prior fiscal year	
f. Total liabilities			c. Second prior fiscal year	

4. RATIOS			5. OTHER PERTINENT DATA
a. CURRENT ASSETS TO CURRENT LIABILITIES	b. ACID TEST (Cash, temporary investments held in lieu of cash and current receivables to current liabilities)	c. TOTAL LIABILITIES TO NET WORTH	
:	:	:	

6. FISCAL YEAR ENDS (Date)	7. BALANCE SHEETS AND PROFIT AND LOSS STATEMENTS HAVE BEEN CERTIFIED	a. THROUGH (Date)	b. BY (Signature)

SECTION II – PROSPECTIVE CONTRACTOR'S FINANCIAL ARRANGEMENTS

Mark "X" in appropriate column.	YES	NO	4. INDEPENDENT ANALYSIS OF FINANCIAL POSITION SUPPORTS THE STATEMENTS SHOWN IN ITEMS 1, 2, AND 3
1. USE OF OWN RESOURCES		.	☐ YES ☐ NO (If "NO," explain)
2. USE OF BANK CREDITS			
3. OTHER (Specify)			

SECTION III – GOVERNMENT FINANCIAL AID

1. TO BE REQUESTED IN CONNECTION WITH PERFORMANCE OF PROPOSED CONTRACT			2. EXPLAIN ANY "YES" ANSWERS TO ITEMS 1a, b, AND c
Mark "X" in appropriate column.	YES	NO	
a. PROGRESS PAYMENT			
b. GUARANTEED LOAN			
c. ADVANCE PAYMENTS			

3. FINANCIAL AID CURRENTLY OBTAINED FROM THE GOVERNMENT

a. PROSPECTIVE CONTRACTOR RECEIVES GOVERNMENT FINANCING AT PRESENT	b. IS LIQUIDATION CURRENT?	c. AMOUNT OF UNLIQUI- DATED PROGRESS PAY- MENTS OUTSTANDING	Complete items below only if item a., is marked "YES."		
			DOLLAR AMOUNTS	(a) AUTHORIZED	(b) IN USE
☐ YES ☐ NO	☐ YES ☐ NO	$	a. Guaranteed loans	$	$
			b. Advance payments	$	$

4. LIST THE GOVERNMENT AGENCIES INVOLVED	5. SHOW THE APPLICABLE CONTRACT NOS.

SECTION IV – BUSINESS AND FINANCIAL REPUTATION

1. COMMENTS OF PROSPECTIVE CONTRACTOR'S BANK

2. COMMENTS OF TRADE CREDITORS

3. COMMENTS AND REPORTS OF COMMERCIAL FINANCIAL SERVICES AND CREDIT ORGANIZATIONS *(Such as, Dun & Bradstreet, Standard and Poor, etc.)*

4. MOST RECENT CREDIT RATING	a. DATE	b. BY

5. OTHER SOURCES *(Business and financial reputation and integrity of the prospective contractor, or, if not established, of the principal executions, as determined by other sources.)*

6. DOES PRICE APPEAR UNREALISTICALLY LOW? ☐ YES ☐ NO

7. DESCRIBE ANY OUTSTANDING LIENS OR JUDGMENTS

SECTION V — SALES		
CATEGORY	CURRENT DOLLAR BACKLOG OF SALES (a)	ANTICIPATED ADDITIONAL DOLLAR SALES FORECAST FOR NEXT 18 MONTHS (b)
1. Government *(Prime and subcontractor)*	$	$
2. Commercial	$	$
3. TOTAL	$	$

SECTION VI — RECOMMENDATION

1. RECOMMEND

☐ a. COMPLETE AWARD ☐ b. PARTIAL AWARD *(Quantity:* _____ *)* ☐ c. NO AWARD

2. REMARKS *(Cite those sections of the report which substantiate the recommendation. Give any other backup information in this space, on the back, or on additional sheet, if necessary.)*

If continuation sheets attached — mark here ☐

3. SURVEY MADE BY *(Signature and office)*

4. TELEPHONE NO. *(Include area code)*

5. DATE SUBMITTED

PREAWARD SURVEY OF PROSPECTIVE CONTRACTOR ACCOUNTING SYSTEM	SERIAL NO. *(For surveying activity use)*	FORM APPROVED OMB NO. 3090-0110		
	PROSPECTIVE CONTRACTOR			

Mark "X" in the appropriate column	YES	NO	NOT APPLI-CABLE
1. Except as stated below, is the accounting system in accord with generally accepted accounting principles applicable in the circumstances?			
2. ACCOUNTING SYSTEM PROVIDES FOR:			
a. Proper segregation of costs applicable to proposed contract and to other work of the prospective contractor.			
b. Determination of costs at interim points to provide data required for contract repricing purposes or for negotiating revised targets.			
c. Exclusion from costs charged to proposed contract of amounts which are not allowable under terms of FAR 31, Contract Cost Principles and Procedures, or other contract provisions.			
d. Identification of costs by contract line item and by units if required by proposed contract.			
e. Segregation of preproduction costs from production costs.			
3. ACCOUNTING SYSTEM PROVIDES FINANCIAL INFORMATION:			
a. Required by contract clauses concerning limitation of cost (FAR 52.232-40 and 41) or limitation on payments (FAR 52.216-16).			
b. Required to support requests for progress payments.			
4. Is the accounting system designed, and are the records maintained in such a manner that adequate, reliable data are developed for use in pricing follow-on acquisitions?			

5. REMARKS *(Clarification of above deficiencies, and other pertinent comments. If additional space is required, continue on the back or on plain sheets of paper.)*

If continuation sheets attached — mark here ☐

6. SURVEY MADE BY *(Signature and office)*	7. TELEPHONE NO. *(Include area code)*	8. DATE SUBMITTED

NSN 7540-01-140-5529   1408-101   STANDARD FORM 1408 (10-83)
Prescribed by GSA,
☆ U.S. GOVERNMENT PRINTING OFFICE: 1984—432-685   FAR (48 CFR) 53.209-1(f)

ABSTRACT OF OFFERS

SOLICITATION NO.

OPENING DATE

PAGE   OF   PAGES

ISSUING OFFICE

SUPPLIES OR SERVICES *(General Description)*

NO.	NAME OF OFFEROR	DISCOUNT TERMS *(Days)* 10 20 30	AC-CEPT-ANCE TIME* *(Days)*	BUSI-NESS SIZE L S	ITEM NO.	QUANTITY	UNIT				DELIV-ERY TIME**	F.O.B. POINT	REMARKS
							$	$	$	$			

* *Indicate by an X a 60-day acceptance.*
** *Indicate by an X if offer conforms to delivery time specified in solicitation.*

I CERTIFY THAT I HAVE OPENED, READ AND RECORDED ON THIS ABSTRACT (AND CONTIN-UATION SHEETS, IF ANY) ALL OFFERS RE-CEIVED IN RESPONSE TO THE SOLICITATION.

TYPED NAME AND TITLE

SIGNATURE   DATE

NSN 7540-01-142-9844   1409-101

STANDARD FORM 1409 (10-83)
Prescribed by GSA, FAR (48 CFR) 53.214(f)

ABSTRACT OF OFFERS – CONTINUATION

PAGE OF PAGES

ITEM NO.

NO. QUANTITY

UNIT

STANDARD FORM 1409 BACK (10-83)

*Transfer number from face of form.

ABSTRACT OF OFFERS – CONSTRUCTION

| 1. SOLICITATION NUMBER | 2. DATE ISSUED | 3. DATE OPENED | PAGE OF | PAGES |

4. ISSUING OFFICE

I CERTIFY that I have opened, read, and recorded on this abstract all offers received in response to this solicitation.

SIGNATURE | DATE SIGNED

5. PROJECT TITLE

6. NUMBER OF ADDENDA ISSUED

8. GOVERNMENT ESTIMATE
(Check A, B or C and complete D, E and F.)

A. HIRED LABOR

B. REASONABLE CONTRACT (Without Profit)

C. REASONABLE CONTRACT (Including Profit)

9. OFFERS

7A. ITEM NO.	7B. DESCRIPTION OF OFFERED ITEM	7C. EST. QUANTITY	D. UNIT	E. UNIT PRICE	F. ESTIMATED AMOUNT	NO. 1				NO. 2				
						A. OFFEROR	B. BID SECURITY (Type and amount)	C. ADDENDA ACKNOWLEDGED	D. UNIT PRICE	E. ESTIMATED AMOUNT	A. OFFEROR	B. BID SECURITY (Type and Amount)	C. ADDENDA ACKNOWLEDGED	D. UNIT PRICE	E. ESTIMATED AMOUNT

NSN 7540-01-150-0981

1419-101

STANDARD FORM 1419 (10-83)
Prescribed by GSA
FAR (48 CFR) 53.236-1(c)

9. OFFERS (Continued)

NO. 3	NO. 4	NO. 5	NO. 6	NO. 7
A. OFFEROR	A. OFFEROR	A. OFFEROR	A. OFFEROR	A. OFFEROR
B. BID SECURITY (*Type and Amount*)	B. BID SECURITY (*Type and Amount*)	B. BID SECURITY (*Type and Amount*)	B. BID SECURITY (*Type and Amount*)	B. BID SECURITY (*Type and Amount*)
C. ADDENDA ACKNOWLEDGED	C. ADDENDA ACKNOWLEDGED	C. ADDENDA ACKNOWLEDGED	C. ADDENDA ACKNOWLEDGED	C. ADDENDA ACKNOWLEDGED
D. UNIT PRICE / E. ESTIMATED AMOUNT	D. UNIT PRICE / E. ESTIMATED AMOUNT	D. UNIT PRICE / E. ESTIMATED AMOUNT	D. UNIT PRICE / E. ESTIMATED AMOUNT	D. UNIT PRICE / E. ESTIMATED AMOUNT

STANDARD FORM 1419 BACK (10-83)

219

Appendix 2

Government Acronyms and Abbreviations Glossary

ACO: Administrative Contracting Officer
AF: Air Force
AFLC: Air Force Logistics Command
AFSC: Air Force Systems Command
AID: American Industrial Development Agency
AIDE: Automated Item Description Extraction
ALC: Air Logistics Center
AMA: Air Material Areas
APPL: Application or Applicable
AR: Army
ARO: After Receipt of Order (Contract)
ASPR: Armed Services Procurement Regulation (now FAR)
BOA: Basic Ordering Agreement. A PO against the BOA is the contract.
BOD: Bid Open Date or Buyer's Order Date
BPA: Blanket Purchase Agreement—works like a BOA: order as needed
BSL: Bidders' Source List—Procurement's list of possible bidders
CAGE: Commercial and Government Entity code number (was FSCM/CAGE)
CAL: Contractor Alert List
CAO: Contract Administrative Officer
CAS: Cost Accounting Standards
CBD: *Commerce Business Daily*—categorized by 2-digit commodity and service codes
CIP: Contractor Improvement Program
CLIN: Contract Line Item Number—subdivision of the contract
CO: Contracting Officer at the buying activity
COC: Certificate of Competency by SBA to guarantee small business performance
CONUS: Continental United States
CORE: Contract Out Reverse Engineering—to buy items without technical data
CPFF: Cost Plus Fixed Fee (contract)

CPIF: Cost Plus Incentive Fee (contract)

CQAP: Contractor Quality Assurance Program

DAC: Defense Acquisition Circular—incorporated into the FAR annually

DAR: Defense Acquisition Regulation (was ASPR, became FAR)

DARCOM: Army Material Development and Readiness Command

DCAA: Defense Contracts Audit Agency

DCAL: Defense Contractor Alert List

DCAS: Defense Contracts Administrative Services

DCASMA: Defense Contracts Administrative Services Management Area

DCASPRO: Defense Contract Administrative Services Plant Representative Office

DCASR: Defense Contracts Administrative Services Management Region

DLA: Defense Logistics Agency

DMS: Defense Management System—DPS priority assignments within purchase orders

DOC: Department of Commerce

DOD: Department of Defense

DPS: Defense Priority System—places one contract ahead of another

DPSC: Defense Personnel Support Center

DSC: Defense Supply Center—central storage areas for specific stock items

ECP: Engineering Change Proposal

8A: Category of small business that is owned, operated, and certified as a Small Disadvantaged Business

ELIN: Exhibit Line Item Number—line item of attachments

F/A: First Article

FAR: *Federal Acquisition Regulations*

FFP: Firm Fixed Price

FFPEPA: Firm Fixed Price with Economic Price Adjustments (contract)

FIIN: Federal Item Identification Number

F/M/F: Forward/Marked/For

FOB: Freight on Board

FP: Fixed Price

FPR: Federal Procurement Regulations

FSCM/CAGE: Federal Supply Code for Manufacturer's /Commercial and Government Entities

FSC: Federal Supply Code—first 4 digits of FSN and/or NSC

FSG: Federal Stock Group—the first 2 digits of FSN, NSN, and/or FSC

FSN: Federal Stock Number—11-digit unique identification code for stock

FY: Fiscal Year—the government accounting year, October 1 through September 30

GFE: Government Furnished Equipment

GPO: Government Printing Office
GSA: General Services Administration
GSI: Government Source Inspection
IAW: In Accordance With
IFB: Invitation for Bid
IM: Item Manager—the central item controller, often worldwide
IS: Industrial Specialist
JSC: Johnson Space Center
LSA: Labor Surplus Area
MBL: Mechanized Bidders' (source) List—provides potential, registered vendors
MDR: Material Deficiency Report
M/F: Mark For
Mil Spec: Military Specifications
MMAC: Material Management Aggregate Code—2-digit alpha suffix to FSN
MSC: Military Sealift Command—joint services sea shipments
NAV: Navy/Naval
NICP: National Inventory Control Point
NMFC: National Motor Freight Code
NSN: National Stock Number, (FSN when item is used by all government agencies)
NSP: Not Separately Priced
O/A: On or About—used when a date is uncertain or can't be determined
OCE: Office Chief of Engineers
OFPP: Office of Federal Procurement Policy
OMB: Office of Management and Budget
OSD: Office of Secretary of Defense
PAS: Preaward Survey
PASM: Preaward Survey Monitor
PASS: Procurement Automated Source System (maintained by SBA)
PC: Prospective Contractor
PCO: Principal Contracting Officer (usually at the buying activity)
PHE: Procurement History Extraction by Federal Stock Number
PHR: Procurement History Record
PIIN: Procurement Instrument Identification Number—the contract number
PL: Public Law—usually one section of it that applies to a subject
PMC: Procurement Method Code
P/N: Part Number—provides FIIN components made by different companies
PO: Purchase Order—to order goods

PQA: Procurement Quality Assurance
PR: Purchase Request—sent from item manager to the contracting officer
PVI: Product Verification Inspection
QAE: Quality Assurance Evaluation
QAR: Quality Assurance Representative
QDR: Quality Deficiency Report
QIS: Quality Inspection Specialist
QPL: Qualified Products List
R&D: Research and Development funds—related to small business SBIR program
RFP: Request for (competitive) Proposal—may/may not be discussed before award
RFQ: Request for (noncompetitive) quotation—usually discussed before award
RYC: Read your contract
SADBU: Small and Disadvantaged Business Utilization
SBA: Small Business Administration
SBDC: Small Business Development Center—agency that develops small business
SBIC: Small Business Investment Company—federally backed specialized investor
SBIR: Small Business Innovative Research program (PL 92–219, 1982)
SBS: Small Business Specialist
SCORE: Service Corps of Retired Executives—SBA counseling for small business
SDB: Small Disadvantaged Business, certified by SBA. Owned and operated by an economically disadvantaged minority
SF: Standard Form
SIC: Standard Industrial Code
SLIN: Subline Item Number—breakdown of CLIN
SNAPPL: Stock Number Advanced Procurement Planning List
SOW: Statement of Work—defines the services to be provided
SQC: Statistical Quality Control
SUP: Supplement
TFC: Termination for Convenience (government changed its mind)
TFD: Terminated for Default (due to your lack of contract performance)
TSA: Army Troop Support Agency
UCC: Uniform Commercial Code
USPS: United States Postal Service
VC: Vendor Code (CAGE 5-digit code)
VIQ: Variation in Quantity

Appendix 3

A Summary of Major Government Procurement Activity

Approximately 14 departments and 60 major agencies with over 1,200 buying offices award federal contracts. The following is a general description of key departments and agencies and what they buy. (The bibliography in the back of the book will provide additional sources. Also see the *U.S. Government Purchasing and Sales Directory*.) The three largest buyers of your products will not be government departments at all, but the centralized procurement agencies listed below:

1. *General Services Administration.* GSA was created as a central procurement source for the 13 federal departments and various agencies outside the Department of Defense. GSA carries out the government's housekeeping activities, buying administrative supplies and serving as the government landlord. It buys the supplies, services, and buildings to keep the government running on a day-to-day basis. Its commodities range from "adhesive sealers" to "woodworking machinery and equipment." Included are all types of tools, furniture, metalworking equipment, twine, draperies, pipes, and vehicular components. What it does *not* buy are some categories of communications equipment, data processing, electronics, and fuels that are provided by the Defense Logistics Agency, defined below. (See bibliography: *List of Commodities and Services*.)

2. *Defense Logistics Agency.* DLA is the central buyer for the administrative support of the Department of Defense. It also supports the GSA and foreign countries in specialized areas, such as procurement spares for airplanes assigned outside the DOD. DLA is subdivided into six different buying centers:

Defense Construction Supply Center
Defense Electronics Supply Center
Defense Fuel Supply Center

Defense General Supply Center
Defense Industrial Supply Center
Defense Personnel Support Center

Like the other purchasing centers, DPSC publishes a quarterly four-quarter forecast. DPSC procures the clothing, footwear, and personnel equipment required to support the military and government workers. As production of clothing has very rigid quality requirements, it will also be necessary to order the specifications which each item must meet. (See bibliography: *Prospective Clothing, Textile, Equipment and Footwear Bidders* and *Department of Defense, Index of Specifications and Standards, DOD-ISS.*)

3. *Army Corps of Engineers.* This is the primary government agency for the government's architectural, construction, and remodeling services. The Corps is the construction, overhaul, and maintenance manager for the nation's infrastructure *outside* the military fences (and sometimes inside). Its needs are international and range from engineering and design services to quality inspectors at construction sites. (See bibliography: *Architect-Engineer Contracts, EP 715–1–4.*)

There are 14 federal departments in the government. Although the above agencies provide their administration and housekeeping requirements, each department buys specialized goods and services to meet its unique mission. To help you identify a particular customer I've identified each of their goals:

1. The *Department of Agriculture* specializes in food production, preparation, research, and distribution. (See bibliography: *What USDA Buys— Fiscal Year 1988.*)

2. The *Department of Commerce* specializes in expanding and distributing production, including an extensive worldwide network of export sales and marketing information. It supports the application of new technology to production.

3. The *Department of Education* has the responsibility to educate and train the citizens of America. It does a lot of bulk information management and projection.

4. The *Department of Defense* is easily the largest agency, bigger than all the others combined. In addition to the Defense Logistics Agency, it encompasses the subdepartments of the army, navy, and air force. If anyone makes it, somebody in the DOD buys it.

5. The *Department of Energy* is concerned with the development, distribution, storage, and utilization of all forms of energy and their applications.

6. The *Department of Health and Human Services* has all of the responsibilities of medical research, medical care for the aged, and protection of the public's health.

7. The *Department of Housing and Urban Development* provides for city development, high-density housing area, and subsidized housing programs.

8. The *Department of the Interior* is responsible for all federally owned lands and corresponding services, including parks systems, extraction and development of natural resources, and coastal waterways.

9. The *Department of Justice* is responsible for the criminal justice system, encompassing the federal courts, the prison system, and the publication and distribution of laws.

10. The *Department of Labor* is primarily an information-processing organization and has several buy listings in the data field, such as graphics, audiovisual, data processing, library materials, etc. It also utilizes and provides to the public a long list of consultant services. (See bibliography: *What the U.S. Department of Labor Buys.*)

11. The *Department of State* handles international business and offers certain opportunities for international construction, consulting services, and foreign-language document preparation.

12. The *Department of Transportation* redistributes goods and personnel around the world and handles needed security.

13. The *Department of the Treasury* manufactures and distributes money.

14. The *Veterans' Administration* is a major buyer and supplier of government hospital and medical supplies. The VA orders a large quantity of equipment and supplies that other agencies buy from central supply agencies. (See bibliography: *Let's Do Business,* from Hines, Ill.)

Several government agencies below the federal department level do a great amount of business with the public:

1. The *U.S. Postal Service* is no longer a true government agency. Congress has established this quasi-commercial agency as an independent organization. It spends billions of dollars procuring its equipment, services, and real estate, and buys vehicles and repair components for its mechanical systems. (See bibliography: *Let's Do Business,* from Washington, D.C.)

2. *State and city procurement centers* exist in all 50 states and most major cities. You should contact your state Department of Commerce for state markets and city managers or mayors' offices for city opportunities. It is

becoming an increasing point of pride and necessity to keep local tax dollars at home to support local industries. The local businessperson has a hometown advantage.

3. *Research and development* grants and procurements go beyond anything you ever imagined. Forty-two pages in section 5 of the *U.S. Government Purchasing and Sales Directory* give addresses of those who procure R&D activities from the public.

4. Additional agencies include:

Environmental Protection Agency

Government Printing Office

National Aeronautics and Space Administration

Nuclear Regulatory Commission

Small Business Administration

Etc., etc., etc.

In other words, there's enough business for anyone willing to make the effort to capture it!

Appendix 4

Probing the $40-Billion Prime Contracting Market

"I used to contract directly with the Department of Defense, but now I sell to three prime contractors," says Erin McCarty, manufacturer. "The primes resell my products to the government, but I don't mind. It's easier doing business with the primes—easier getting information, less paperwork, less formal."

Other contractors report that doing business with the government gives them an edge in understanding how to do business with the primes, and vice versa. Says Jim Tangdall, a paper manufacturer, "I schedule prime and commercial contracts between federal contracts. That way, I'm in full swing all the time."

You might heed Jim Tangdall's advice. While you're waiting to hear about that lucrative government contract, why not take the time to investigate the subcontracting market? A prime is defined as any company that receives a contract directly from the government, but most people think of prime contractors as companies receiving government contracts for more than $500,000 (more than $1 million for construction). These large-dollar prime contractors are required to establish plans and goals for subcontracting with small and small disadvantaged business firms. And even though primes are not yet mandated to meet subcontracting quotas, the government carefully considers their plans and activities as a basis for awarding future contracts.

Often considered the "forgotten market," prime contractors annually account for over $40 billion in small business subcontracts. (See exhibit A4-1.) It is estimated that primes subcontract from 42 to 48 percent of their total award to small and small disadvantaged business firms.

Don't assume that prime contractors are interested exclusively in defense-related items from local suppliers. In 1987 Rockwell International, maker of the B–1 bomber, used 3,000 subcontractors and awarded contracts to small businesses from forty-eight states. Besides products and raw materials one would normally associate with the building of a bomber,

Rockwell's procurement list also included flashlights, gloves, clocks and watches, cheesecloth, wiping cloths, furniture, distilled water, etc.

===================== **EXHIBIT A4-1** =====================

Top 25 Prime Contractors

AMOUNTS OF GOVERNMENT-AWARDED PRIME CONTRACTS FOR FISCAL YEAR 1987 THROUGH THIRD QUARTER (NINE MONTHS)

Company	Dollars (in billions)
1. General Electric Company	4,968,219
2. McDonnell Douglas Corporation	4,932,594
3. Lockheed Corporation	4,800,716
4. Martin Marietta Corporation	4,197,218
5. General Dynamics Corporation	3,588,814
6. Raytheon Company	3,075,847
7. The Boeing Company	2,925,620
8. Westinghouse Electric Corporation	2,810,433
9. Rockwell International Corporation	2,588,263
10. United Technologies Corporation	2,581,674
11. General Motors Corporation	2,471,416
12. Grumman Corporation	2,354,702
13. University of California	1,839,728
14. American Telephone and Telegraph Company	1,764,893
15. International Business Machines	1,589,069
16. Tenneco Inc.	1,405,275
17. Honeywell Inc.	1,377,828
18. The LTV Corporation	1,117,800
19. Litton Industries Inc.	1,110,195
20. Allied-Signal Inc.	1,096,752
21. E. I. du Pont de Nemours and Company	1,074,110
22. Textron Inc.	1,032,273
23. EG & G Inc.	1,006,010
24. Burroughs Corporation	951,158
25. Sperry Corporation	882,185

LOCATING PRIME MARKETS

Because prime contractors have access to the Procurement Automated Source System (PASS), your registration on PASS gives you automatic entrée to the prime market. (See chapter 5 for an explanation of PASS.) If you plan to wait around until you are discovered on PASS, however, you may never be solicited. Because most prime contractors choose subcontractors from their internal files, and because there is no centralized subcontractors' bidders' list, it is best to contact each prime market individually to establish yourself as an interested and qualified bidder.

One of the best sources for learning about prime contractors' buying needs is the *Small Business Subcontracting Directory,* a list of all the Department of Defense prime contractors, with their corresponding products or services. (See bibliography.) Additionally, every military office and government agency has a small business advocate who can provide you with a list of the prime contractors supplying products and services.

CONTACTING PRIME CONTRACTORS

Once you identify potential prime markets, you should do some homework, even before your introductory contact. Although you want them to know *you,* don't overlook the importance of knowing *them*—their past, present, and future. Your introductory contact will be enhanced if you can show the company you are interested in it and have a working knowledge of its business.

Start by obtaining a copy of the prime's annual report or company brochures from the library or chamber of commerce, or from the company itself. Since each prime contractor has different subcontracting procedures, you might ask the prime to send you any brochures or written information on subcontracting procedures. You can obtain additional information by reading the business section of the newspaper and professional, trade, or in-house publications, or by attending professional organization meetings—including chamber of commerce committees.

The second thing you should probably do to prepare for your first contact is compile information about your company that succinctly explains your qualifications and experience. Include such items as a list of your products and services, the names of past and current customers, and a description of your equipment and facility capability and quality assurance program. Perhaps the best way to present this material is in the form of an illustrated company sales brochure. (See exhibit A-2.) This brochure is particularly important if you want to "prequalify" to bid on technical products or services or on products with observable qualities, in which case pictures of the products or services would demonstrate your technical capabilities.

======================= **EXHIBIT A4-2** =======================

Elements of a Sales Brochure

The objective of a sales brochure is to sell your product or service to a prime contractor or other customer. Whether it is an inexpensive black-and-white presentation or an expensive four-color presentation, your brochure should follow the ABCs of Accuracy, Brevity, and Clarity and include the following elements:

• *Business identification.* The first section of your sales brochure should define your company's federal supply code (FSC) and its product or service. Use a picture of your products or personnel performing your service. Don't forget to include your company's name, address, phone number, and any other basic information.

• *Facility capability.* A picture of your facilities with a description of space available, transport docking capabilities, and railroad or interstate connections should be presented in this section.

• *Equipment.* Provide a listing of your specialized production and support equipment, tooling, and test equipment that make your product/service possible. Use pictures to present any specialized equipment or production.

• *Personnel qualifications.* Describe your personnel availability and configuration, including a breakdown by job category. List any special certifications and specialties.

• *Contract history.* List your current and recent contracts categorized by other primes, government, and commercial contracts.

• *Achievements.* Describe any industry achievements, awards, or special commendations. Use this section to discuss your quality control program and commitment to timely production and deliveries, as well as any prequalifications that you have earned. (See chapter 7 for prequalification information.)

Even though business transactions with prime contractors are less formalized and more personalized than with government agencies, most primes advise that your first contact be in writing. A letter of introduction establishes your seriousness and professionalism as a potential bidder. Also, since the primes must report their subcontracting activity to the federal government, a written query helps the prime document its contacts with small and disadvantaged businesses. Limit your letter to one page, and include the following:

- Identify your product or service by category.
- Briefly highlight your qualifications and experience.
- Ask to be placed on the prime's list of qualified sources.
- Briefly establish that you know about the prime's business, by referring to either present projects or future goals.
- State that you will follow up with a personal phone call or personal contact seven days after sending your letter.
- Include a sales brochure and/or attachments that detail your qualifications and experience. If applicable, include lists of equipment and customers, and any other helpful catalogs or product lists.

Knowing to whom to send your letter is almost as important as what you say. Most primes request that you write to the small business advocate. I recommend that you call the advocate's *secretary* to confirm the advocate's correct name and address. I also think it's a good idea to send a similar letter addressed to the purchasing agent.

FOLLOWING UP

The most important advice I give subcontractors attempting to penetrate the prime market is "Be persistent." "Keep on . . . keep on" is the advice one prime small business advocate offers to subcontractors who become frustrated waiting for a prime's reply. She candidly admits, "The subcontractors who keep pestering us are often the ones who win the contracts— provided they are qualified."

You must follow up with a personal contact within a week after you send in your letter. *And make this personal contact count.* Arrange an appointment to talk to the business advocate and the purchasing officer. Seize the opportunity to find out what else the prime requires so that you also can become qualified to bid on those contracts. Then follow up promptly to provide what is required.

SOLICITATIONS AND AWARDS

While each prime has its own methods for soliciting and awarding contracts, their procedures are largely governed by the Federal Acquisition

Regulations (FAR), especially if military or highly technical items are being procured. For the most part, the prime makes a Request for Quotation (RFQ) or Request for Proposal (RFP) to at least three qualified bidders on a rotation basis. Depending on the technical scope of the procurement, the prime may then follow up with a quality survey. The prime subsequently awards the contract on the basis of cost, responsibility, and responsiveness.

FOLLOWING UP AFTER THE AWARD

It is important that you maintain a good relationship with the prime and inform the prime of your achievements or new product developments, even long after you are firmly established as a prime subcontractor. Publicize your product, exhibit in trade shows, attend procurement seminars, and do all the things you need to do to keep your product in the forefront. Do everything, that is, except trying to influence buyers with gifts or remunerations—which is *absolutely illegal*. The best way to win prime subcontracts is to produce a quality product in a timely manner.

Small Business Innovative Research (SBIR) Grant Opportunities

Ray Yard, the owner of a civil engineering construction company, has an idea for developing an electrical device to measure load stresses on bridges. Research and development, however, will cost more than $50,000—an expense his company cannot afford, even for what promises to be an extensive market.

Elaine Greenspan, a reading teacher and part-time inventor, has an idea for an optical device to correct visual discrimination problems in learning-disabled children. When she approaches her local university for financial support, she is told that her idea has promise but that the school doesn't have the research funding to help her proceed.

Curtis Mitchell, an engineer for an environmental testing company, has developed preliminary drawings for a device that can detect asbestos fibers in air-circulation systems. He knows the idea has tremendous commercial potential, but he does not have the financing to quit his job and start his own company.

Common stories, even in the land of opportunity: individuals with great ideas, commercially viable ideas, but no resources to launch their inventions. So the ideas languish until one day big companies with big capital can develop them. Right?

Not necessarily. These individuals discovered a new source of capital: Small Business Innovation Research (SBIR) government grants. Reserved for the little company with a promising idea in science or technology, SBIR offers unique opportunities. Awarded by eleven government agencies (see exhibit A5-1), SBIR grants were established

- To stimulate small businesses to participate in technological research

- To utilize small business to meet special federal research needs

- To increase private sector commercialization of research derived from federal research funds

======================= **EXHIBIT A5-1** =======================

Agencies offering SBIR Grants

Department of Agriculture
SBIR Coordinator
USDA-CSRS-CRGO-SBIR
U.S. Department of Agriculture
Justin Smith Morrill Building, Rm. 112
Washington, D.C. 20251

Department of Commerce
Director, Office of Small and Disadvantaged Business Utilization
U.S. Department of Commerce
14th and Constitution Ave., N.W.
Washington, D.C. 20230

NOAA/NESDIS
SPC, Rm. 307
Mail Stop L
Suitland, Md. 20233

Department of Defense
Deputy Director
OSD/SADBU
U.S. Department of Defense
The Pentagon, Rm. 2A340
Washington, D.C. 20301–3061

Department of Education
SBIR Program Coordinator
U.S. Department of Education
555 New Jersey Avenue, N.W., Rm. 602B
Washington, D.C. 20208

Department of Energy
SBIR Spokesperson
c/o SBIR Program Manager
U.S. Department of Energy
Washington, D.C. 20545

Department of Health and Human Services
Director, Office of Small and Disadvantaged Business Utilization
Office of the Secretary
U.S. Department of Health and Human Services
Washington, D.C. 20201

Department of Transportation
Chief, University Research and Technology Innovation Office
(DTS-23)
U.S. Department of Transportation
Transportation Systems Center
Kendall Square
Cambridge, Mass. 02142

Environmental Protection Agency
SBIR Program Manager
Research Grants Staff (RD–675)
Office of Research and Development
Environmental Protection Agency
401 M Street, S.W.
Washington, D.C. 20460

National Aeronautics and Space Administration
Director, SBIR Office—Code IR
National Aeronautics and Space Administration
600 Independence Avenue, S.W.
Washington, D.C. 20546

National Science Foundation
SBIR Program Managers
National Science Foundation
1800 G Street, N.W.
Washington, D.C. 20550

Nuclear Regulatory Commission
SBIR Program Representative
Program Management, Policy Development and Analysis Staff
Office of Nuclear Regulatory Research
U.S. Nuclear Regulatory Commission
Washington, D.C. 20555

The SBIR program accounts for more than six thousand research contracts worth over $600 million since its establishment in 1983. SBIR grants consist of three incremental phases, providing up to $550,000 to develop a single idea:

• Phase One awards up to $50,000 for six months of applied research on a topic of interest to any of eleven government agencies. Phase one is usually a "paper study" that proves a concept is feasible without actually developing a prototype.

- Phase Two awards up to $500,000 for twenty-four months of continued research and development for Phase One projects that the government deems promising. This phase usually generates a prototype that will lead to a commercial product and a *plan* to implement Phase Three—the commercial application of the idea.

- Phase Three monies come from the private sector or, in rare instances, from government small business procurement contracts, and are used to commercialize the new technologies created in Phases One and Two.

QUALIFYING FOR SBIR GRANTS

You can qualify for an SBIR grant if your company meets the government's qualifications for a small business. This means that the business:

- Is independently owned and operated
- Is a for-profit company
- Has 500 or fewer employees
- Is a U.S. company
- Is the primary source of employment (at least twenty hours per week) for the entrepreneur or person who is chiefly responsible for conducting the project

To apply for Phase One, you must first have an idea that coincides with one of the eleven agencies' technological or research needs. Each agency publishes Presolicitation Announcements on a regular basis. (See exhibit A5-2 for topic examples.) To get on the mailing list, contact the agency (see exhibit A5-1 for agency addresses) and request that you be added. If an item in one of these presolicitation announcements sounds like a project you might want to pursue, ask the agency for a more detailed description of the topic and proposal instructions, available in a booklet entitled "Solicitations Contract Proposal." If you require technical information in addition to this one- to two-paragraph synopsis, then ask the agency for more information.

─────────────────── **EXHIBIT A5-2** ───────────────────

SBIR Solicitation Topic Teasers

To give you an idea of the breadth and latitude of potential SBIR grants and contracts, I extracted the following SBIR solicitation research topics from one month's SBIR Pre-solicitation Announcements:

- National Aeronautics and Space Administration: aeronautical propulsion and power; aerodynamics and acoustics; aircraft systems, subsystems, and operations; materials and structures; teleoperators and robotics; human habitability and biology in space; quality assurance, safety, and check-out for ground and space operations
- National Science Foundation: atmospheric sciences; ocean sciences; advance scientific computing; molecular biosciences; earth sciences; chemical, biochemical, and thermal engineering
- U.S. Department of Transportation: passenger/baggage tracking; glass bottle contents verification system; development of an instrument/system to measure, record, and analyze aircraft cockpit visibility; airborne instrumentation for locating radio interference; effects of rotational shifts on operational errors; entrepreneurial and small business participation in mass transit; overhead infrared vehicle detector
- Department of Health and Human Services: biomedical and clinical research on aging, digestive diseases and nutrition, periodontal diseases, test methods for assessing the biological effects of environmental agents, genetics, communicative disorders; (through the National Institutes of Health) employee assistance programs evaluation package on drug abuse and prevention program assessments

THE SBIR PROPOSAL

Now you are ready to prepare your proposal, which must follow—to the letter—the individual agency's guidelines outlined in the "Solicitations Contract Proposal" booklet. However, if you wait until you receive the booklet before beginning work on your proposal, you will probably miss the proposal deadline. I suggest you get a head start by acquiring any number of publications that describe the standard proposal format and evaluation criteria for SBIR proposals. (See exhibit A5-3 for sources of SBIR information.)

Sources of SBIR Information

If you would like more information on SBIR grants, there are a number of good sources:

- The *U.S. Small Business Administration* (1441 L Street, N.W., Rm. 500, Washington, D.C. 20416), or your local SBA office, provides several publications that may help you, including *Proposal Preparation for Small Business Innovation Research.*
- *Local libraries, colleges, and vocational technical institutions* may also provide pamphlets and forms.
- *Accounting firms,* especially large national firms, offer publications on SBIR proposal writing.
- *Individual agency publications* such as the ones cited in this appendix are also obtainable by writing to specific agencies (addresses provided in exhibits A5-1).
- *SBIR mailing list.* You can receive SBIR Presolicitation Announcements by sending your name and address to the Office of Innovation, Research and Technology, U.S. Small Business Administration, 1441 L Street, N.W., Washington, D.C. 20416.

After receiving your proposal, the agency "prescreens" it to determine whether it meets certain basic criteria. Even technicalities such as page length and binding requirements can be reasons for prescreening disqualification. If your proposal passes prescreening, then it will be evaluated for:

- Scientific/technical quality
- The qualifications of the principal investigator
- The anticipated technical and/or economic benefits of the proposed research
- The ability of the Phase One effort to progress toward proving the feasibility of the idea

QUALIFYING FOR PHASE TWO

You can get information on how to prepare Phase Two proposals from your Phase One government project manager during Phase One. Phase Two proposals are usually more comprehensive than Phase One proposals, and are also evaluated by the same criteria as Phase One. In addition, the agency considers how well the applicant has met Phase One objectives by the time the Phase Two proposal has been submitted, and also more carefully analyzes the potential for commercialization of the research. Agencies give extra consideration to proposals that demonstrate a private-sector commitment for Phase Three funding. Your best source of information for preparing Phase Two proposals will probably be your government project manager.

If you think SBIR grants will never apply to you, consider the case of Orville Mott, a weekend computer and electronics hobbyist, who tinkered his way into an SBIR grant. Mott got tired of the time it took to repair his, and his friends', television sets and computers. So he developed a diagnostic computer software program to test his circuit boards to identify bad circuit board components.

Orville's program worked so well, he wondered why he couldn't apply what he had learned to other circuit boards. The government thought it was a good idea, too, and awarded him an SBIR grant (Phase One and then Phase Two) of $550,000 to develop a circuit board component tester. Now the government can inexpensively identify and replace components, instead of replacing an entire circuit board. Who says the government isn't interested in saving money?

And who says SBIR can't help you turn your invention into a commercial success? SBIR could very well be the answer to your search for venture capital.

Appendix 6

Discovering the Trillion-Dollar Market of Construction and Architecture-Engineering Contracts

The fact that our nation's infrastructure is crumbling is hardly new—or good—news to most Americans. But what *may* be good news for small businesses is the way in which this problem translates into billions of dollars of procurement opportunities. (See chapters 2 and 10 for examples of contracting opportunities.)

Since construction and architecture-engineering contracts involve different contracting procedures from the ones we have discussed, it behooves you to understand these variations to take full advantage of the $3.3 trillion worth of procurement opportunities predicted for the 1990s.

CONSTRUCTION CONTRACTS

To comprehend the breadth of this $3.3 trillion market, consider the government's definition of *construction*. More than the construction of buildings, it includes the "construction, alteration, or repair (including dredging, excavating, and painting) of buildings, structures, bridges, dams, highways, streets, sewers, water mains, power lines, railways, canals, channels, and other similar property."

There are two ways you can receive a construction solicitation. First, you can request a solicitation. If the contract is for $25,000 or more, the buying agency must advertise in the *Commerce Business Daily*. Contracts for under $25,000, however, are merely posted at the buying agency and require some personal contact on your part.

The second way to receive a construction solicitation is to get on the bidders' list by submitting a Standard Form 254 to your target agencies. If the contracting officer requires additional information to determine your qualifications, you may be asked to fill out a supplemental Standard Form 255, detailing past experience on similar projects. While not as formal as a preaward survey, this information, coupled with your past performance record, is usually enough to determine your qualifications. (See table A-1 for a summary of construction contracting procedures.) If you want to be considered for international contract awards, send a copy of your SF 254 to the Department of the Army. (See bibliography: *Department of the Army.*)

For all contracts over $100,000 (and for some of lesser amounts), the government will also send prospective bidders a Standard Form 1417, Presolicitation Notice, before sending the solicitation. This notice will include a description of the project, including where to obtain plans, and the deadline for requesting copies of the solicitation.

When a contract opportunity develops, a contracting officer will send solicitations to a selected number of contractors that have submitted an SF 254 on a rotational basis.

Depending on the type and amount of the contract, the government uses two types of solicitations with a description of the project:

• For contracts of $25,000 and over, the agency issues an invitation for bids (IFB sealed-bid soiicitation) or a negotiable Request for Proposal (RFP). Both will include the *range* of the government's estimated cost.

• For contracts of less than $25,000, the agency issues an RFQ.

If you receive an IFB or RFP, prepare and submit your bid according to the standard procedures outlined in chapter 8 and any special instructions included in the solicitation. If you do not care to bid on the solicitation, decline the opportunity in writing, stipulating that you would like to be considered for future solicitations.

With a few exceptions, the government will process and evaluate construction IFBs and RFPs by using the same procedures as for standard contracts. (See exhibit A6-1 for exceptions.) Likewise, the prospective contractor will respond similarly, with one major exception: The bidder must submit a bid bond certification that states he or she will not withdraw the bid. Upon winning the contract, the contractor must furnish a performance bond guaranteeing contract performance by surety(ies) and payment of employee and materials bills.

================ **EXHIBIT A6-1** ================

Construction Contract Idiosyncrasies

Besides procedural differences in the procurement process, construction contracting is subject to some other requirements, which include

• *Inspection.* Bidders may inspect the construction site and examine all government data pertaining to it, including records and plans of previous construction, boring samples, etc. The solicitation will stipulate the time and place for site and data inspection.

• *Construction estimates.* If the projected value of the contract is more than $25,000, the government must prepare its own construction estimate. If the contractor's bid is more than 30 percent higher than the government's estimate, the project must be reexamined and the solicitation reissued to obtain responsive bids.

• *No double awards.* Unless the rule is waived by a higher authority, no construction contract can be awarded to the architecture-engineering firm that designed the project. The rule and its reversal also apply to construction companies.

• *Price adjustments.* Construction contracts include a "differing site conditions" clause that provides for a price adjustment if the contractor discovers that physical conditions at the site differ materially from those described in the contract or from those ordinarily encountered.

• *Subcontracting quotas.* For all contracts of more than $1 million and for designated contracts of any amount, the prime contractor is required to complete from 12 to 20 percent of the work; that is, no more than 80 to 88 percent of the work can be subcontracted.

• *Delinquency assessment.* Contracts may include a "liquidated damages clause," which assesses financial damages to contractors that fail to complete the project on time.

• *Adherence to labor laws.* Labor laws stipulating such things as minimum and overtime wages for employees (Davis-Bacon Act, Contract Work Hours, and Safety Standards Act) or anti-kickback policies (Copeland Act) apply to construction contracts. Equal employment opportunity regulations may also apply. Contact the U.S. Labor Department for information on these laws.

• *Projects completed in such a way as to protect the environment.* This includes not only saving trees and existing vegetation to prevent erosion, but also disposing safely of toxic chemicals such as cleaning solutions and lubricants.

Every construction and architecture-engineering contract for more than $200,000, as well as selected "problem" contracts greater than $10,000, must be evaluated by the agency's contract administrator. The results become a matter of government record, thus establishing a contractor's performance record.

ARCHITECTURE-ENGINEERING CONTRACTS

The procedures governing architecture-engineering contracts vary so much from other procurements that they are considered in a class by themselves. For starters, architecture-engineering contracts do not use the standard competitive bidding procedures, and they do not use IFB or RFP solicitations. If possible, they are usually awarded to firms in the local area of the project.

The government defines architecture-engineering contractors as planners, architects, engineers, consultants, interior designers, and all similar or related professionals. To be considered for an architecture-engineering contract, you must submit a Standard Form 254 to local government purchasing agencies that have the *authority* to issue A + E contracts. For instance, the Army Corps of Engineers not only contracts for its own A + E projects, but it also contracts for other agencies such as the army and air force, and even for selected civilian firms such as flood control and hydroelectric projects. The General Services Administration contracts for other agencies, including many nonmilitary projects such as the design and engineering of federal buildings.

A + E projects of $10,000 or more are advertised the same way as construction contracts. But that's where the similarity ends. (See appendix table A-1 for a description of contracting procedures.) Instead of issuing a *written* IFB or RFP to selected contractors based on standard contract procedures, the agency's evaluation board begins by reviewing all SF 254s and checks any other information available (performance records, evaluations by occupants of buildings designed by the firm).

For contracts estimated at $25,000 and over, the evaluation board conducts oral or written discussions with at least three qualified firms regarding their qualifications, experience, organization, capacity, current work load—virtually any relevant information *except* the fee.

After evaluating the contractors' qualifications, the board recommends *at least* three prospective contractors, in order of preference, to another evaluation board for final selection. Called the selection authority, this higher authority will then rate these three contractors in order of preference and forward the findings to the contracting officer. (See exhibit A6-2 for a list of evaluation criteria.) The only exception to this evaluation procedure is contracts of $10,000 or less. These contractors are selected by the agency head from the evaluation board's recommended list—without a higher selection authority's review.

EXHIBIT A6-2

Evaluation Points for A + E Contracts

Since A + E contracts are not awarded on the basis of standard competitive bidding procedures, it is important to know the evaluation board's selection criteria. The board considers

- Professional qualifications necessary for satisfactory performance of the project
- *Specialized* experience of the firm in the type of work required
- Capacity of the firm to accomplish the work in the required time
- Past performance and experience (if any—none is required) on other civilian and/or government agency contracts
- Location of the firm in the geographical area of the project, *if* there are an appropriate number of local qualified firms for consideration
- Government cost estimates (for contracts projected to exceed $25,000)
- Volume of work previously awarded by the agency to the firm—the goal being to distribute contracts equitably among qualified architecture-engineering firms, including small businesses and small disadvantaged businesses and firms that have not had prior agency contracts

---

Negotiation, the last step in the selection process, begins when the contracting officer requests a proposal from the highest-rated firm. If the contracting officer cannot negotiate a satisfactory contract with the first firm, then the same procedure will be followed with the second-rated firm, and so on until a satisfactory agreement is reached.

The rewards of A + E contracts are well worth the effort of learning how to compete in these markets. The future needs in these two areas are so phenomenal, in fact, that once you establish yourself as a reputable contractor actively seeking contract work, you will be well on your way to winning some long-term government business.

TABLE A6-1.
ARCHITECTURE/SERVICES AND CONSTRUCTION FORMS

Contract Value	Bidders Required	Type Solicitation	Advertisement	Solicit Form	Contract Form	Contract Types
Supplies & Services						
<$25,000	3	Verbal/RFQ	None	DD 1155	DD 1155	FFP
>$25,000	3	RFP/IFB	CBD	SF 33	SF 33	FFP
Construction						
<$25,000	3	Verbal/RFQ	None	DD 1155	DD 1155	FFP
>$25,000	>3	RFP/IFB	CBD	SF 1442	SF 1442	FFP

Common Forms for Both Construction Categories

SF 254 (Architect-Engineer and Related Service Questionnaire). SF 254 is a 7-page document that establishes the types of contracts the company has completed in its last 30 representative jobs.

SF 255 (Architect-Engineer and Related Services Questionnaire). SF 255 is an 11-page document to establish technical skills available in the company for proposed projects.

SF 24   (Bid Bond). Provides documentation with a bond to guarantee that the bidder doesn't withdraw the bid at the last minute (or else the bidder forfeits the bond).

SF 25   (Performance Bond). Provides documentation with a bond to guarantee the performance of the contractor (or else the bidder forfeits the bond).

SF 25A (Payment Bond). Provides documentation with a bond that guarantees the contractor will pay labor and materials bills. This avoids construction-related lawsuits.

Appendix 7

A Summary of Federal Acquisition Regulations (*FAR*) Topics

Subchapter A—General

1. Federal Acquisition Regulations System
2. Definitions of Words and Terms
3. Improper Business Practices and Personal Conflicts of Interest
4. Administrative Matters

Subchapter B—Competition and Acquisition Planning

5. Publicizing Contract Actions
6. Competition Requirements
7. Acquisition Planning
8. Required Sources of Supplies and Services
9. Contractor Qualifications
10. Specifications, Standards, and Other Purchase Descriptions
11. Acquisition and Distribution of Commercial Products
12. Contract Delivery or Performance

Subchapter C—Contracting Methods and Contract Types

13. Small Purchase and Other Simplified Purchase Procedures
14. Sealed Bidding
15. Contracting by Negotiation
16. Types of Contracts
17. Special Contracting Methods
18. Reserved

Subchapter D—Socioeconomic Programs

19. Small Business and Small Disadvantaged Business Concerns
20. Labor Surplus Area Concerns

21. Reserved
22. Application of Labor Laws to Government Acquisitions
23. Environment, Conservation, and Occupational Safety
24. Protection of Privacy and Freedom of Information
25. Foreign Acquisition
26. Reserved

Subchapter E—General Contracting Requirements

27. Patents, Data, and Copyrights
28. Bonds and Insurance
29. Taxes
30. Cost Accounting Standards
31. Contract Cost Principles and Procedures
32. Contract Financing
33. Protests, Disputes, and Appeals

Subchapter F—Special Categories of Contracting

34. Major System Acquisition
35. Research and Development Contracting
36. Construction and Architect-Engineer Contracts
37. Service Contracting
38. Federal Supply Schedule Contracting
39. Management, Acquisition, and Use of Information Resources
40. Reserved
41. Reserved

Subchapter G—Contract Management

42. Contract Administration
43. Contract Modifications
44. Subcontracting Policies and Procedures
45. Government Property
46. Quality Assurance
47. Transportation
48. Value Engineering
49. Termination of Contracts
50. Extraordinary Contractual Actions
51. Use of Government Sources by Contractors
52. Solicitation Provisions and Contract Clauses
53. Forms

Appendix 8

How to Prepare an Unsolicited Proposal

YOU WANT UNCLE SAM!

Occasionally a small business or individual has a useful product or service that the government does not solicit. This occurs particularly for products that are not commercially available, such as new inventions or unique services.

My friend Karen Cook, a scriptwriter, recently pursued this relatively untapped market after she told me about a script on dog-bite prevention she had completed for a local utility company. The company had intended to produce it to train their meter readers, but at the last minute funding fell through. The company paid Karen for the script and reassigned the copyright to her.

"It's such a wasted effort," she complained.

"Why not try to sell it to the federal government?" I suggested.

"Why would *they* want it?" she asked.

"Maybe the U.S. Postal Service could use it to train mail carriers," I said.

You can guess the rest. There were no solicitations for Karen's unique script, and she was ready to give up when I suggested submitting an unsolicited proposal. Karen is now eagerly awaiting the Postal Service's response.

Perhaps, like Karen, you have a unique product or service that you think the government—or a prime contractor—might need. If after researching the market you discover that your product or service is not being solicited, you should consider submitting an unsolicited proposal to the agency you think will be interested.

Before you write your proposal, call an official at your targeted agency or prime contractor to confirm that it might require your product or service. Then request written instructions on its policies and procedures for preparing an unsolicited proposal.

PREPARING AN UNSOLICITED PROPOSAL

While there is no standard format for an unsolicited proposal, *FAR* states that it should contain the following:

Basic Information

- Offerer's name and address, type of organization, and small business status
- Names and telephone numbers of technical and business personnel to contact for evaluation or negotiation purposes
- Identification of proprietary data (to be used only for evaluation purposes)
- Names of other federal, state, and local agencies receiving the proposal or funding the proposed effort
- Date of submission
- Signature of person authorized to sign the offer obligating the small business

Technical Information

- Concise title or proposal
- A 200-word abstract (summary) describing the proposed effort
- A complete presentation of the effort's objectives, method of approach, and extent; the nature and extent of the anticipated results; and the manner in which the work will support the agency's mission
- Names and biographical information of key personnel
- Type of technical or other nonfinancial support needed from the agency

Support Information

- Proposed price or total estimated cost
- Period for which the proposal is valid
- Type of contract preferred
- Proposed duration of the effort
- Brief description of your organization, experience, and facilities
- Signed affidavits on applicable security clearances, environmental impacts, and any "organizational" conflicts (for example, a conflict of interest would be the submission of an unsolicited proposal for a project or product you are already producing for the government)

EVALUATION OF THE UNSOLICITED PROPOSAL

Generally, an unsolicited proposal is evaluated by whether or not the product/service or proposal:

- Is innovative and unique
- Has been independently originated and developed by the offerer (this includes a project or service devised in response to publicized *general statements,* such as those advertised in the "Sources Sought" section of the *Commerce Business Daily*)
- Has been prepared without government supervision
- Contains sufficient detail to prove that the product or service can benefit the agency's research and development and/or other mission responsibilities
- Is not available by competitive methods

FOLLOW UP

After you submit your unsolicited proposal, call the agency within seven days to verify that it has been received. Even though the agency's written instructions should say when you will be notified of a decision, reverify the date by which you will learn whether you have received a contract award.

If your targeted agency rejects your proposal, don't give up. There may be another agency that will be interested. With the exception of the SBIR grant program, most agencies accept unsolicited proposals. So if your product or service is unique and fulfills a government need, there should be a government agency that is interested in your proposal. The government awards contracts for unsolicited proposals all the time.

A List of *Commerce Business Daily* Federal Supply Group, Services, and Construction Codes

These codes are used for locating advertisements in the *Commerce Business Daily*. Alphabetical codes are used for services and construction industries, and numerical codes (the first two digits of the FSC number) are for commodity groups of the Federal Supply Classification.

Services and Construction Indexes
A. Experimental development
F. Natural resources management
G. Social services
H. Expert and consultant services, quality control, and inspections
J. Maintenance, repair, and rebuilding of equipment
K. Modification of equipment
L. Technical representative services
M. Operation and/or maintenance of government-owned facility
N. Installation of equipment
O. Funeral and chaplain services
P. Salvage services
Q. Medical services
R. Professional, technical, and management services
S. Housekeeping services (includes utilities)
T. Photographic mapping, printing, and publication services
U. Training services
V. Transportation and travel services
W. Lease or rental of equipment (except transportation)
X. Miscellaneous
Y. Construction of structures and facilities
Z. Maintenance, repair, and alterations of real property

Federal Supply Group (FSG) Indexes

10. Weapons
11. Nuclear ordnance
12. Fire control systems
13. Ammunition and explosives
14. Guided missiles
15. Aircraft and air-frame structural components
16. Aircraft components and accessories
17. Aircraft launching, landing, and ground-handling equipment
18. Space vehicles
19. Ships, small craft, pontoons, and floating docks
20. Ship and marine equipment
21. Reserved
22. Railway equipment
23. Ground effect vehicles, motor vehicles, trailers, and cycles
24. Tractors
25. Vehicular equipment and components
26. Tires and tubes
27. Reserved
28. Engines, turbines, and components
29. Engine accessories
30. Mechanical power-transmission equipment
31. Bearings
32. Woodworking machinery and equipment
33. Reserved
34. Metalworking machinery
35. Service and trade equipment
36. Special industry machinery
37. Agricultural machinery and equipment
38. Construction, mining, excavating, and highway maintenance equipment
39. Materials handling equipment
40. Rope, cable, chain, and fittings
41. Refrigeration, air-conditioning, and air-circulating equipment
42. Fire-fighting, rescue, and safety equipment
43. Pumps and compressors
44. Furnace, steam plant, drying equipment, and nuclear reactors
45. Plumbing, heating, and sanitation equipment
46. Water purification and sewage treatment equipment
47. Pipe, tubing, hose and fittings
48. Valves
49. Maintenance repair shop equipment

50. Reserved
51. Hand tools
52. Measuring tools
53. Hardware and abrasives
54. Prefabricated structures and scaffolding
55. Lumber, millwork, plywood, and veneer
56. Construction and building materials
57. Reserved
58. Reserved
59. Electrical and electronic equipment components
60. Fiber optics
61. Electric wire and power and distribution equipment
62. Lighting fixtures and lamps
63. Alarm, signal, and security detection systems
64. Reserved
65. Medical, dental, and veterinary equipment and supplies
66. Instruments and laboratory equipment
67. Photographic equipment
68. Chemicals and chemical products
69. Training aids and devices
70. General-purpose automatic data processing equipment
71. Furniture
72. Household and commercial furnishings and appliances
73. Food preparation and serving equipment
74. Office machines, test processing and visible record equipment
75. Office supplies and devices
76. Books, maps, and other publications
77. Musical instruments, phonographs, and home-type radios
78. Recreational and athletic equipment
79. Cleaning equipment and supplies
80. Brushes, paints, sealers, and adhesives
81. Containers, packaging, and packing supplies
82. Reserved
83. Textiles, leather, furs, shoes, tests, and flags
84. Clothing, individual equipment, and insignias
85. Toiletries
86. Reserved
87. Agricultural supplies
88. Live animals
89. Subsistence
90. Reserved
91. Fuels, lubricants, oils, and waxes

92. Reserved
93. Nonmetallic fabricated materials
94. Nonmetallic crude materials
95. Metal bars, sheets, and shapes
96. Ores, minerals, and their primary products
97. Reserved
98. Reserved
99. Miscellaneous

Appendix 10

Sample Quality Manual*

This Aid presents a sample quality control system closely prepared from one developed by Honeywell Inc., Minneapolis, Minnesota. It may be used as a guide in initiating your own quality assurance system, whether you sell to consumers, industrial users, or government.

A SAMPLE MANUAL

Introduction

This manual describes for our employees and customers our quality control system. The system applies both to the items we produce and to the items we buy from our suppliers.

As dictated by the complexity of product design, manufacturing techniques used, and customer requirements, more specific written procedures may be required to implement the policies set in this manual.

No changes may be made to this manual or any supplementary quality control procedures unless approved by the plant manager or an authorized representative.

Table of Contents

* Taken from the Small Business Administration's Aid #243, *Setting Up a Quality Control System*, U.S. Government Printing Office: 1979, 0-297-068.

Assembly Inspection and Functional Testing   8.0
Faulty (Discrepant) Material Control   10.0
Tool and Guage Control   11.0
Overrun Stock Control   12.0
Packing and Shipping   13.0
Identification   14.0
Appendix A   Organization Chart   (PAGE 7 of this Aid shows the
                                         organization described in the
                                         sample manual.)

Appendix B   Purchase Order Form
Appendix C   Inspection Data Form   Each company should use its
                                         own forms for the Appendices.

Appendix D   Identification Tags
Appendix E   Travel Card

1.0 Scope

1.1   The quality control system includes: receiving, identifying, stocking
      and issuing parts and material; all manufacturing processes; pack-
      ing; storing; and shipping.
1.2   The system is designed to ensure customer satisfaction through qual-
      ity control management of supplies made and services performed
      here, and by our suppliers at their facilities. It is designed to spot
      processing problems early so we can correct them before we've pro-
      duced a lot of faulty items.
1.3   Written inspection and test procedures will be prepared to supple-
      ment drawings and other specifications, as necessary.

2.0 Responsibilities

2.1   The supervisor of quality assurance reports directly to the plant
      manager.
2.2   The quality assurance supervisor's responsibilities include:
      2.2.1   Planning how to meet customers' quality requirements.
      2.2.2   Reviewing customer drawings and specifications.
      2.2.3   Determining inspection points.
      2.2.4   Writing inspection and test instructions.
      2.2.5   Establishing (and making sure employees follow) the most
              effective and efficient quality assurance procedures possible.
      2.2.6   Keeping adequate quality assurance records.
      2.2.7   Reviewing quality assurance records and overseeing follow-
              up for correction and prevention of defects.
      2.2.8   Assuring that our suppliers' quality control and follow-up are
              adequate.

2.2.9 Inspecting all special and standard gages, test equipment, and tooling used to manufacture products when we acquire them and calibrating them on a regularly scheduled basis.

2.2.10 Coordinating in-plant correction of items rejected by customers, explaining to customers what action will be taken, and evaluating the actions for effectiveness.

2.2.11 Making sure inspectors make unbiased decisions to accept or reject items.

3.0   Purchase Order Control

3.1   All of our purchase orders to suppliers must be approved by the plant manager or an authorized representative.

3.2   When the purchase order is released, our buyer will send our supplier all required drawings, specifications, and other customer requirements (such as material or process certifications, physical or chemical analysis, source inspection) with the purchase order.

3.3   If there is a drawing or specification change after our order is placed with the supplier, our buyer will send the supplier a purchase order change, including our latest Engineering change and the latest drawings or other specifications.

3.4   Copies of all purchase orders will be kept on file for our customers to review.

4.0   Drawing and Specification Change Control

4.1   We manufacture to customer drawings and specifications. Sets of these are filed in job number folders in Production Control files.

4.2   Production Control is responsible for charging out and keeping track of drawings and specifications.

4.3   The Sales Department receives Engineering changes from our customers and is responsible for sending these changes to Production Control immediately.

4.4   Production Control is responsible for issuing the latest Engineering changes, drawings, and specifications to departments that need them and for voiding outdated Engineering changes, drawings, and specifications.

4.5   A standard procedure will be set up to control changes by effective date or serial/lot number.

5.0   Receiving Inspection

5.1   All parts and materials will be received and logged in by the Receiving Department.

5.2 All parts and materials will be sent to Receiving Inspection after logging in.

5.3 Receiving Inspection will assure that proper certification, physical and chemical test data, special process certifications, or source inspection certifications are with the items to be inspected.

5.4 The receiving inspector must document the complete results of all inspections and tests.

5.5 Inspection will identify accepted lots and send them to stock.

5.6 Rejected lots will be identified and set aside in Receiving Inspection until the buyer and Production Control decide on disposition.

5.7 The Receiving Department will send a copy of each rejection report to the Purchasing Department and the supplier.

5.8 The Purchasing Department has the responsibility of assuring that a pattern of continually receiving faulty items from any supplier doesn't develop and assuring supplier corrective action.

5.9 The Quality Department will follow up to see that a supplier who has sent us items we reject has effectively corrected what it has been doing wrong.

5.10 Receiving Inspection instructions will be written with consideration given to the complexity of the parts, material received, and customer requirements. Follow customer instructions (if any) for inspection.

5.11 Sample according to customer requirements (if any) or MIL-STD-105D (available from Superintendent of Documents, Washington, DC 20402).

5.12 The Quality Department will review Receiving Inspection records periodically to see if any suppliers are consistently failing to meet standards.

5.13 All inspection records will show the number inspected, the number rejected, and the name of the inspector.

5.14 Inspection records will also show the disposition of supplier-provided records and data.

6.0 Raw Material Control

6.1 Raw materials, bar stock, sheet stock, and castings will be marked so they can be traced to their certification, and stored in an area apart from the normal flow of in-process material.

6.2 Copies of all certifications will be filed in the job order number folder by job order number and available for customer review.

6.3 Only raw material accepted by Receiving Inspection will be released for production.

6.4 Certified stock will be issued from its storage area only for job order requirements.

6.5 Verification of suppliers' certifications will be ordered from independent testing laboratories when deemed necessary by the Quality Department or to meet our customers' requirements.

6.6 All certifications will be traceable to purchase order, date of receipt of the material, and the inspector of the material.

7.0 In-Process Inspection

7.1 The Quality Department will make first piece inspection after set up is completed and approved by Production.

7.2 No production runs will be made until first piece inspection is accepted.

7.3 After first piece inspection acceptance, in-process inspections will be made by the Quality Department at intervals adequate for early detection of processes producing material that doesn't meet standards.

7.4 The Quality Department will keep records of all first piece and in-process inspections.

7.5 The inspection records will be stored in the job number folder and will be available for customer review.

7.6 Tag or otherwise identify rejected items and move them to an area apart from the normal flow of in-process materials.

7.7 The Quality Department will follow up to prevent recurrence of faulty material.

7.8 Inspection records will list: the number of pieces accepted, the number rejected, kind of defects and basic causes of rejection, date of inspection, and the inspector's name.

7.9 Attachment ——— shows the locations of fabrication and inspection stations. For each station, it lists the types of items subject to inspection, the kind of inspection done, and the applicable drawings and specifications.

7.10 Special processes will require appropriate inspections and controls, including qualification and certification of personnel and equipment.

8.0 Assembly Inspection and Functional Testing

8.1 Production personnel will make assembly inspections and do functional testing, as required.

8.2 The Quality Department will check functional tests under an established sampling plan.

8.3 The Quality Department will keep the inspection records.

8.4 The inspection records will be kept in the job number folder and will be available for customer review.

8.5 All faulty (discrepant) assemblies will be marked and set apart so they won't be accidentally used.

8.6 The Quality Department will initiate corrective and follow-up action to prevent recurrence of faulty material.

8.7 Inspection records will list: the number accepted, the number rejected, the date of the inspection, and the inspector's name.

9.0   Final Inspection and Testing

9.1 Final inspection and tests will be performed either on 100 percent or on a sample of the items. The number of items sampled will depend on the complexity of the items and customer requirements. Inspection will follow customer-supplied procedures, when available, or MIL-STD-105D.

9.2 Each end item will be inspected/tested 100 percent, unless the customer asks otherwise.

9.3 The Quality Department will keep all final inspection and test records.

9.4 Inspection and test records will be filed in the job number folder and will be available for customer review.

9.5 The Quality Department will follow up to see that processes producing faulty materials are corrected and to prevent recurrence of faulty material from those processes.

9.6 All faulty material will be marked and set apart from the normal flow of finished material.

9.7 Faulty material will not be shipped to the customer without specific customer instructions to submit such nonconforming material.

9.8 Rejected material which has been repaired, reworked, or sorted must be resubmitted to final inspection to make sure it meets requirements.

9.9 Inspection records will list: the number of pieces accepted, the number rejected, the date of inspection, and the inspector's name.

10.0   Faulty (Discrepant) Material Control

10.1 All faulty (nonconforming) material, supplies, or parts will be placed in a "DO NOT USE" area. The items will be clearly marked with job number, part number, revision letter, lot size, defect, inspector's name, and any other information necessary.

10.2 The specific reason an item(s) has been rejected will be clearly written on a rejection tag attached to each part or container.

10.3 No one may remove items from the "DO NOT USE" area until disposition is determined by a Material Review Board made up of the plant manager and representatives of the Production and Quality Departments.

10.4 Nonconforming material will not be shipped unless the customer's buyer approves it. The shipping documents will be marked with what's wrong with the items.

10.5 The Quality Department will control all lots submitted for acceptance inspection. Each lot will be kept as a unit, apart from other lots, and out of the normal flow of material.

10.6 During the processing of material all production and inspection operations must be kept in proper order. Each step must be completed before the next step is begun.

10.7 The Quality Department will set up a system so that the stage of inspection each item is in can easily be identified.

10.8 Unidentified material will be taken out of the normal flow of production until it is inspected to insure that it meets all specifications.

10.9 Reworked material will be segregated from other material until the Quality Department determines its status.

11.0   Tool and Gage Control

11.1 All special tools, jigs, fixtures, gages, and measuring equipment must be properly identified.

11.2 Each new or reworked tool, jig, fixture, gage, and item of measuring equipment will be inspected before issue for use.

11.3 All gages, measuring and test equipment will be calibrated to standards set by the National Bureau of Standards.

11.4 A written schedule for calibrating gages, measuring and test equipment will be set and strictly followed. Frequency of calibration will be based on type and purpose of the equipment and severity of usage.

11.5 A restricted area for storing and calibrating gages, measuring, and test equipment will be set up.

11.5.1 A strict system of issue, control, and return will be set and followed.

11.6 If the customer supplies special gages, they will be checked at the intervals the customer sets. If the customer supplies no inspection schedule, the equipment will be checked according to a schedule that takes into account type, purpose, and severity of use.

11.7 Calibration will follow the written procedures kept in the calibration area.

11.8   Obsolete or out-of-service tools and gages will be tagged.

11.9   Decals or stickers will be put on tools and gages or their containers to show the last date of calibration and the due date of the next calibration.

11.10   Personal, as well as company-owned production and inspection tools, must be properly and regularly calibrated.

12.0   Overrun Stock Control

12.1   The Quality Department will oversee overrun stock.

12.2   The Quality Department will insure that any overrun parts sent to stock are properly marked "accepted." The part number, latest drawing number and specification revision, date of inspection, job number, and quantity of parts will be shown. The Quality Department will periodically check to see that the parts are properly packed to prevent deterioration and damage.

12.3   No overrun parts will be shipped to a customer until they are reinspected and found in acceptable condition and to meet the latest drawing and specification revisions.

13.0   Packing and Shipping

13.1   No order will be shipped to a customer until all shipping papers are stamped or signed and dated by the final inspector.

13.2   No order will be shipped until all required certifications, test reports, special samples, etc. have been packed with the material in accordance with the customer's requirements and accepted by the final inspector.

13.3   All material will be packed to prevent damage, deterioration, and substitution.

13.4   The customer will be identified on the packaging, parts, and as otherwise necessary to prevent lost and misdirected shipments.

13.5   The order will be packed as directed by the customer, if applicable.

14.0   Identification

14.1   All materials and articles will be identified by a basic part number and revision letter.

14.2   Critical materials and articles will also carry a serial or lot number. If required, a list of materials and articles by identification numbers will be attached.

Appendix 11

How to Read a Solicitation and Contract

The following is a summary of the sections of the uniform contract format, used for both solicitations and contracts. Once you know what to expect in these thirteen sections, you should have no trouble submitting a responsive bid or proposal.

PART I. THE SCHEDULE

The Schedule explains the solicitation's specifications and requirements. While much of this section's information is standardized, it also includes information that is individualized for each procurement and blank spaces for the prospective contractor's response to the government. Generally, this section includes the following information:

Section A. Solicitation/Contract Form

The Solicitation/Contract Form is actually a Standard Form 33—the cover sheet and first page of the solicitation. The first page summarizes the proposal, providing information such as:

- A table of contents
- The time, date, and place for the bid opening or proposal acceptance
- Blank spaces for the *legally empowered* contractor and contracting officer to sign/countersign the bid or offer
- A blank space for the bidder to record the acceptance period during which the bid or proposal is valid (the standard response is sixty days, unless otherwise noted in the solicitation)
- A blank space that the offerer must sign to acknowledge any solicitation amendments
- A blank for the contractor to record any prompt-payment discounts for the government. (Since discounts are not considered in evaluating a bid or proposal and the government is required to pay within thirty days of

receiving a qualified invoice, I can't imagine why anyone would offer the government such a discount.)

- Bid or proposal submission requirements (including the deadline and location)
- A blank to indicate your reason for nonresponse if you decide not to make a bid or offer

Section B. Supplies or Services and Prices/Costs

This section includes

- A brief, "line-item" description of the item(s) or service(s) being procured, with corresponding blanks for the contractor to enter unit price(s)
- Quantities being procured
- Government-required marking information and delivery schedules
- Blanks for contractor's proposed delivery schedule (RFP only; see section F for information on how to respond)
- An explanation that clauses and provisions from *FAR* and the DOD *FAR* supplement are incorporated in the solicitation by reference number only, and that they will be as legally binding as if they were included in their entirety. (See part II, section I of the solicitation for information on referenced clauses.)

Section C. Description/Specifications/Work Statements

This section provides a detailed numerical reference to production drawings or specifications that the contractor may send for or that may be attached to the solicitation. Do not assume, however, that the referenced specifications listing is inclusive, since the drawings often reference other documents not included in the listing.

Section D. Packaging, Packing, and Marking Requirements

Packaging, packing, and marking requirements are detailed in this section, including a listing of referenced FAR clauses. In order to understand the detailed levels of packaging, you may need to send to the superintendent of documentation in Washington, D.C., for the military standards (MIL-STD-794) that detail these requirements.

Section E. Inspection and Acceptance

Section E specifies inspection and acceptance locations and requirements for items or services. Specifically, the government will state sampling criteria, first-article test requirements, and the special requirements that inspection programs must have to meet product standards, such as testing the first five items to come off a continuous production line.

Section F. Deliveries or Performance

In this section the government states the delivery or performance schedule, location, and shipping method. It says that "offerers that propose delivery that will not clearly fall within the applicable required delivery period specified above, will be considered non-responsive and rejected in the case of an IFB and may be rejected in the case of an RFP." In the case of an IFB this clause reiterates that a contracting officer cannot negotiate delivery terms with the seller. But in the case of an RFP the clause opens the possibility of negotiation.

For example, if you cannot meet the government's required delivery schedule, you might call the contracting officer, and if necessary the SBA, and ask for consideration of a partial award. A partial award allows you to perform on part of the procurement and/or extend the delivery on a portion of the procurement. Even if you cannot meet the required schedule, submit your best schedule. Partial awards are made every day—especially to small businesses.

The scheduled delivery date listed in this section is established relative to the assumed award date (five days after the government sends the contract). *If either the award date or contract receipt is delayed, the delivery schedule may be adjusted accordingly—provided you correctly document the government-caused delay.* If one of these delays occurs, *immediately* send a copy of the late-arriving contract cover page (Standard Form 26 or 33) to the contract office, the SBA, DCASMA, and anyone else listed on the cover page. Boldly note on the page when you received it (use a date/time stamp if you have one). Also state that while you will perform on the contract, the production status records should be changed to reflect a revised delivery date so that you will not be penalized for a government delay.

This section also explains procedures for transportation or transit credits (wherein the contractor's shipment costs are rebilled to and paid by the government) and the maximum/minimum shipping weights and dimensions. Read these clauses carefully, because they explain the most economical shipment method. If you do not comply with these recommended shipping procedures, you will be billed for the cost difference.

Section G. Contract Administration Data

An explanation of accounting and appropriations computer codes is presented in this section, as well as an explanation of DCAS contract administration assignments and other information stipulating how the government will administer or monitor the contract. (See chapter 9 for a detailed discussion of contract administration.)

Section H. Special Contract Requirements

This section includes any specialized provisions that may apply to the procurement, ranging from information on economic price adjustments or multiyear contracts; to documentation required for inspection, insurance, contract work hours, labor disputes, and handling of hazardous materials; to government distribution of DD 250 receiving reports.

PART II. CONTRACT CLAUSES

Section I. Contract Clauses

Section I provides the sequential listing of *referenced FAR* clauses and agency amendments. Look up complete clauses in your copy of *FAR*, section 52. (See bibliography: *Federal Acquisition Regulations* for ordering information.) If you do not have a copy of *FAR*, locate a copy at your local library, small business development center, or nearest DCAS office. Photocopy applicable clauses to study. (Some agencies provide a one-time free photocopy service of clauses for your review.)

PART III. LIST OF DOCUMENTS, EXHIBITS, AND OTHER ATTACHMENTS

Section J. List of Documents, Exhibits, and Other Attachments

Here you will find a listing of all the documents that are too long to be included easily in the solicitation. When you receive your IFB or RFP, check this section to confirm that you have all of these attachments.

PART IV. REPRESENTATIONS AND INSTRUCTIONS

Section K. Representations, Certifications, and Other Statements

Section K—and L and M following—appear in the solicitation, but appear in the subsequent contract only by reference.

Representations, certifications, and other statements refer to documentation that the contractor must complete to establish eligibility for the contract award. After completing all certifications for one contract, a contractor need only check off the blocks on subsequent contracts. Certifications may confirm such items as:

- Size of the business
- Qualification as disadvantaged, minority, or other special status
- Fulfillment of the government's requirements of an "authorized" dealer or manufacturer as stipulated in the Walsh-Healey Law (see bibliography: *Major Laws Administered by U.S. Department of Labor*)
- Certification that a contingency fee will not be paid to any broker or person outside your company contingent upon your winning a contract
- Notification that you have ever filed any equal opportunity compliance reports (for suspected infractions) or have ever been listed on the Environmental Protection Agency List of Violating Facilities
- Certification that you buy American supplies
- Acknowledgment that you have read all the amendments of laws relating to government procurement
- Certification that you will use precision components for certain manufacturing processes procured in the U.S.
- The address of the manufacturing facility producing the product being procured
- The product weight, dimension, and method of shipment so that the buyer can calculate freight shipments as part of the total cost (for evaluating the bid)
- Name of parent company (if applicable) and identifying data and sales history for the division or subsidiary supplying the procurement

Make sure you understand the meaning of every certification, because failure to comply may result not only in termination for default but also in charges of misrepresentation or fraud. If you do not understand a certification, look it up in *FAR* or ask the contracting officer.

Section L. Instructions and Conditions, and Notices to Bidders (or Offerers)

Here the government instructs the contractor on how to prepare the bid (or proposal) and explains various situations and conditions that may affect the submission, including:

- The use of government materials and property for production of government items and services

- Government procedures for handling late submissions, modifications, and withdrawals
- Affiliated or joint bidders, such as two or more bidders joining to provide all of the items on the solicitation; in this situation the government requires clear identification of assigned responsibility for each item or service
- Shipping instructions
- Factors that may be monitored if a preaward survey is required
- Terms for accepting bids submitted by telegraph or bids proposing alternate conditions
- The addresses of the offices providing specifications and drawings incorporated by reference
- Terms for authorizing progress payments (see appendix 12 for a discussion of progress payments)
- Any other applicable notices and instructions

Section M. Evaluation Factors for Award

Section M stipulates the proportional importance of the methods that the government uses to select the contractor for this procurement. Besides the "lowest cost," other factors might include transportation costs, the rental cost paid to the government for government-supplied tools or test equipment, and proposed prices bid for additional (optional) buys that the government might want. For RFPs, the government may also list technical or managerial factors that will be evaluated along with the cost. The government is not allowed to evaluate individual solicitations using criteria other than what is listed in this section.

Appendix 12

Procuring Progress Payments: Using the Government to Finance Your Contract

If you are a small business bidding on an IFB or an RFP fixed-price contract extending over four months and for $100,000 (more than $1 million for large businesses), you may be eligible for progress payments. Progress payments allow the contractor to be paid an interest-free percentage of contract costs before delivery, as those costs are incurred. The percentage is usually 90 percent of incurred costs for small businesses and 80 percent for large businesses.

Before you are eligible for progress payments, the government must first make sure your accounting system can segregate and account for contract costs.

The time to ask for progress payments is before the contract is issued. If your procurement is a negotiated RFP, simply ask if progress payments can be included during the negotiation interval. If the solicitation is an IFB, you should check section L carefully to see if progress payments are authorized. If they are not mentioned, ask the contracting officer if they are authorized, and proceed according to the officer's instructions. If you make your IFB offer contingent upon progress payments that are not allowed, you will be disqualified for nonresponsiveness.

See *FAR* subpart 32.5 for further information.

Bibliography

The name of the publication is followed by the address at which it can be ordered. If the Superintendent of Documents is the major supplier, see that listing for the address. Those books known or thought to have a cost are preceded by an asterisk. Agencies are increasingly charging a price for them as the volume demand keeps rising.

The Superintendent of Documents (U.S. Government Printing Office, Washington, D.C. 20402) maintains a catalog of documents available and the price of each. To obtain the latest list of documents and prices, call 1–202–783–3238 and ask for the current catalog, or check with your local public library.

Aerospace Material Specifications
Microfiche SAE, Customer Service Department, Publications Group
400 Commonwealth Drive
Warrendale, Pa. 15096

Air Force Prime Contractors, AFCMD 70-3
Small Business Office
Air Force Contract Management Division
Kirkland Air Force Base, N.M. 87117

Alphabetical/Numerical Cross-Reference Procurement List
Identifies federal stock classes for product/service names. Published by individual buying activities—no central source known.
DLAs available from DLA, Cameron Station, Alexandria, Va. 22314. AFLCs available from all Air Logistics Centers

Architect-Engineer Contracts, EP 715-1-4
U.S. Army Corps of Engineers
Office of Chief of Engineers
20 Massachusetts Avenue, N.W.
Washington, D.C. 20314-1000

Automated Item Description Extraction (AIDE)
Computer-extracted description of items and related data. Published by individual buying agencies.

Basic Guide to Exporting, A
  U.S. Department of Commerce
  International Trade Administration
  Superintendent of Documents

Bidders' List Catalog, OCALC/PMXDM
  Oklahoma City Air Logistics Center
  Tinker AFB, Okla. 73145

Business America—The Magazine of International Trade
  U.S. Department of Commerce (biweekly)
  Superintendent of Documents

Catalog of Available Forms and Publications
  Superintendent of Documents

Catalog of Federal/Domestic Grant Programs
  Superintendent of Documents

Commerce Business Daily (Information)
  Call the Superintendent of Documents

Competition Catalog, Competition and Pricing Office
  Defense Industrial Supply Center (DISC-PV)
  700 Robins Avenue
  Philadelphia, Pa. 19111-5096

Competition: Hit List
  DGSC-PAC
  Defense General Supply Center
  Richmond, Va. 23297-5000

Construction/Architect Evaluations and Performance Histories
  Office, Chief Engineer, Attn.: DAEN-PR
  Paulaski Building
  Washington, D.C. 20314

Contracting and Acquisition Unsolicited Proposal Guide
  Department of the Air Force, AFSC Pamphlet 70-5
  Headquarters, Air Force Systems Command
  Wright-Patterson Air Force Base
  Dayton, OH 45433

Contracting Opportunities with GSA
  U.S. General Services Administration
  75 Spring St., S.W.
  Atlanta, Ga. 30303

Contract Management Engineering Manual for DLA, DLAM 4800.2
   DLA, Cameron Station
   Alexandria, Va. 22314

Defense Logistics Agency Handbooks, HB–4/HB–8
   (Cross References; Contractors to Manufacturers Federal Codes)
   Defense Logistics Services Center
   DLA, Cameron Station
   Alexandria, Va. 22314

Defense Logistics Studies Information Exchange (DLSIE)
   U.S. Army Logistics Management Center
   Fort Lee, Va. 23801-6043

Defense Standardization Manual, M200
   Superintendent of Documents

Department of Defense, Index of Specifications and Standards, DOD-ISS
   Superintendent of Documents

Department of Defense Single Point, DOD-SSP
   (Specifications and Standards)
   Naval Publications and Forms Center
   5801 Tabor Avenue
   Philadelphia, Pa. 19120

Department of the Army—Central Listing of Construction Contractors
   North Pacific Division
   Army Corps of Engineers
   P.O. Box 2870
   Portland, Oreg. 97208

Directory of Buying Activities of the South Central Small Business Council
   Small and Disadvantaged Business Utilization Office
   Oklahoma City, Air Logistics Center (OCALC)
   Tinker AFB, Okla. 73145-5990

**Directory of Federal and State Business Assistance Centers, PB 86–100344:
Guide to Services, Facilities and Expertise*
   U.S. Department of Commerce, National Technical Information Services
   5285 Port Royal Road
   Springfield, Va. 22161

Directory of Federal Laboratory and Technology Resources, PB88–100011:
Guide to Services, Facilities and Expertise
U.S. Department of Commerce
National Technical Information Services
5285 Port Royal Road
Springfield, Va. 22161

DOD/A-E Selection Procedures
Office of the Assistant Secretary of Defense
Manpower, Reserve Affairs, and Logistics
Superintendent of Documents

DODISS, Department of Defense Index of Specification and Standards
Superintendent of Documents

DOD Small and Disadvantaged Business Utilization Specialist
Superintendent of Documents

Evaluation of a Contractor's Inspection System, DOD Handbook H–51
Superintendent of Documents

Federal Acquisition Regulations (FAR)
Department of Defense Supplement to the FAR
Superintendent of Documents

Federal Procurement Data System, Standard Report
U.S. GSA, Federal Procurement Data Center
4040 N. Fairfax Drive, Suite 900
Arlington, Va. 22203   (1-703-235-1326)

Federal Supply Classification, Cataloging Handbook
Department of Army Supply Bulletin, Handbook H2-1, SB708-21
DLA, Defense Logistics Service Center
Battle Creek, Mich. 49016

Forecast of Planned Competitive Procurements
National Aeronautics and Space Administration
Johnson Space Center
Procurement Operations Office, Mail Code BD35
Houston, Tex. 77058

Government Production Prime Contractors Directory, 1987–88
Government Data Publications
1120 Connecticut Ave., N.W.
Washington, D.C. 20036

Guide to the Defense Contracting Regulations for Small Business, Small Disadvantaged Business, Women-Owned Small Business: Directorate of Small and Disadvantaged Business Utilization
Office of the Secretary of Defense
Washington, D.C. 20301-3061

Guide for Private Industry, A: How to Obtain Information on Specifications and Standards
Naval Publications and Forms Center
5801 Tabor Avenue
Philadelphia, Pa. 19120

*Guide for Small Business, A
Oklahoma Department of Commerce
6601 Broadway Extension
Oklahoma City, Okla. 73116-8214

Guide to the Preparation of Offers for Selling to the Military
Directorate of Small and Disadvantaged Business Utilization
Headquarters USAF
Washington, D.C., 20301

HB–4, Alphabetically Organized CAGE Numbers
HB–8, Numerically Organized CAGE Numbers
(See Defense Logistics Agency Handbooks.)
H–51, Evaluation of a Contractor's Inspection System
Superintendent of Documents.

Handbook for Small Business: A Survey of Small Business Programs of the Federal Government
Superintendent of Documents

How to Prepare Bids
Department of the Air Force
Office of Small and Disadvantaged Business Utilization
Headquarters USAF
Washington, D.C. 20301

How to Sell to the State of Oklahoma
Central Purchasing
Rm. B4, State Capital
Oklahoma City, Okla. 73105

Identification of Commodities and Services Purchased by the Defense Logistics Agency
Cameron Station
Alexandria, Va. 22314

Index of Aerospace Material Specifications: Industrial Specifications Applicable for Government Contracting
   Society of Automotive Engineers
   F400 Commonwealth Drive
   Warrendale, Pa. 15096

Index of Selected Procurement Assignments
   Air Force Logistics Command, Aeronautical Systems Division
   U.S. Printing Office, Superintendent of Documents

Labor Standards for Federal Service Contracts
Title 29, Part 4, Code of Federal Regulations
U.S. Dept. of Labor, WH Publication #1267
   Wage and Hour Division
   Superintendent of Documents

Let's Do Business
   Procurement Policies and Programs Division
   U.S. Postal Service
   Washington, D.C. 20260-6201

Let's Do Business
   Veterans' Administration Marketing Center
   P.O. Box 76
   Hines, Ill. 60141

List of Commodities and Services
   Federal Supply and Services, GSA Form 1382
   GSA, Business Service Center, your local area

Major Laws Administered by U.S. Department of Labor Which Affect Small Businesses
   Director, Office of Small and Disadvantaged Business Utilization
   U.S. Department of Labor, Rm. S-1004
   200 Constitution Avenue, N.W.
   Washington, D.C. 20210

Military Specifications, Attn. NCD 105
   Naval Publication and Forms Center
   5801 Tabor Ave
   Philadelphia, Pa. 19120-5099

NASA, Johnson Space Center
   Subcontracting Opportunities
   Procurement Operations Office, Mail Code BD35
   Houston, Tex. 77058

Nation's Public Works, May 1987: National Council on Public Works Improve-ment
   Superintendent of Documents

Nation's Public Works, The—Defining the Issues
   National Council on Public Works and Infrastructure Improvements
   Superintendent of Documents

Navy Ships Parts Control Center Buy Requirements Listing
   Competition Advocate Office
   Code OOC, P.O. Box 2020
   Mechanicburg, Pa. 17055-0788

Procurement Automated Source System (PASS)
   P.O. Box 700
   Menominee, Mich. 49858-0700

Procurement History Extraction/Records (PHE/PHR)
   Computer-extracted listing of contract buys by stock number order.
   Published by individual buying agencies.

Production Manual for Contract Administration Services
   Defense Logistics Agency, DLAM 8300.1
   Cameron Station
   Alexandria, Va. 22304-6100

Proposal Preparation for Small Business Innovation Research (SBIR)
   Office of Innovation, Research, and Technology
   U.S. Small Business Administration
   Washington, D.C. 20416

Prospective Clothing, Textile, Equipment and Footwear Bidders
   Defense Personnel Support Center (DPSC)
   2800 South 20th Street, P.O. Box 8419
   Philadelphia, Pa. 19101-8419

Quality Control System and Written Procedures, Guide
   GSA Region 7, Quality Control Division
   819 Taylor Street
   Fort Worth, Tex. 76102

Reverse Engineering Handbook, U.S. Army
   Naval Publications and Forms—MIL-HDBK-115(ME)
   5801 Tabor Avenue
   Philadelphia, Pa. 19120

Selling to Air Force Prime Contractors
  Small Business Office
  Air Force Contract Management Division
  Kirkland Air Force Base, N.M. 87117

Selling to the Military
  Superintendent of Documents

Selling to the United States Air Force, AFP 800-41
  Office of Small and Disadvantaged Business Utilization
  Headquarters, USAF
  Washington, D.C. 20301

*Selling Your Products to AVSCOM & TROSCOM, AVSCOM & TROSCOM
Pamphlet 715-1*
  Headquarters, U.S. Army Aviation Systems Command
  Headquarters, U.S. Army Troop Support Command
  Small and Disadvantaged Business Utilization Office
  4300 Good Fellow Boulevard
  St. Louis, Mo. 63129-1798

*Setting up a Quality Control System, MA-243, Management Aids for Small
Manufacturers*
  U.S. Small Business Administration
  Washington, D.C. 20416, or any SBA regional office

Small Business Guide to Federal R&D Funding Opportunities
  National Science Foundation
  Office of Small Business Research and Development
  Superintendent of Documents

Small Business Preferential Subcontract Opportunities—Monthly
  Government Data Publications
  1120 Connecticut Ave, N.W.
  Washington, D.C. 20036

*Small Business Specialists
  Department of Defense
  Office of the Secretary of Defense
  Washington, D.C. 20301

Small Business Subcontracting Directory
  Directorate of Small and Disadvantaged Business Utilization Office
  Office of the Secretary of Defense
  Washington, D.C. 20301-3061

Small Contractor's Assistance Program (SCAP)
U.S. Army Corps of Engineers, Office of Chief Engineer
20 Massachusetts Avenue, N.W.
Washington, D.C. 20314-1000

Standard Industrial Classification (SIC) Codes
National Technical Information Services
U.S. Department of Commerce, FIPS Pub. 66
Springfield, Va. 22161

State Technical Assistance Centers and Federal Technical Information Centers
National Technical Information Center, Brochure PR–767
U.S. Department of Commerce
Springfield, Va. 22161

Stock Number Advanced Procurement Planning List (SNAPPL)
Projections of what will be bought over next one to two years, by stock numbers, required to meet congressional budgeting process. Published by individual buying agencies.

U.S. Government Purchasing and Sales Directory
U.S. Small Business Administration
Office of Procurement and Technical Assistance
Superintendent of Documents

What the U.S. Department of Labor Buys
U.S. Department of Labor/OASAM
525 Griffin Street, Rm. 622
Dallas, Tex. 75202

What USDA Buys—Fiscal Year 1988
U.S. Department of Agriculture
Office of Advocacy and Enterprise
Small and Disadvantaged Business Utilization
South Building, Rm. 1567
Washington, D.C. 20250

Index